BEARDED BRIGANDS

FRONT COVER: Official T Patrol photograph taken just outside Cairo in March 1941, after the seige of Giarabub. Frank Jopling is at far left, wearing his customary goggles.

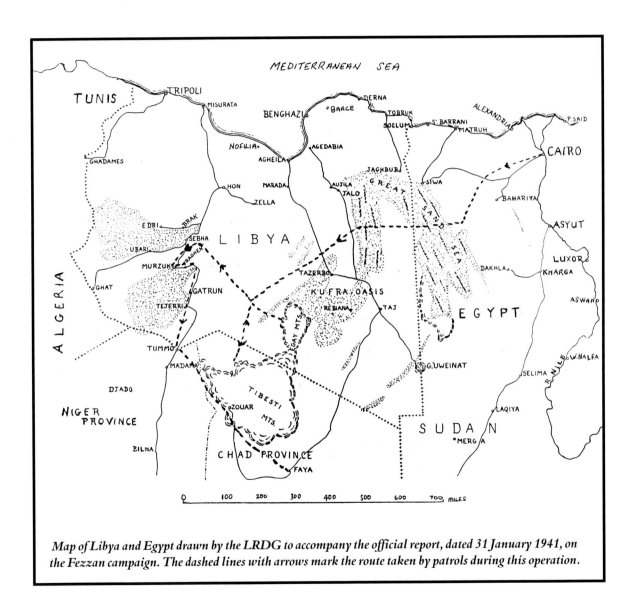

Map of Libya and Egypt drawn by the LRDG to accompany the official report, dated 31 January 1941, on the Fezzan campaign. The dashed lines with arrows mark the route taken by patrols during this operation.

BEARDED BRIGANDS

The diaries of Trooper Frank Jopling
Edited by Brendan O'Carroll

LEO COOPER

Also by Brendan O'Carroll:

Kiwi Scorpions, the story of the New Zealanders in the
Long Range Desert Group during the Second World War

First published in New Zealand in 2002 by Ngaio Press

First published in the United Kingdom in 2003 by
Leo Cooper, an imprint of Pen & Sword Books Limited,
47 Church Street, Barnsley, South Yorkshire, S70 2AS.

© Brendan O'Carroll, 2003

ISBN 0 85052 955 7

A CIP record for this book is available
from the British Library

Printed in China by Everbest Printing Co. Ltd.

All rights reserved. No part of this publication may be
reproduced, stored in a retrieval system or transmitted
in any form or by any means, electronic, mechanical,
photocopying, recording or otherwise, without prior
written permission from the publisher.

Design, typesetting and additional editing by John MacGibbon

CONTENTS

Editor's preface	7
The Long Range Desert Group	9
About the diarist	13

THE DIARIES:

Early days	16
Fezzan campaign	48
Attack on Muzurk	59
Guests of the Free French	71
Attack at Gebel Sherif	82
Siege of Giarabub	92
To Kufra	102
Tazerbo	110
Reconnaissance and charting	115
To Siwa	123
With the Eighth Army	136
The road watch	150
Convoy attacks	166
Barce raid	188
Postscript	204
Appendix I — Letter to Irene Gwyer re Guardsman Easton's death	206
Appendix II — Letter to Irene Gwyer re the Long Range Patrol badge	207
Appendix III — Names of T Patrol trucks	208
Appendix IV — Members of T, T1 and T2 Patrols, who Frank Jopling served with between July 1940 and September 1942	209
Index	214

ACKNOWLEDGEMENTS

I wish to thank the following people for their help in making this book possible:

Irene Jopling, and her sons *Bill* and *Bruce*, for kindly permitting me to edit and publish Frank's diaries and photographs.

Ian and Peggy Judge of the LRDG (NZ) Association for their generous support in loaning photographs and references held by the Association.

Merlyn Craw, for permission to publish his wartime photographs. Merlyn served in T Patrol, and for a time was Frank Jopling's NCO. Both were captured following the Barce raid in September 1942.

Jonathan Pittaway and *Craig Fourie* of South Africa, for permission to republish several photographs from their most comprehensive book, *LRDG Rhodesia*.

Graeme Rutherford for contributing photographs from his family collection.

Owen Gillingham for the photo of his sun compass.

David Ellis for contributing photographs from the albums of his late father Eric Ellis, T2 Patrol.

Shona MacGibbon for allowing me to use some of her father Struan MacGibbon's photos.

To my daughter *Diana*, for the many hours spent transcribing the original work onto my computer and to my son *Patrick*, for advice on computer application. Also, to my wife *Margaret* and younger daughter *Michelle*, for their encouragement in this project.

Brendan O'Carroll

EDITOR'S PREFACE

While researching for my book *The Kiwi Scorpions, the story of the New Zealanders in the Long Range Desert Group*, I came across the diaries of Trooper Frank Jopling, who had served in the LRDG's 'T Patrol'. I used several Jopling entries in Kiwi Scorpions, and felt at the time that the complete diaries were a great story in themselves.

Jopling kept a meticulous daily journal of his service, initially with the Long Range Patrol and then with the Long Range Desert Group, as the unit became known in December 1940. This fascinating personal account of desert life, activities and operations with T Patrol was recorded as events unfolded until September 1942, when Jopling became a prisoner of war. He also took many photos with his personal camera and had hopes of producing a book about his experiences after the war. But only now – nearly 60 years later and 15 years after his death in 1987 – has his dream been realised, thanks to his widow Irene Jopling kindly giving me permission to edit and publish Frank's diaries and photographs.

To my knowledge, this vivid chronicle of one man's experience in the LRDG is the most comprehensive insight into the daily workings of the force ever published. Studying the entries, the reader can share in Frank Jopling's wartime escapades as a member of one of the Second World War's foremost special force units, from the first pioneering trip in July 1940, until his capture in 1942 after enduring an incredible 12-day desert trek while suffering gangrene. Jopling's simple narrative reflects the thoughts, attitudes and observations of an ordinary New Zealand soldier travelling and fighting in Libya, an arid land of climatic extremes in stark contrast to the temperate climate of his South Pacific home. This account also serves as an unofficial history of LRDG's T Patrol (later split into T1 & T2 Patrols), with whose members Jopling shared two years of grand adventure and camaraderie.

Initially the keeping of diaries was prohibited, as the LRDG was a covert behind-the-lines organisation. However, Jopling had a passion for writing and defied the ban by keeping a secret journal. In early 1941 his notebooks came to the attention of his superiors, who, as it transpired, were so impressed with them, that instead of putting him on a charge, they made him the official diarist and photographer for the NZ War Office, Middle East War Office, and the London War Office. Also, by February that year, the unit was no longer considered secret and journalists began to seek stories about the men they saw as swashbuckling desert pirates. Jopling's diaries and photos were a ready source of information and colour and were the basis of many magazine and newspaper articles. The diaries were also considered to be important war history and copies were sent to the Archives Section of the New Zealand Army Headquarters.

The New Zealand Broadcasting Unit in the Middle East talked Jopling into narrating his own work in a programme called *Frank's Diary*, for radio audiences back home.

Introducing him during the Sunday night programme, *Radio Magazine from Egypt*, the announcer said:

"Over here in the Middle East we have recently come across a young New Zealander who kept a detailed account of various trips made by his patrol across the unexplored desert country of Egypt, Libya, and Equatorial Africa. The story is so vivid, and so intensely interesting, that in itself it is a piece of valuable war history. In broadcasting extracts from this diary we have persuaded the writer himself to recount to you the words written day by day, in many cases, hundreds of miles away from any form of civilisation."

Though Jopling wrote a complete day-to-day account of his activities, both in the field and while on leave or at base, a full transcription of this might prove a little tedious or repetitive to the general reader. Accordingly, I have summarised some of the quieter and more routine periods. From time to time I have also added comments within square brackets to identify people, weapons, equipment etc, and to help explain the broader picture of the military situation happening at the time. Apart from this, and some editing of grammar to aid clarity, what you read is what Jopling wrote.

Few of the photographs in this book are technically equal to the work of official war photographers, and some of the prints were in poor condition. However, these images are less 'posed' than most official photographs and and their honesty and immediacy makes them an invaluable record of life at the business end of things. Nearly all were taken by amateurs - the LRDG soldiers themselves. Most were by Frank Jopling, who was eventually issued with a good Contax camera to record LRDG activities for army publicity purposes.

Brendan O'Carroll
Editor
Auckland, August 2002

THE LONG RANGE DESERT GROUP

The war in North Africa came to an end with the Axis surrender in May 1943. For almost three years, while the main war between the opposing armies had been waged along the Mediterranean coast, the Long Range Desert Group operated behind enemy lines and dominated the vast inner deserts of Egypt, Libya and Tunisia.

This special intelligence gathering and reconnaissance unit, first known as the Long Range Patrol, was conceived in June 1940 by Major Ralph Bagnold, a British Army signals officer, geographer and desert explorer of the 1920s and 1930s. Its initial purpose was to assess the threat to Egypt from the Italians in south-eastern Libya. For the first six months the patrols were nearly entirely manned by especially selected volunteers from the Second New Zealand Expeditionary Force (2NZEF). These self-reliant, hardy men were already accustomed to outdoor life and the handling of vehicles, as they came from farming or practical trade backgrounds. Therefore they were well suited to the task ahead of them and had successfully adapted to desert conditions. They were to become the first Kiwi troops to see action in World War II.

In December 1940, recruits from the British Guards Regiment joined the force, and it became known as the Long Range Desert Group. Later reinforcements came from Southern Rhodesia and the British Yeomanry Regiments.

This small, but extremely effective force of Empire troops went on ground reconnaissance patrols in especially adapted trucks and were experts in navigation, desert warfare, and survival. Their principal objective was to provide detailed charting of Libya (most its the interior was unmapped) and information about enemy dispositions from deep behind the lines in the Libyan desert. Each patrol was a completely self-contained independent body, capable of operating for hundreds of miles and weeks on end over some of the most difficult and arid terrain in the world.

They ran regular reconnaissance and survey patrols between Cairo and Tripoli, and provided the Eighth Army, via radio, with much of its information about enemy movements. By the summer of 1941, the LRDG's Heavy Section had established a chain of supply dumps which greatly extended the range of operations.

In January 1943, the New Zealand T1 Patrol, under Captain N P Wilder, crossed the frontier and became the first troops of the Eighth Army to enter Tunisia. They found an uncharted pass south through the Matmata Hills which became known as Wilder's Gap. Two months later the New Zealand Division used this route, marked by the legendary 'black diamond' signs, to execute its 'left hook' round the enemy's fortified Mareth Line. This was one of the key actions that eventually led to the defeat of the Axis forces in North Africa.

By 1942 the strength of the LRDG had peaked at about 350 personnel, spread over two squadrons, A and B. The New Zealanders comprised A Squadron, and the British and Rhodesians made up B Squadron. Supporting sections included headquarters air, signals, survey, repair, and heavy transport.

The New Zealand patrols were designated 'W', 'R' and 'T', and their vehicles bore Maori names starting with that letter. The other patrols were the Guards ('G') Yeomanry ('Y') and the Southern Rhodesians ('S'). Initally the patrols consisted of 27 to 32 personnel travelling in 11 especially adapted 30cwt trucks – either Chevrolets or Fords. However by 1942, the patrol sizes were reduced so that each had 18 to 20 men, in five or six vehicles. They were accompanied by a commander's pilot vehicle which was usually a Ford 15cwt, or a Willys jeep.

As experts in desert navigation and survival, the LRDG were often asked to guide others to their objectives. These groups included the Special Air Service, Popski's Private Army, the Free French and the Sudan Defence Force. The LRDG also enjoyed success in other activities such as inserting, supplying, and collecting British and Arab undercover agents, rescuing Allied prisoners of war, and recovering downed airmen.

ORGANISATION

The units were organised so they could be act offensively if required. A variety of heavy and light machine-guns were mounted on the vehicles and each patrol had a heavy truck-mounted gun. Initially this was a single shot 37mm Bofors anti-tank gun. Later it was replaced by the more versatile Italian semi- automatic 20mm Breda gun.

The unit harassed the enemy by attacking its forts, supply dumps and airfields. They disrupted convoys by mine-laying and machine-gunning. This forced the Axis forces to withdraw badly needed troops, armour and aircraft from the front to protect their rear areas, as they never knew when or where the raiders were going to strike next. The LRDG came and went so quickly that the Italians called them Pattuglia Fanatasma (Ghost Patrols). Contemporary newspaper reports helped build a romantic swashbuckling image of these men, calling them 'bearded brigands' and 'desert highwaymen'.

Appropriately, the insignia chosen for the LRDG was a scorpion. It was a potent symbol for power in a small unit, capable of striking suddenly and with deadly effect. The sting was its firepower and this was combined with the element of surprise. Part of the LRDG's success was due to their small size. They could easily conceal themselves behind enemy lines in the shadows of dunes and wadis, or widely disperse to become difficult to find.

Between December 1940 and April 1943, there were only 15 days on which a patrol was not operating behind, or on the flanks of the enemy. The unit had lived up to its unofficial motto, as penned by Dr. F B Edmundson, New Zealand Medical Corps and LRDG medical officer: "Not by strength, by guile."

The qualities of the New Zealanders in the LRDG are perhaps best described by the British soldiers they served with. Captain Bill Kennedy Shaw explained in his book on the LRDG how he viewed the 'Kiwis'.

"There can be no doubt whatever that much of the early and continued success of the LRDG was due to speed and thoroughness with which the New Zealanders learned desert work and life."

Kennedy Shaw also felt the New Zealanders were fitter and possessed a maturity and independence not found in British soldiers of a similar age.

Lieutenant Colonel Vladimir Peniakoff wrote in his book, *Popski's Private Army* (1950): "A free, cheerful, tireless, efficient body of bearded men, they were the most pleasant companions I have ever had. I graded their squadrons, drawn from various parts of the Empire, on a scale of human excellence, which ranged from the New Zealanders high on top through the Rhodesians and the British Yeomanry down to the squadron drawn from the Guards Regiments. The New Zealanders, farmers in civil life, took easily to the roaming life in the desert. They had from the first a resourceful, happy assurance and set a standard which the others tried to follow."

Recruiting

The LRDG was never short of recruits and many dropped rank so they could join. For example, in December 1940 Bagnold asked General Freyberg, commander in chief of New Zealand Division, for further volunteers. Eight hundred applied for 40 positions, so the Group was always in a position to choose the best. The New Zealand Squadron seemed to attract more mature experienced practical men with rural backgrounds and their numbers included several brothers and cousins.

One appeal of the LRDG was the almost complete freedom from drill, guards, and fatigues, plus the best army food in the Middle East. It was interesting and often exciting work, with the opportunity to prove oneself without the usual regimental constraints. If an individual showed particular aptitude for the work there was a good chance for promotion. A number of men who had joined as privates finished their service with the Group as senior NCOs or officers.

On the debit side there was the strain of operating for long periods behind enemy lines with very little leave. They suffered from climatic extremes of heat and cold, sandstorms, thirst, anxiety, malaria and desert sores. If they became sick or wounded, captured or lost, there was little chance of assistance apart from what could be provided from their own resources. Losing their transport due to enemy action, or more rarely through serious mechanical failure, became a matter of survival. LRDG annals record a number of occasions where men trekked great distances, successfully navigating their way to safety while sick or wounded or with very little water or rations. Frank Jopling was one of those men.

The New Zealand Squadron's last operation was in the Mediterranean, September to November 1943, on the Dodecanese Islands. This sometimes overlooked and ill-fated campaign resulted in more New Zealanders being lost in three months, than after three years in the desert. They had been committed without the knowledge of the New Zealand Government and when the operation ended, General Freyberg ordered the Kiwis back to the New Zealand Division. They had been 'on loan' to the British for three and a half years. Even so, a handful continued to serve with with the LRDG in Europe until its disbandment in August 1945.

Approximately 325 New Zealanders passed through the LRP or LRDG. They were a major element in the force and they contributed significantly to its success. While some only served a few months, others stayed on for several years. Four of their number were killed in action, one died of wounds, one was listed as missing, and four died while they were prisoners of war. The LRDG's total roll of honour for all its members was 37 men.

Despite the anxieties and hardships of serving in the desert or the Dodecanese Islands, the men displayed their usual tenacity and stoically got on with the job. The determination and success of this small force was reflected in the fact that nearly a third of its members won decorations. The dangerous nature of LRDG operations, along with the high quality of its personnel, meant a good level of esprit de corps always prevailed.

The LRDG 'ran out of desert' with the Axis surrender in Tunisia, in May 1943. Frank Jopling's war ended earlier, when he was captured by the Italians in September 1942. Yet it was men like him, who, far from the coolness of home, ventured into a remote and arid land and through their own ingenuity and indefatigable spirit, achieved incredible results that were out of all proportion to the size of their force. Their success was reflected in a comment made during the desert campaign by the commander of the Afrika Korps, Field Marshall Erwin Rommel: "The LRDG caused us more damage than any other British unit of equal strength."

ABOUT THE DIARIST

Frank W Jopling was born in Sunderland, Northumberland, England, on 15 April 1913. In 1930, aged 17, he travelled alone to New Zealand on the vessel RMS Rangitata. Disembarking in Auckland, he was supposed to journey on south to Wellington to stay with his uncle. However, he wanted to seek his fortune, so instead boarded a train and went north where he found work as a farmhand. After several years he settled down farming at Okoroire near Matamata. In his spare time he served in the New Zealand Territorial Forces as a trooper in the 4th Waikato Mounted Rifles, which later became part of the Second New Zealand Divisional Cavalry.

On 12 September 1939, a few days following the British declaration of war against Germany on 3 September, the New Zealand Government called for volunteers for overseas service. Jopling, having already enjoyed part-time military life, didn't hesitate to take up the call to arms and on 5 October was sent to the Army training camp at Hopu Hopu near Hamilton. He was placed with the HQ Squadron of the NZ Divisional Cavalry as a driver/mechanic.

After two months training, his final leave came on 14 December, when he made his way to Devonport, Auckland, the home of his girlfriend, Irene Gwyer. On 27 December they became engaged to marry. However, the next day Jopling had to return to camp as his regiment was making final preparations for their overseas departure.

With the First Echelon being formed on 4 January 1940, Trooper F W Jopling went to Wellington by train and boarded the same vessel that brought him to New Zealand ten years earlier. On 6 January, the Rangitata and five other troopships, escorted by HMS

1940: Jopling's first army vehicle, No. 33, a 30cwt Morris Commercial. He spent five months based at the 2NZEF training camp at Maadi, just outside Cairo. Only the truck kept him from going mad with boredom during that period, Frank wrote.

Ramillies, Canberra and Leander, transported New Zealand's first troops to foreign shores since the Great War. Travelling west to Fremantle, the force added five ships with Australian troops, plus another cruiser. After a stop in Colombo, they arrived safely at the Egyptian port of Tewfik on 13 February. From there the soldiers moved to the Second New Zealand Division's base at Maadi, near Cairo.

Jopling's diary describes five months of basic training at Maadi camp before joining the LRDG in July 1940. Later, reflecting on that time, he wrote:

"Of my five months in Maadi I will only say a little, as I was bored stiff from start to finish, though shortly after we arrived there we experienced a number of dust storms for the first time. On 29 February I took over my first army vehicle, a 30cwt Morris Commercial, and if I hadn't had that to keep me occupied, I am sure I would have gone mad with boredom long before the five months were up.

"On 3 July came the news that some sort of desert patrol was going to be formed from the NZ Division and that some of the men would be picked out from the Divisional Cavalry. The next day I was given the great news that I was one of the drivers chosen. The nature of the job was still a mystery, but one thing seemed certain and that was that it would be a risky job, as we were told that if we had any good friends we ought to say goodbye to them before we left, in case we never saw them again. After hearing I was selected, I didn't hear any more for some weeks.

"It wasn't till July 25 that we eventually left Maadi for Abbassia, on the outskirts of Cairo, to undergo training before starting on the job. The next morning our Commanding Officer, Major Ralph Bagnold, gave us a talk as to what the job was all about. We gathered that there were going to be three patrols: T, W, and R, and we would be travelling over thousands of miles of unmapped desert. Our trucks were 30 cwt Chevrolet WBs and our base would be at Abbassia. The job would be mainly reconnaissance, but we might meet up with a small Italian force, who we would endeavour to deal with. If the force was too large, we would make a run for it. We have to carry enough benzine for at least 1,200 miles, sufficient food etc. for three weeks and we are only allowed one gallon of water per day. If the truck needs any, it has to come out of that gallon per day.

"After putting in two weeks' training and work on the trucks, we set off on a three-day manoeuvre to give us an idea of what we would have to put up with.

Maadi Camp, 1940. This vast tented expanse was the desert base for 2NZEF.

A MK V1 Vickers light tank of the NZ Divisional Cavalry at Maadi 1940. It had a crew of three, were lightly armoured, and mounted .303 and .50 machine guns. They were only useful as reconnaissance vehicles.

"We headed towards a place known as Mushroom Rock, where naturally enough, there is a rock in the shape of a mushroom. It is about 220 kilometres from Cairo and we felt we were in the middle of enemy territory, but actually we were in the middle of Egypt. We dumped our benzine at Mushroom Rock and on our way back we stopped at the Ramak Dunes, which are a row of dunes about 120km from Cairo. (The trucks' speedometers are in kilometres.) We were told to try and cross the Ramak Dunes, as we would have to cross plenty of that terrain later on. So three trucks took a run at it, and were travelling at about 40 mph when they came to the top. The result was that they took off like aeroplanes. My truck landed on the radiator and damaged it, along with the fan and the axle. Two men were injured. One cut an eye and the other his leg; however they weren't serious. After that we gave the idea up, did a few more manoeuvres, then headed for Cairo.

"The first job we did when we got back was have a wash and shave. We still had a lot of work to do before we set off on our first real trip. On August 27 we were inspected by General Wavell, C in C *[Commander in Chief]* Middle East. After inspecting all our trucks he said, "Well good morning men, good luck and good hunting." He then got into his car and drove away. On September 4 we were all prepared for our first trip. The following day we set off. We didn't know where or for how long, but we were all looking forward to what lay ahead of us."

What follows is Jopling's diary account of the first operational trip of the Long Range Patrol, written as events unfolded.

Irene Gwyer, Frank's fiancée, dressed in the uniform of of a nurse aid in the Women's War Service Auxiliary (WWSA). Frank was a regular letter writer and numbered all the letters he sent to Irene. The couple married in August 1945.

The LRDG's 'classic' vehicle – the 1942 Canadian Chevrolet 30 cwt truck with its cab cut off. Mounted on the back is a .50 Browning machine gun. The drawing is from a wartime Italian identification manual.

EARLY DAYS

5 SEPTEMBER 1940 Well, well, well, what organisation!! And what a start to a history making trip. We were all lined up and ready to move off when they suddenly decided that the Ford 15cwt V8s were no good the way they were, as when they loaded them up, the tyres hit the mudguards, so it was decided that they would have to be taken to Ordnance and get them altered. We were told that we wouldn't be leaving until 4pm.

2.00pm The V8s are back and W Patrol has just moved off. We *[T Patrol]* will be moving off shortly. An Air Force officer is travelling with us to pick out potential landing grounds for aeroplanes. So the Air Force must be working in conjunction with us. We're all more or less thrilled with the trip and anxious to get going. Not necessarily because we want to have a go at the Italians, but more for the adventure and excitement of the trip. We are going where no trucks have ever been before, over country that has never been mapped and we will probably see things that have never been seen by white men.

4.00pm We have halted for a while, 37km from the barracks. We have caught up to W Patrol and R Patrol has just caught up with us. We have been over this bit of desert before and it has been pretty rough going for a while anyhow. W Patrol is moving off now, so I don't suppose we will be long after them. We are not allowed cameras or diaries out on this trip, so I have to be careful when and where I write this.

6.00pm We have halted again and the radiator was boiling, but she was cool again only a matter of seconds after we had faced the truck into the wind and switched off. We have now gone 80km and so far no-one has got stuck. I suppose we will be travelling right until it gets dark, seeing as we started late.

7.30pm It is just getting dark and we have stopped for the night after doing 123km. Arthur Spedding *[Corporal A J Spedding]* and Don Ormond *[Sergeant A R W Ormond]* got the tea on. We are having bully beef, spuds, onion, peas and curry, all made into a stew. R Patrol stopped by some dunes further back and I don't know where W is. Well it is getting too dark to write now, so I will close down.

6 September 1940 *12 noon* I am afraid I have had neither time nor opportunity to write this sooner. We got up at 6am and set off at 8am. We couldn't start any earlier, as clouds hid the sun and it is very slow going without the sun compass. We have now done 134km over very rough going. I hope it is better this afternoon. They are putting the scrim and nets over the trucks now and it looks very effective. W, R and ourselves are all here, but we will be parting from W Patrol any time now. We are having sardines and tinned fruit for lunch, which sounds all right to me just at present.

6.00pm We have again stopped for the night near some sand dunes after having travelled 257km since breakfast – the biggest mileage in one day since there was such a force as an LRP. I have put in 20 gallons of benzine today.

It has been very rough and soft all day except the last 20km, which has been very good. The poor old truck has had to work hard today and has been boiling most of the time. There is another stew on tonight, but I like them very much. Well, I must stop writing now before I get caught.

7 September 1940 *7.00pm* We have just finished a breakfast of sausages and bacon, filled our water bottles and we are all loaded up and ready to go. There is not nearly so much wind this morning and not so much dew. Nor is it as cold.

9.30am It may have been warmer when we were standing still, but it wasn't too warm travelling at 60 kilometres per hour with no windscreen in front. We travelled 43km in the first hour which was very fast going, but very cold.

10.30am Another halt. We had a bit of excitement watching a truck chase a gazelle and try to shoot it. It seems a pity to shoot them as they are beautiful animals, but fresh meat is fresh meat out in

Trooper Frank Jopling taking a 'shot' with his theodolite. He studied navigation and went on to lead the 22nd Guards Brigade across the desert. Later he navigated by the stars during a 12-day desert trek when his truck was destroyed after the Barce raid in September 1942.

the desert. However it got away, so we won't get any fresh meat for a while yet.

12 noon We have been travelling through some wonderful country, mostly sand dunes etc. It has been very pretty and good going, except for some soft patches. In one place we all got stuck, including myself, but it didn't take us long to get out again. We are now waiting for two trucks which have got stuck in another place, but they will be here shortly. We have travelled 100km this morning so far.

1.30pm I have plenty to write about now. We have been crossing sand dunes ever since we left at 12 noon and talk about thrills, it was great!! Travelling at 80kph up and down smooth sand dunes. I had to keep looking at the speedo to see if we were moving, because to look at the sand in front, you would think we were standing still. The next bit of excitement we had was a lake! Naturally we all thought it was a mirage, but it wasn't long before we found it was actually Lake Sitra. We are now stopped beside it and have had lunch. Before that, three of us went in and had a swim, but it wasn't very deep. It was very salty – far saltier than sea water. At least it was wet and we got some of the dust off us. There are quite a few footprints like a dog which Captain Clayton *[Captain P A Clayton, T Patrol commander]* reckons are cheetahs. I would like to see one.

Mushroom Rock, a distinctive LRDG landmark.

We have done 137km so far and we have another 140km to go to get to Siwa and our benzine is running pretty low. I have only 12 gallons left besides what is in the tank, but that will be enough to get us there.

5.30pm Well, this afternoon we drove across the roughest country I have ever driven over. Anyone standing on the edge and looking across would have said it was impossible to cross with a truck, yet we did it without damaging any vehicles. We have now stopped for the night after having crossed the roughest part. We have done 213km today and about 613km since we left Abbassia, and we have approx. 100km to go to get to Siwa.

8.00pm We have finished lunch and had two issues of rum. We had bully beef, vegetables and curry made into a stew, and believe me those stews are good. While waiting for the second boil-up of tea, Captain Clayton gave us a bit of a speech. He told us we would arrive in Siwa tomorrow and that the place just leaks information to the enemy. As our benzine dump is in Siwa, we will have go in and collect it. If anyone asks any questions, we are taking it back along the Sitra road.

A huge rock stands alone in a flat desert plain. (Ellis)

8 September 1940 *2.00am* I have just been woken up to go on lookout. It is fairly cool, but alright with an overcoat on. There are some weird sort of noises going on which are made by desert foxes. I am on watch for an hour.

8.00am We have just had breakfast of herrings mixed with rice. It was a welcome change from the usual plain herrings. We are waiting for R Patrol to catch up with us.

12.30pm I said yesterday that it was the roughest country I had ever been over. So it was, but we went over it slowly. Today it was rough and we had to fly over it flat out in third gear or else get stuck. Believe me, things were flying. At one stage my tail board became unhooked and a whole lot of rations and stores fell out the back. I have been stuck twice, but finished up here in the lead except for the Captain, who led the way. We are now at a sort of halfway dump between Siwa and our main dump and we are now unloading everything from the truck and going into Siwa to get some water and benzine. We are about to have lunch now, of meat loaf and pickles, followed by tinned fruit and lime juice. We have been here for an hour now and six of T Patrol's trucks have still not arrived.

7.00pm All the other trucks eventually arrived here about 3pm. They all unloaded their stores, except the cases of empty water tins. We then went into Siwa with a Rhodesian guide leading the way. I started off sixth in the convoy and I was the only one who got to our destination without getting stuck. The guide took us straight to the swimming pool, and the three of us in the truck had the pool to ourselves for about two hours, before the guide came and led us to where the benzine was. The swim was great! While we loaded with benzine the others had their swim. We then filled ourselves up with dates and picked a few more to put in the truck. Shortly after that, the rest of the men came back and we set straight off for where we had dumped the rest of the gear. 'Mary' *[Lieutenant R B McQueen, 2IC, T Patrol]* said he would come with me and we would be the last truck and help anyone who got stuck. After assisting two vehicles we arrived back at dusk and tea was just about ready.

Siwa is a purely native village with no means of communication with the outside world. The houses are made of some sort of mud and are in poor state of repair. The population is about 5,000 and they earn their living by growing dates. The whole of the cultivated land around is dates and a few pomegranates. There are about half a dozen Rhodesian soldiers there, including a Lt. Colonel, and they are hidden in the date palms. There are also a few 'Gyppo' soldiers. The drinking water here isn't too good. It is hard to describe and is totally different from any I have tasted. It certainly doesn't quench one's thirst nearly so well, and it tastes salty to me. However, I suppose we will get used to it. We were the first New Zealanders to have been to Siwa.

We are now only about 50 miles from the Libyan border (Siwa is about 700km from Abbassia.) Every night we listen to the news, and the Germans seem to be doing a lot of damage

After a long patrol the men enjoyed a welcome swim in the cool bubbling springs at Siwa. These had brought relief to desert travellers for centuries. This pool was known as the 'Figure 8'.

over London – 400 casualities and 1,300 seriously wounded. Although they keep stressing how wonderful the morale of the people is, I don't think they will stand too much of that. However, if reports are correct, they seem to be getting a lot of German planes.

9 SEPTEMBER 1940 This morning I was told I was going with the Captain in his truck on a reconnaissance trip to find a way over the dunes for our 22 30cwt trucks. We set off at 9.30am and went over country that few white men have been over and certainly no New Zealanders. I thoroughly enjoyed the trip. I saw all sorts of weird shaped rocks and in one place there were acres of oysters. It is a pity there were no oysters inside or we would have had a great feed. We arrived back at 6pm and much to our surprise, we found our cook making mutton broth and some cold boiled mutton and pumpkin, which apparently Mary had bought out of the 20 piastres each we put into a fund at the start of trip. He also bought some dates and pomegranates.

8.00pm Well, we have had the feed and it was very nice too. The remainder of the trucks have been into Siwa again and brought out some more benzine and water. They also had another swim, which unfortunately we missed.

10 SEPTEMBER 1940 *7.00pm* Talk about thrills!! We are now about 35km from where we camped last night. We loaded up with benzine and water and left our private gear behind. Only one truck got through without getting stuck and I am afraid that wasn't mine. I got stuck in one place and it was just about looking as though I would never get out. We couldn't even get the wheels to grip on the sand channels, and each time we tried to move her, she sank further down, until the tailboard was just about touching the sand. Then someone suddenly had a brainwave that we should put a bit of cotton waste in the channels to make the tyres grip.

After that it was no trouble. We eventually arrived here just at lunch time – four hours to do 35km! We unloaded the trucks, had lunch and then went back for another load as well as our personal gear. That trip was the best I have had so far. I travelled at 85kph and sometimes I didn't know if the truck was going to roll over sideways or, at other times, if she was going to roll over backwards. However I got there without getting stuck and only two other trucks did the same. The next trip I had a heavier load on than the first. It was very heavy going, but I only got stuck once. This time it was only for a couple of minutes and then I was out. I arrived back here at 5.30pm and started to get tea ready. I am very thirsty after a hard day's work and the sooner I get a cup of tea the better.

We heard today that the 'Heads' *[senior army officers]* reckon we are taking on a job that is

A heavily loaded Marmon-Herrington truck of the Heavy Section deeply bogged in the sand. These six-wheel drive vehicles were essential in keeping the forward dumps and bases supplied.

absolutely impossible. When Major Bagnold decided who to take on the trip, he wanted good daring drivers who could use their initiative and could be told things. So they picked the New Zealanders and I was one of them. Well, it is a wonderful experience and I am glad I didn't miss. The time now is 7.30pm. and there are still only five out of 11 T Patrol trucks here. I hear them yelling out that tea is ready, so I better go and get it.

11 SEPTEMBER 1940 Apparently they had a bit of fun last night: one truck got stuck even deeper than I was. They reckon if you stood away you could hardly see the truck, as it was buried so deep that you couldn't see the tailboard. However, they eventually got it out and the next episode was when a truck turned over on a corner. The driver was fairly well bruised and scratched, but he had no broken bones. The man with him got off free except for a lump out of his topee.

The next episode was when the wireless truck came over the same hill too fast and took off at the top and never touched the earth until it landed at the bottom, just missing another truck by about five yards. It would have been too bad if he had hit. One man flew out the back and on to the bonnet where Mary hung on to him until the truck stopped. Luckily he only got a shaking. The driver bent the steering wheel, but didn't do any damage to himself. Mary got a slight cut on the hand. The truck itself escaped with a slightly bent axle. They brought it in this morning and it was marvelous how little damage was done. About the only real problem was a bent axle which they replaced. The rest was just minor and didn't affect the running of the vehicle.

Today has been more or less a day of rest. We are a day ahead of time, so after doing maintenance on the trucks we lay under them all day. One man has malaria, but apparently he has had it before in the West Indies, so it was just a recurrence which you always get when you have had it before. He will probably be alright in a day or two.

Lt R B 'Mary' McQueen, 2IC, T Patrol

We are now in the middle of the Sand Sea, which only about six white men have ever crossed before, and then only in light cars – so you can quite understand why the 'heads' reckoned we were taking on an impossible job. This morning we followed a snake track, but we couldn't find the snake. Except for sand snakes, the snakes here are deadly poisonous. This evening we loaded up with enough benzine, water and rations to last for 28 days. From here we go to our main base and R Patrol, which is a sort of a HQ will pick up anything we leave behind and take it to the main dump after we go into Libya. We expect to go there in about three days time.

12 SEPTEMBER 1940 *8.00am* We have set out to our main dump, carrying the biggest load we have ever had. We have about two and a half tons on a 30cwt truck and considering there have only been about six light cars over here before, our effort is almost incredible. We have done 16km and are waiting for two or three trucks that got stuck further back.

7.30pm We have had a great trip today. The going has been soft nearly all the way and the Captain reckons that we have got a lot further than he had expected us to. He personally congratulated our truck, because we were first by about half an hour at one halt this afternoon and we were second here, which wasn't bad, seeing that we always start off 8th in the convoy. The only time we overtake another truck is when they get stuck. We have been between 30 and 50km away from the Libyan border all day.

13 September 1940 *7.00pm* We are now at our main dump, about 30km from the border. It was a wonderful trip today. We got up to 95 kph. When we arrived here R Patrol dumped their load and went straight back to our last dump about 35km from Siwa. They have three trips to make while we are over the border. We have done 1,137km since we left Abbassia and we have arrived here a day ahead of time. The Captain reckons we have done wonderfully well, having achieved what the 'heads' thought was impossible.

W Patrol are about 27km away and are also ahead of time. We are 347km south of Siwa now. We are all enjoying this trip and not one of us would change places with any man in any army. I have since found out that as far as is known, the first 60 km from Siwa has never been crossed by white men before

14 September 1940 *10.00am* This morning I have started doing maintenance on the truck, but the wind got up and started a sandstorm. The sand is a sort of fine pebbles and believe me, when we are travelling at 30 or 40mph it can sting. We had to give up the maintenance and rigged up as good a shelter as possible, so we are now going to have a rest. The sand still seems to come through, but it is better than nothing. The sandstorm is getting worse, so we are going to move away from the sand areas.

7.00pm We set off shortly after 4pm and travelled 66km further south. The ground is more stony down here and the wind seems to have dropped. Major Bagnold and Lieutenant Ballantyne *[Lt. L B Ballantyne, LRP adjutant and quartermaster]* both came down to visit us today.

9.00pm Mary gave us a lecture after tea while we were sitting over our rum issue. He said we would be crossing the border tomorrow and explained our procedure according to what we meet.

15 September 1940 *10.00am* We have now crossed into Libya and are travelling south. We are ten kilometres inside Libyan territory, but have seen nothing yet. We have now halted, I don't know quite why, but the Captain seems to be looking for something, as he has been standing on top of a truck with his field glasses. Now he has gone off in the 15cwt.

3.00pm Well of all the cheek. The Captain was away looking for a suitable rock to 'attack'.

When he found one he came back and we attacked it with the Lewis guns, firing two magazines at it. Fancy coming over to Libya to have a practice with the LMG.

9.00pm I have just gone on picquet *[guard duty]* again. We have run fairly well into Libyan territory, but haven't seen any of the enemy. We travelled 131km today.

11.00pm I was supposed to have wakened the next man at 10pm, but I have been over listening to the wireless. Lord Haw Haw was on and he is making a big fuss of the capture of Sollum, which is in Egyptian territory. Actually no-one was there to argue the point with him, as they want to draw the Italians to Mersa Matruh if possible. The reason the wireless was going was that the Captain was very particular about getting the time signal, as we are passing close to enemy-held Kufra tomorrow. If he is the slightest bit out in his bearing he might run into Kufra, which would probably be just too bad for us. Well, I better go and wake up 'Skin' Moore *[Trooper R J Moore]*.

16 SEPTEMBER 1940 *3.00pm* We are now about latitude 25 and well into Libya. The Captain reckons that it is too hot to travel so we stopped at 10.30am and are starting again at 4pm. The temperature is at least 130° in the shade and it is too hot to sleep. We are all thirsty too.

The Naaten Bisciara well, dug in 1897. It was surrounded by the scattered bones of dead animals. The men on the left are carrying standard-issue four-gallon 'flimsies'. These were greatly inferior to German 'jerry-cans' which the Allies captured and used later in the North African campaign.

7.00pm We have stopped for the night near some high hills which are not marked on the map, so probably no white man has been here before. The Captain is going to mark the hills on the chart. Tomorrow we will be getting near Kufra, so we might see something. Nearly everyone is feeling the heat, but are still quite cheerful.

17 September 1940 *9.00am* Things are starting to look up. We have travelled just on 100km this morning and about an half an hour ago we came across a whole lot of tracks, mostly from dual-tyred vehicles, which were made within the last week. After thoroughly inspecting them, we carried on for a while and came across some posts which look as though they marked a route. Then over to our right we saw a white object that looked like a tent, so as we got closer it looked like buildings of sorts. We then got the action signal and having put the magazines on the guns we charged at about 70mph, but there was no sign of life. The things we thought were tents were some sort of markers for an emergency landing ground for aircraft. There was a wind indicator in the centre. We looked around for a dump, but none was to be seen. However, we were now all keyed up and were scanning the horizon for anything that might come over the top.

11.30pm We have stopped for our midday halt of five hours. We have had our lunch, and as it was too hot to eat canned fish, we just had fruit. I have just started half an hour's picquet and there are more of those posts marking another road. I am sitting on a rock on a bit of a rise and I have just finished scanning the horizon with a pair of field glasses, but there is nothing to be seen. It is important to watch the direction from which we came as we might have been followed. It we see anything we are to fire a shot to wake the rest of the patrol.

3.30pm On picquet for another half an hour. It is very hot. Mary reckons he wouldn't advocate another trip down here in this heat, but it won't be the heat next time, as it will be near winter. We are now only about 64km from a well called Naarten Bisciara and we are going to take it. They have been discussing how to attack it – whether to attack it tonight, then fill up our water tins and be away at dawn, or wait until dawn and attack it then. But I should say wait until we see it and how many enemy are there etc. I think that is what they will do.

6.00pm We have halted to cool the engine down and are now about 28km from the well. We are keeping our eyes wide open, watching for any form of enemy.

7.00pm We have halted for the night about 15km from Naarten Bisciara. The Captain has decided not to attack till the morning. We are looking forward to a good wash and a bellyful of water. It means a lot to us, as we will have about as much water as we like once we get to the well.

18 September 1940 *7.00am* We have now halted and are within 5km of the well, although we can't see it. Don Ormond has just come back from a talk with the Captain and the orders are not to fire until he gives the action signal. We are to aim straight and not over their heads.

8.00am Once again we made a spectacular charge only to find that there was no one there and we had the well all to ourselves.

10.00am Naturally we all made for the well to see if there was any water in it, if it was fit to drink and able to be got at. When we opened up the lid we could see the water 180 feet below. There was a long rope tied to the lid and a pulley to run it on. It was not long before we had cut the top off a water tin and made a bucket to hang on the end of the rope. The next item on the programme was to taste it and it turned out to be beautiful water. So we all swallowed as much as we could, got all the available empty water tins we could lay our hands on and set about filling them up. In addition, we have filled a benzine tin per man so we can have a good wash when we get away.

The Captain is rather anxious to get moving again as he reckons that our tracks are sure to have been seen, and if so, they are almost certain to send an aeroplane out to look for us. The wells are the most obvious places to look, so we are about to move off. But before we do, I will describe one or two things here. First the place is absolutely covered in bones of camels, goats, sheep and probably several other sorts of animals that I don't recognise. The goats and sheep have most likely been used as food by Arabs passing through, whereas the camels have either been killed because they were unfit to travel any further or else they drank too much on an empty stomach and got gripes like horses do. Secondly, there are fresh tracks of about 30 or 40 camels which can't be more than a day or two ahead of us. The Captain says that he is going to follow them and try to get information out of the Arabs concerning Kufra, as that is where he reckons they have come from. According to the Captain, the well was dug in 1897. The boys are all feeling pretty refreshed now, and are ready to move off again.

7.00pm We have stopped for the night about 100 miles from the well. Today we halted between 12.30 and 4pm and the boys felt a lot better than they had for the last few days.

10.00pm I have just come on picquet again for an hour. There is no doubt the Captain has a lot of confidence in himself – or perhaps I should say contempt for the enemy. Every night so far we have been allowed to light fires to boil up and make tea etc. Last night, being only 15 miles from the well, we thought we certainly wouldn't be allowed to light one, but he came along and said we could light a fire providing we didn't take too long. So tonight, with the danger of aircraft following our tracks we thought we certainly wouldn't be allowed to light a fire, but sure enough he comes along and says we can light as many fires as we like, as he wants to attract the attention of anyone around here. He also said tonight that there are only about two Italian pilots in Libya that they could send down here and he didn't think they would bother.

It is just about time for me to wake up Skin Moore, so I will get my bed ready. The well is approximately 800km from Siwa and we have travelled 1,654km since we left Abbassia.

19 SEPTEMBER 1940 This morning we were up bright and early and were on the move by 6am. The travelling was very rough and soft going, and when the sun got a bit of heat in it we had to have frequent halts to cool down the engines, especially the Ford V8. We eventually stopped for our midday halt at 10.30am, as the stops were becoming more frequent. We had travelled 106km and we were about 4km from the Sarra wells which we intended to get to. We had seen nothing all morning except some old truck and camel tracks. This afternoon was hotter than than any afternoon we have had yet. Perhaps it didn't seem much worse as we had plenty of water, but it must had been at least 135° in the shade. We are now well into the tropics and this morning we crossed the old Egyptian-Libyan boundary, but about ten years ago, Egypt gave Italy a lot of waste desert which included the Sarra wells, so we are actually still in Libya.

We started on the move again at 4pm and stopped at the top of the next rise. From there we could see the Sarra wells, but what caught our eye more than the Sarra well were some buildings around it. So we thought, "here goes for some real action this time." We had made the previous two charges from the artillery formation, but this time we spread out in extended order. On the signal from the Captain we all charged down on the buildings with all guns loaded and arrived only to find, once again, no one in possession.

After searching the buildings, which were apparently only shelters for Arab camel trains etc., and scouting all round in a radius of a couple of kilometres, we pulled up at the well. And what a well! We lifted the lid and looked down and we could just see faintly in the

The Sarra well was so deep that Jopling said the men had to walk out nearly 500ft to pull up the rope to recover the water.

distance the reflection of the water. After getting a rope and tying a tin on the end of it, we let it down and when it hit the water we pulled it up and it seemed as though it was never coming to the top. The men who were pulling it walked out at least 500 feet. How far below that the bottom of the well was, I don't know. Considering the tools the Arabs had in 1897, with the well being only 3 feet 6 inches in diameter, one wonders how it was ever made. However, we got all the spare water tins out again and set about filling them. Naturally there weren't nearly so many this time. By 5.30pm we had filled them all up while the Captain kept watch in a hill close by. Although not as good as the water in the last well, the water was better than that at Siwa. We carried on south for about ten kilometres, where we are now camped for the night.

The Captain said there was an aerodrome 25km from the well which we are going to investigate, but even that didn't prevent us from lighting fires because he reckons they won't send any planes up at night, as they don't have any landing facilities.

While at the well I found a dead snake which I took to the Captain and he said it was a horned viper which was near enough to being deadly poisonous. We are now 200km from Bisciara and 1,800km from Abbassia.

20 September 1940 *8.20am* As soon as we had breakfast we had to count and make sure that all our water and benzine tins weren't leaking. We have 19 cases of benzine and seven cases of water. Mary and his troop went back toward the well to see if he could find any trace of these camels, as there weren't any tracks of any kind near the well. The rest of us carried on south. We have now travelled 22km and the Captain is apparently searching for the landing ground. He has now gone away in his V8, but I don't know what he is doing as he is out of sight. We have to wait here till he comes back.

11.00am The Captain didn't arrive back until 10.30am and we then carried on for about 4km and we have now stopped for our midday halt after doing 26km altogether this morning.

2.15pm I have just come on picquet for half an hour and believe me it is warm. There are mirages all round and you could swear it was water. Apparently the Captain was looking for a landmark, including a tree, that was indicated on the map, but he was unable to find it. Three palm leaves are leaning against each other in the shape of a pyramid and the Captain reckons they mark the route to somewhere, so we are going to follow them.

7.00pm We are still at the same spot and are staying here the night. The Captain came along at 3.30pm, asked us to make a cup of tea and said he had decided to stay here the night as it would probably be dark by the time Mary got back. He eventually arrived at 5.30pm, having seen no sign of the camels. After we had a cup of tea, the Captain decided to give the gunners some Boys anti-tank gun practice. While they were shooting I cut up a pumpkin and started to get tea ready. They didn't shoot too well, only hitting the tin twice out of ten shots, but most of them had never fired the gun before.

Crossing the Harug. This rocky terrain was difficult to negotiate and had to be done very carefully in low gear. The risks were punctures, cracked sumps, exhaust systems or differential housings.

21 SEPTEMBER 1940 *7.00pm* We set off again at 6am and for the first 40km it was lovely driving, travelling at 60kph all the way, but after that we struck the longest and stoniest patches so far. It was 150km long and very hard work driving through it. We had our midday halt about 12 noon. It wasn't nearly so hot as there were a few clouds around. We set off again after our cup of tea at 4.30pm. After travelling 40km we struck some light car tracks which the Captain said were Major Bagnold's when he was here in 1932 – which shows how long the tracks last in some kinds of sand. Over to our right was a big beacon which turned out to be the boundary between Libya and French Equatorial Africa (Chad). So we are now in F.E. Africa and out off enemy territory, as Chad joined up with De Gaulle about a month before we started on this trip. At present we are about 15km into Chad and so far haven't seen anyone. We are wondering how we are going to explain to them that we aren't Italians.

11.00pm I have just come on an hour's picquet again, but if I see or hear anything this time, instead of firing a gun or tooting a horn I have to go and wake the Captain and he will decide what to do.

This morning, just before we got on to the rocky ground, we stopped near some tracks which the Captain reckoned were ostrich tracks. They were very similar to man tracks, only the steps were longer. I thought ostriches were just about extinct in this part of the world, but apparently they are not.

The map of this part of Africa is just a white sheet of paper with no markings on it at all, so I don't suppose there has been anyone here except Major Bagnold in 1932. Our navigator, Tony Browne, *[Cpl. L H Browne]* is making a map as he goes along. We are now heading for an oasis where we will rest for a couple of days before going to Uweinat, which is a large Libyan benzine dump for planes travelling to and from Abyssina. We are meeting W and R patrols and the Marmon-Herringtons *[LRP Heavy Section trucks used for supplying the dumps]* there.

At 1.00am last night, our wireless operator, Jack Shepherd, *[Cpl. J R Shepherd]* got in touch with W Patrol. They are asking the Marmon-Herringtons to bring some diesel fuel, so they must have captured one or more Fiat diesel trucks. Well, we have travelled 830km into Libyan territory and we haven't even seen an animal, let alone a man. We saw a few birds and insects which I don't know the names of, but otherwise all we have seen are camel and a few car and truck tracks.

22 September 1940 *7.00am* We have had breakfast and are all loaded up ready to go. The Captain has gone on to Tekro with the wireless truck to try and explain that we weren't Italians. We are to follow in a half hour's time.

8.30am We followed the Captain's tracks for about 20km and met him coming. He said

Getting stuck, a common problem with desert travel, and certainly not a pleasant experience when under enemy fire, as T Patrol was while retreating from the Umm el Arenab fort (see page 64). Extracting vehicles was hot, hard work. Sand would be dug away from the wheels and metal sand channels or canvas mats inserted to give the tyres traction. Note the Boys .55 cal anti-tank rifle mounted in the rear of the truck.

it wasn't there at all. We are in some stony hills and the Captain has gone to look for the place. We are going to do some maintenance on the trucks.

12.30pm The Captain and the wireless truck have just returned from having found the place about 31km west of where the map showed it. He said he wouldn't bother to take us there. Apparently the only population there were three Senegalese soldiers who were guarding the wells. As soon as they saw the trucks they put their rifles to their shoulders, but the Captain called out in Arabic and French that they were friends not enemies and they lowered their rifles. The Captain gave them some cigarettes and bully beef and they were quite satisfied. They had a little garden where they grew everything they ate, but they had no fruit to sell and anyhow, our money wouldn't be any good to them. One well was only 12 feet deep and had lovely water in it. There was also a reserve well about 100 feet deep.

7.00pm We left here at 4.30pm, but before we did, the Captain explained that we are now as far away as we are going, and so we will now travel east-north-east until we get near Uweinat, which is about 450km from here. We will meet W and R Patrols there and have a go at taking the place. We are supposed to meet W in about three days time. We have travelled 2,245km *[1,404 miles]* since we left Abbassia, but we probably won't travel as far as that going back. By the way, I forgot to mention that Dan Ormond, our sergeant and troop leader, brought me my morning tea in bed. What a war!!!!

23 SEPTEMBER 1940 *8.00pm* We went off E.N.E. at about 6.15am and travelled 112km until lunch time, over wonderful going. We are now taking things fairly easy as we have nothing to do until we meet the rest of the LRP near Uweinat on Wednesday (today being Monday), so we have plenty of time. This morning we found an old stone bowl and a stone about half the length of a rolling pin and about twice as thick. The Captain thinks it was used for grinding corn and this must be the site of an ancient village. This afternoon those who carried revolvers had a bit of shooting practice (again in Libyan territory). We also tried out some hand grenades which had been captured from the Italians in previous fights. They explode on impact, but are not much good.

This evening the pots were boiling for the first cup of tea. I made the tea. One of the pots had a broken handle and while carrying it to the truck the broken handle slipped out of my hand, with the result I got boiling tea over both legs from just below the knee downwards. However, Dan Ormond set about putting some stuff on them and bandaged them up and at present they don't feel as bad as they might have been. After we finished tea, the Captain wanted to see what the flare grenades were like when fired. When one of those goes off it shows for 100 miles or more and yet the Captain calmly asked Cyril Hewson *[Cpl. C D Hewson]* to fire one in the middle of Libya, only about 200 miles from Uweinat which we are going to attack. However, he was very pleased with it. It stayed alight for a long time and lit up the countryside wonderfully well.

24 September 1940 *5.30am* My legs aren't very sore this morning and I slept quite well. There was a bit of excitement this morning. We were just finishing breakfast when one man reckoned he saw a flare go up. He reported it to the Captain, who gave orders to pack up immediately – not even to issue water. While we were packing up, another flare appeared about 20km away and shortly after that, a third one. After that it was too light for flares. The Captain has gone away in his truck and the wireless truck to investigate. Meanwhile, we have scattered out and are waiting for their return.

We are quite keen to meet up with an Italian patrol or something, as W Patrol have captured one or more trucks and some prisoners. We don't like the idea of returning with nothing.

9.00am The Captain and the wireless truck have now been away three and a quarter hours. So Mary has decided that two troops will go and look for him. Our troop is stopping behind. T9 is the only truck left with a sun compass, so it will stay behind. My truck is going instead. Well, our guns are ready for action, so off we go.

1.00pm We travelled about 2 kilometres before we met the Captain returning. So once again we had got all ready for action for nothing. He had gone about 100 kilometres and hadn't seen any sign of tracks, so we reckon the man who thought he saw the flares had better not have so much rum in the future. Well, we have travelled 98km this morning and are now about 130km from where we have to meet W at noon tomorrow. We didn't stop for lunch until 12.30pm today, as we were late starting. At 12 o'clock we tried out the machine-guns to make sure they were all firing properly.

12 midnight I have just come on picquet for an hour. We travelled another 73km after 4pm, over good going, making a total of 171 for the day. We are about 60km from our rendezvous and only about 90km from Uweinat, the place we hope to take and where we know are two aerodromes. Yet when we stopped here, the Captain said we could light a fire to boil up. We don't quite know how we plan to take this place, but it appears that there will be one patrol for each aerodrome and the other for the village itself. The RAF is going to take some part in it, but how, we don't know yet. My legs aren't too bad tonight. I see by the bandage that one blister had burst, but as long as I keep the bandage on it will be OK.

25 September 1940 *3.00pm* Things are starting to get interesting now. A message came through from W last night which didn't make sense when decoded. Presumably our operator received it wrong or the W Patrol operator sent it wrong, so every hour today, our operator has been trying to get W – so far with no success. We set off this morning at 7.30am and could see Uweinat Mountain, which is 6,000 ft high. We travelled for a while on good going, but as we got nearer to Uweinat, the Captain decided we would be less conspicuous if we kept to the sand dunes. However, we weren't in there long before he decided it was too soft. I got stuck twice. When we came out, we seemed very close to the mountain, as we could see the jagged surface quite plainly. You can imagine my surprise when Mary told me that there was an aerodrome between us and the mountain. They were relying on the mirages to hide us from the enemy.

Well, we came on again and at 11.45am arrived at our rendezvous, which is in plain view of the mountain, but amongst a few bushes. We parked the truck by the biggest bush we could find and set about putting the camouflage over it. When we had done that we got lunch ready and after that we settled down in a shady spot for a smoke before going to sleep. I had just about finished my cigarette when I saw a movement in the bush about a yard away from me. I looked up and saw a snake coming towards us. I called, "Look out, snakes!" to the two who were with me. Fred Kendall *[Tpr. F Kendall]* picked up a shovel and made a single swipe at it and cut off its head with the first blow. We then grabbed it by the tail and pulled it out into the open. It was 4 feet 6 inches long and about 2 inches across and sandy in colour. We took it to the Captain, but he didn't know what it was. I asked him if it was poisonous and he said, "I don't know, but you had a chance to find out." We went back and looked at its head and saw that it had two fangs inside its mouth. I wouldn't care to have been bitten by it. No one could sleep on the ground after that.

It is now 3pm and there is still no sign of W or R Patrols. They were due here midday. I suppose they have struck some soft stuff like we did. I hope nothing has happened to them. They may have said something about it in that message last night, but we couldn't get them on the air again. We got W on the air at 6pm and they repeated the same message over again, so the Captain signalled back in plain English: "Your message is indecipherable!" So they are going to check it at the other end and call up at 10pm.

Lt F B Edmundson, LRDG
medical officer

26 SEPTEMBER 1940 There was a bit of excitement at 11pm last night. I was awakened by a yell: "Hey, wake up everyone, the truck's on fire!!"

I sat up and looked round and saw the camouflage on Tom McGarry's *[Tpr. T J McGarry]* truck burning. There was a rush to get slippers, as there were too many prickles to go barefooted. We grabbed a shovel and rushed over to the truck, still yelling. As McGarry continued to sleep on the top of his truck, some started beating the flames with the shovels, others throwing sand on the tyres. One man grabbed McGarry's blankets, pulled them off and started beating the flames with them, yet McGarry slept on. When the fire was nearly out, he suddenly woke and was out of that truck before you could say "knife!" It certainly takes a lot to wake McGarry. However, we got the fire out before the truck was damaged.

They got W Patrol on air again last night and received the message: "Originator's apologies, message indecipherable", and gave a new rendezvous on the other side of Uweinat, in Egyptian territory. So at 6am this morning we set off round the mountain and while doing so, we travelled in three countries: Libya, Sudan and Egypt. We arrived at the new rendezvous at midday, after travelling 189km in four hours including several stops, one being about 20 minutes. We averaged about 45 kph which was very good going.

We then had lunch and our siesta, and were just about to have our afternoon tea when W and R came over a rise. They camped about a kilometre away. After I had my tea, I went over and met them, and of course they told us about the capture of the trucks etc. They captured four trucks carrying 2,500 gallons of benzine, a lot of medical supplies and some shirts and mats etc. They were not Army trucks, but merchant trucks supplying the Italians. They also found two bags of mail which will be of high value to the authorities. Nearly everyone got souvenirs. One man had the front number plate and another the rear plate of the truck, whose registration number was Libya 1314, which is my regimental number. I will try and get it off him. They got four prisoners who seemed quite happy except one who was married, but he will be allowed to write and explain his absence to his wife.

The back of Tom McGarry's truck after the fire. It was fortunate the flames were put out before the stored fuel and ammunition exploded. A Boys anti-tank rifle is mounted on the crossbar.

The prisoners informed them that the Italians had just sent 6,250 soldiers to Uweinat, including a battalion of machine-guns. Major Bagnold has decided not to attack it, but reckons that it will be more to our advantage to attack their convoys. The indecipherable message they sent us was, "Keep clear of rendezvous," and there we were – for a day and a night. We even lit a fire at night, only 20km from the aerodrome. W Patrol saw two planes which also saw them, but didn't drop any bombs. They know we have been there and it will probably cause them a bit of worry.

Two of the Italian trucks which were big 6-wheeled Fiats have gone to Cairo. Major Bagnold came along their tracks and reckons he saw some Italian trucks near them, so we have to follow their tracks tomorrow to make sure they get home. On my way back from W Patrol I called in at R and saw the doctor *[Dr. F B Edmundson]* about my legs. He was very pleased with their condition, for although they had blisters and burst, the skin still covered them. He reckons I was very lucky as they could have been a lot worse.

27 SEPTEMBER 1940 *7.00pm* We set out this morning for Abbassia. W and R are going home direct. We set out to pick up the tracks of the trucks that have already gone home just to make sure they get there. We travelled about 100km north before we picked up their tracks, and shortly after that we had to go through a mountain range via a pass. It was the only way through without going a long way around the mountains. It was where the Captain thought the Italians might have waited in ambush for the other trucks to come through, but the three sets of tracks were still going when we got through. That pass was about the roughest place we have been yet. It was a steep climb with soft going and boulders strewn all over the track. Twice we had to back down a hill to get a good run at it before we could get up. We eventually stopped for lunch at 12.45pm. after doing 150km. We had lunch with lime juice, then had a cup of tea and set off again at 2pm, still following the three tracks. We stopped again at 5.15pm, and as one truck with carburettor trouble hadn't arrived yet, the Captain decided to stop for the night.

◦ **28 SEPTEMBER 1940** ◦ *1.00pm* We struck W and R tracks at about 9am and have followed them all morning. If the Italians had seen those marks after we had passed, they would have thought the whole British Army were coming. Actually there are only 35 trucks, but it looked as though there were a lot more. We have now stopped for lunch after travelling 218km over fairly rough country, and at the speed we were travelling, I would call it very rough. 218km is the largest morning mileage we have ever done and we ought to break our daily record quite comfortably too. We are leaving again at 2pm.

8.00pm We have stopped for the night after doing 336km, which is easily our biggest mileage for one day. The Captain reckons that we will get to Dalla by lunch time tomorrow. It is about 240km, so it sounds like a pretty late lunch time. He says it is all good going from now on, so it may be all right yet.

◦ **29 SEPTEMBER 1940** ◦ *11.00am* We have now done 168km and I've seen none of the Captain's "good going" yet. The first half was soft stony country and we were in 3rd gear all

Filling 4-gallon water tins at Ain Dalla. This was a regular water re-supply point for all the patrols

the way. The last 80km was over good hard sand dunes, but every now and then they had huge ripples which you couldn't see till you were right on top of them. There have been a few soft patches too and we are now waiting for a truck that got stuck.

3.00pm After stopping for lunch, we set off again at 1.30pm and did another 40km in about ¾ hour over great going. It was like riding on a 'switchback railway.' Up and down at 80 to 90km. However, the last two kilometres were very soft and flat going, and five out of the 11 trucks got stuck. I wasn't one of them. We are now at Dalla. There is no population here – only a couple of date palms and only one of them has dates on it and they aren't ripe. There is plenty of water and we don't have to lower a bucket to get it, as there is a pipe leading from the well, which is on top of a rise. It comes halfway down the hill, so we have running water all the time. Of course there was a rush for the water, not because everyone was thirsty, but because they wanted a wash. I must say we had the best wash since we left Abbassia, as we could use the pipe as a shower by kneeling down. I feel miles better now.

The Captain has taken his own and two other trucks about 30km away to get some

Difficult 'going' through the mountains; also good country for both hiding and setting ambushes. The LRDG used the term 'going' to describe the nature of the terrain.

benzine from a camp that the Marmon-Herringtons made. I suppose they will be back about 4.30pm. When he comes back, he wants to leave here and travel about 20km, so as to get on top of some hills and have straight going in the morning. But because there is some soft sand between here and there, he reckons we may have trouble getting through.

8.00pm It was about 5.00pm when they came back with the benzine and it was about 5.30 before we got going. We have travelled 26km over soft going all the way, but didn't strike any trouble until the final climb of the day. Then only three trucks got struck again and I wasn't one of them. Well, we have had our tea and I am now off to bed.

30 SEPTEMBER 1940 *12.30pm* This morning was the roughest riding we have had yet. How the trucks stood up to it I don't know. We have now done 120km and we have been bumping and twisting ever since we left this morning and we have been travelling far too fast for the condition of the track. We have now stopped for lunch and I sincerely hope that this afternoon will be better going.

8.00pm We have now finished our tea after travelling another 110km over country very nearly as bad as this morning, but not quite. I am now very tired after doing what I consider to be the hardest day's work since I have been in the Army and believe me, I am ready for bed.

A Cairo street. Jopling enjoyed his leave by going to the pictures, learning Arabic and sightseeing. (Ellis)

1 OCTOBER 1940 *12.30pm* This morning we travelled 267km, which is our record morning mileage. Last night we camped near Mushroom Rock, the place we went to on the five-day stunt and we left there at 6.15am this morning. It was fairly rough going for a while and then got fairly good, but not for long. The last 100 kilometres have been very good going and we have been able to do 60km in an hour. We have now stopped for lunch on a hill from where we can see the three pyramids. We were all glad to see them, as we are just about ready for a spell. We are now going to have a quick lunch and then carry on again.

7.00pm We arrived in Abbassia at 2.30. Everybody stared at our beards as we came through Cairo. When we arrived in Abbassia we had to look for our new barracks, which are in the Isolation Hospital. We eventually found it and parked our trucks on the ground already provided. We got our kit bags and we were shown to our quarters, which turned out to be pretty good. We sorted ourselves out, one troop to a room, and got our beds ready. We then collected our letter mail. I received 19 letters. We don't get our parcels till tomorrow, but I hear there are several for me. It took me about four hours to read all the letters and it was great after being out in the desert for four weeks to come back to all that.

Narrow street in the Muski Bazaar area, Cairo (MacGibbon)

Well, as anyone would gather from reading this, we have all thoroughly enjoyed the trip and are looking forward to the next one, although the next will probably not be as free from action as that one. We had of course broken a lot of records and done what the 'Heads' reckoned would be impossible. No 30 cwt truck had ever crossed the Sand Sea, yet our patrol with R had 20 trucks between us, as we went over as one convoy.

We travelled 2,000km into enemy territory which is also a record, and while there, we travelled where no white man has ever been before, over country that had never been mapped. Between them, Tony Browne our navigator and the Captain made a pretty precise map. You would imagine the surprise the Italians would get when they saw our tracks and when they found that four of their trucks were missing.

We have just been paid £1 at the orderly room and Major Bagnold gave a speech and said that the General had asked him to convey his thanks to the LRP for the wonderful work they had done. The General will write a personal letter of thanks which will be posted on the notice board.

I am now going to have a hot bath, then to go to the barber to get a haircut, shave and shampoo, after which I will feel a lot better. We will probably have a lot of work to do on the trucks during the next few days, then have a couple of days' leave before we go off to war again.

2 October 1940 This morning we had to take all the benzine and water off the truck and then set about cleaning the Lewis gun, the Boys gun, rifles and revolvers. At lunch time they issued the parcels. I got four parcels and some newspapers from home. This afternoon we went down to the store and unloaded everything off the truck. This evening I went to the pictures and saw 'A Man to Remember', which was a very good serious picture.

3 October 1940 This morning we took our trucks down to the store and cleaned them out and then checked over all the tools etc. This afternoon 11 trucks went to Cairo to Universal Motors to have one or two things done to them and I took my truck in to bring the drivers back. This evening I went to an Aussie show at the Slade Club and it was very good, but I had to come away at half time to go on picquet from 10 to 12pm.

4 October 1940 This morning I started to take the head off my truck and at 11.30 we got paid and had the rest of the day off. I went into Cairo to look for some suitable presents to send home, but came back without anything.

5 October 1940 12 months today since I went into camp at Hopu Hopu and I haven't seen an enemy yet. This morning I finished taking the head off the truck and it will be all ready to start on Monday. We had this afternoon off, so I went into Cairo again. I arrived back in camp at 10pm.

6 October 1940 There were no parades today and we heard that we were getting four days leave – 10 from each patrol on Tuesday, another 10 on Saturday and the rest the following Wednesday. This afternoon I went into Cairo again and when I came back there were three letters waiting for me, one with 10/- in it.

7 October 1940 This morning I ground the valves of my truck and in the afternoon I cleaned the engine. This evening I went to bed early. They decided to send us on leave in two lots instead of three, but as the head is still off my truck I couldn't go with the first lot.

8 October 1940 Today I put the truck together again and, strange as it may seem, it went. But I haven't finished it yet. This evening I decided to go into Cairo and look for somewhere to stay on my leave. I decided I would like to stay at an expensive hotel for a couple of nights to see if I would still be a 'gentleman'. I enquired at three hotels and they all said that no soldiers were allowed, only officers. When I asked them why, they said, "Because they drink too much and make too much noise." It didn't make any difference when I told them that I didn't drink. I suppose they couldn't believe that a man could be a soldier and not drink.

9-20 OCTOBER 1940 *Jopling spent time on leave and carrying out base duties. As a personal interest while on leave, he started to learn Arabic, because he wanted to get to understand the locals better. This was to prove very useful out in the desert, and two years later it probably saved his life when Arabs rescued him after a long foot trek. Truck maintainance was continued and preparations were made for their next trip.*

⁌21 OCTOBER 1940⁌ Today we finished everything that needed to be done to the truck and we are all ready to load up tomorrow. Ever since Freyberg *[Maj.Gen. B C Freyberg, C-in-C NZ Division]* arrived back from England on September 30th, he has been trying to get us back to the NZ Division, but Captain Clayton reckons we needn't worry – we won't be going back.

⁌22 OCTOBER 1940⁌ We were all very busy today loading our trucks to be ready to move off tomorrow. We are putting 35 cases of benzine on, which is about 25 cwt for a start. Major R Bagnold is now a Lt. Colonel, Capt. E Mitford, W Patrol, is now Major, and Lt. D G Steele, R Patrol, is now Captain.

⁌23 OCTOBER 1940⁌ We were supposed to leave Abbassia at 2pm, but didn't get started until about 4pm. Lt. Col. Bagnold spoke to us just before we left and said General Wavell

A HQ Chevrolet WB 'Matai' stuck in soft sand. Note the contrasting camouflage pattern often found in the early trucks.

always takes a very keen interest in our work. Well, naturally we didn't get very far, as it was 4pm when we started. We travelled 41km, which was far enough to get out of sight of the pyramids.

This evening Captain Clayton gave us a lecture on what we had to do on the trip. We are going north of Kufra – between Kufra and a place called Jalo. There we are to find a narrow part of the road and lay some mines. Then we will look for the most likely alternative route, where they would probably go after they found the road was mined, and lay more mines there. We will then pass close to Jalo and travel north to two more wells which have a small force guarding them. These we will probably take, and capture as many prisoners as we can. We will then make our way home as fast as possible, arriving in Abbassia on November 7th.

One of our aeroplanes will join us when we get to the other side of the Sand Sea. If possible, they don't want to get into combat with an Italian plane, as our plane is more a troop transport and will be used for taking prisoners or any wounded back to barracks. So we are apparently going to see a bit of excitement on this trip. Captain Clayton read a letter from the Italian C.O. at Jalo. This letter was in the mail on the trucks we captured last trip. It described in detail the number of troops and armaments they had there, right down to two Very pistols, one of which was broken.

The Vickers Valentia flies over an LRP radio truck. On the right of the vehicle is the Wyndom aerial, which much improved radio communication over long distances.

⌐**24 October 1940**⌐ This morning the Captain reckoned that he wasn't in any hurry, so we did a bit of navigation training on our way. But this afternoon went as fast a ever and we finished up by travelling 240km for the day. We are now not very far N.E. of Mushroom Rock.

⌐**25 October 1940**⌐ The Captain is still apparently in no hurry because this morning he and the wireless truck went on about three kilometres and for practice we had to attack them from three flanks. It turned out to be a victory for us!

8.00pm The news is on, so I will grab the opportunity to write this up. We have travelled 196km today over rough country, practically the same country as we travelled over on September 30th. We are now about 90km from Dalla.

⌐**26 October 1940**⌐ *12 noon* Well, we are now at Dalla once again and thank goodness for that. Gosh, it's rough from Mushroom Rock to Dalla. We are filling up all available water tins and will be away again at about 2pm.

There is no sign of W Patrol this trip. They have been split up between T and R patrols and a few to Lt. Kennedy Shaw. He has four trucks in his party and they are going to climb a hill near Uweinat and sit and watch for a day or two. R Patrol is going to lay some mines south of Kufra and then they will drive the Italians trucks they had previously hidden back to Cairo.

7.00pm We are now on the edge of the Sand Sea and we will at last get a bit of smooth travelling. We are crossing the Sand Sea on practically the same route that W took last trip.

27 October 1940 We fired the anti-tank guns and the machine-guns before we started off this morning, just to make sure they were working all right. By the way, one of the machine-guns is a heavy Vickers. It is mounted on the Captain's truck. Well, we set off again at about 8am, intending to travel about 300km, which is the distance from where we started this morning to the place where W made a dump on the other side of the Sand Sea. I am afraid there have been too many sticks, including myself. I got stuck three times. However, we did 165km and from here to the dump is a lot better going, according to the Captain. Tonight I am on picquet.

28 October 1940 Today we travelled 60km over real good going and arrived at Big Cairn dump at 10am. We filled up the trucks with a load of benzine and marked out a landing zone for the aeroplane. We then camped near the landing ground, camouflaged the trucks and sat down to wait for the aeroplane to arrive. It was due at 3pm, and sure enough on the tick of three the plane appeared in sight and made a perfect landing. It had brought out some mail for us and that is the first time mail has ever been delivered in the Sand Sea. Incidentally, a letter written to me on Sept. 8th was the first one handed out, so I actually received the first letter ever delivered in the Sand Sea.

We all went out and inspected the plane *[a Vickers Valentia of 216 Squadron, RAF]* and at 4.30pm we had to make the tea. The plane followed our tracks at an altitude of 600 feet and spotted our trucks 15 miles away, which shows that our camouflage isn't very effective. We are staying here the night and moving off in the morning. At 8pm we listened to the news and heard that Italy had invaded Greece. It is quite good news, as it will probably bring Turkey into the war and possibly Russia. However, things must start popping now.

29 October 1940 I found out today that yesterday was the first time that the Sand Sea had been crossed by plane. We set off this morning over – to use the Captain's own words – "The best going God made." We did 120 kilometres in the first two hours and got into the Libyan Sand Sea by lunch time. From then on the progress was pretty slow, as the going was soft and there was a sandstorm blowing. We finished up the day doing 275km.

30 October 1940 The maps of this part of the world are total blanks. There is absolutely nothing on them except the longitudes and latitudes and as far as is known, no human being has ever crossed here and I don't blame them. Today has been the hardest travelling we have had yet, and at one place at lunch time the Captain thought we would have to give it up and try further south. However, some of the men managed to pursuade him to let us have another go at it after lunch. Six of us got through without getting stuck and, by using eight sand trays, we managed to get the others through also. Today we have travelled 130km and we are only 30km nearer to Jalo than we were this morning . The Captain says we will be a day late getting there, but the Italians won't mind that. He wants to get there at the end of Ramadan, after which the Muslims feast. While they are feasting, the Captain reckons they will be tired and half drunk.

31 October 1940 We got through the Sand Sea at about 10am and from then on, we had some wonderful travelling and finished up by doing 324 kilometres. We travelled north-west nearly all day and arrived at the main road that runs north and south just as it was getting dark. We saw a signpost which said 180 miles to Jalo and we were that far north of Jalo – even north of Aujila. We then cut back on our tracks for about five kilometres and camped for the night. There was a strong icy cold wind blowing which made things rather unpleasant, and for the first time since we have been on this job we weren't allowed to light a fire. However, having put one tarpaulin up the side of the truck to act as a wind break and another spread above between two trucks to prevent aircraft from spotting us, we got three primus stoves going and it didn't take us much longer to get the tea ready than when we had fires.

1 November 1940 Well, we have started off the month with a day full of events and I will try and put the time down with them.

5.00am We have had breakfast and we are just about to move off. The cold wind is still blowing and everyone is wearing all the warm clothing they brought with them including overcoats, and we are still cold.

7.00am We set off for the road again and when we struck it, we headed north. We travelled for about 80km and laid some mines across the road. At this point we were only about 60 miles off the coast and could smell the sea air. When these mines are discovered the Captain reckons the Italians will think a landing party has landed off one of the battleships. While we were laying the mines a cry went up of, "Two trucks coming over the hill!!" When we looked up, we saw two black objects going away from us over a hill. So the Captain ordered Mary to take his troop and circle round and try and come in behind them. He was away for about half an hour and when he came back he said he had seen plenty of camels, but no sign of any trucks.

10.00am We travelled west for a while and then turned south. Once again we came on the road and travelled south. We were then heading for an oasis called Aujila which has quite a large Arab population. We knew there was a fort there, but we didn't know how many soldiers there were or what weapons they had. However, we carried on down the road, crossing many new tracks. Some were from cars and some were dual tyred tracks, mostly from trucks. We then came slowly over a rise and saw acres and acres of trees and palms.

We carried on, keeping out of range of any guns that might be hidden there. We saw some Arabs with their camels on our left, but we were more interested in the scores of tracks made by dual-tyred trucks. We followed them and they led down to the bottom of the basin where there was a road crossing it. A beautiful place to lay mines. We all got on to the road and laid mines behind our last vehicle, in full view of what we then thought was a fort, but later discovered was someone's tomb. It was in full view of the village and the camel train that was coming towards us. So you can quite imagine we didn't waste any time in putting the mines down.

We then went to the other end of the road and did the same there. After that, we went to the top of the rise and waited for the last trucks to come up. While we were waiting, an Arab came over the hill. Of course a yell went up to the Captain and he went forward to meet him, while we were ready for any treachery. They talked for about 20 minutes and it was then that we found out that what we had thought was a fort, was someone's tomb. When they had finished talking, the Captain called for my truck and we gave the Arab some tea. He told the Captain that the fort was about 10 kilometres west of where we were. He used to be in the army and although he no longer was, he had to report any vehicles that passed through there. He noticed that we had stopped on the road and said that it was an easy road to get stuck on. I don't know whether he believed our story or not.

1.30pm From there we headed north west for about five kilometres and came upon another road, so we laid some mines there. We then carried on south and before very long we came upon another basin of trees and palms and some more Arab buildings. We stopped before we went over the ridge because a lot of dual-tyred tracks had converged into a narrow roadway. So once again we put some mines down. The Captain knew we had been spotted from the fort, so naturally he was in a hurry to lay the mines.

We had just finished and were starting to move forward when a native soldier came over the ridge giving the Italian salute, thinking we were an Italian colonel and his escort or something. As soon as he got close to the truck, 'Clarrie' Roderick *[Cpl. L Roderick]* fixed his bayonet and jumped off, pointing rifle and bayonet at the soldier who nearly dropped with fright, but managed to put his hands above his head.

The Captain first put the soldier up on his truck, but afterwards put him on mine. He told us there were five men in the fort, but only two soldiers, both Italian sergeants. So we went to the top of a rise which was about 600 yards away, and opened fire on the fort with the

Bofors gun, Boys rifles and machine-guns. Believe me, I wouldn't have wanted to be in the fort while that bombardment was on. We fired seven shells with the Bofors gun and every one was a hit. We then saw the occupants of the fort run down into the palms and then into the village.

Three trucks went to the fort and collected two machine-guns, three rifles and one revolver. There were also about twenty swords, but they only took two of the best. The Captain reckoned he could have captured the two soldiers down in the village by holding the head of the village hostage until they were handed over. However, he said that would take some time and now that job had been done he wanted to get out of it. His orders were to bring a prisoner back if possible, and now that we had one we ought to be satisfied.

We left there at 1.30pm and headed for home until 4.30 when the V8 broke a back axle. Rather than fix it, the Captain got another truck to tow it until 6pm. We camped for the night, having travelled 404km. It has been very cold all day and I didn't have my jersey off at all. I had my greatcoat on most of the day. The prisoner wouldn't eat anything except a dry biscuit and a cup of tea. R Patrol was bombed today, south of Kufra

2 NOVEMBER 1940 I was wakened out of my slumber at 1.15am this morning and told that breakfast was ready, which consisted of a cup of tea and a biscuit. The fitters had fixed the V8 during the night and we were on our way again by 2.15am. It was bitterly cold. We used our headlights all the way and arrived on the edge of the Libyan Sand Sea just as the sun was rising over the top of the dunes. Just inside the Sand Sea we boiled the billy and had a proper breakfast. After the meal we set off across the Sand Sea and did we have some thrills!!

We went down a few hills that were very nearly perpendicular and on one occasion I went over a low one too fast and took off, but the only damage I did was to bend the tie rod. I put a jack under it and it straightened out pretty well. We crossed the Sand Sea and did about another 50km before we camped for the night. We finished up doing 356km – wonderful going, considering we had crossed the Libyan Sand Sea.

3 NOVEMBER 1940 The Captain's truck, the wireless truck and Cyril Hewson's truck left us this morning. The Captain wanted to find out just where the south end of the Sand Sea ended. He reckoned he would meet us where we camped for the night. So Mary took charge of us and led us to the dump we had established on our first trip out. We arrived there at 12 noon, dumped some of the benzine we had kept on board and kept just enough to get us to the Dalla dump. We travelled on about 20km and stopped for lunch, then set off across the Egyptian Sand Sea. By sundown we were well over half way across and camped for the night. The three trucks that left us this morning didn't turn up. Today we travelled 300km.

◦**4 NOVEMBER 1940**◦ We set off again this morning at 7am and decided to get as far as the Dalla dump and wait there for the Captain and his party. We arrived at 11am after being stuck once, then loaded with six cases of benzine and filled the tank. The Marmon-Herringtons had delivered this while we had been in Libya. Mary sent three trucks on to Dalla with 50 gallon tins to fill with water while we waited for the Captain and his party to turn up. Meanwhile, we greased up the trucks and tightened all nuts ready for the rough trip we had ahead of us between Dalla and Cairo.

The Captain turned up at 12 noon minus the V8, which had broken the new axle in exactly the same place as the other one. As there were no more new axles, we decided to leave the vehicle there camouflaged, and pick it up some other time. It had only travelled about 30km from where they left us, so it was well inside Libya, but they reckon the Italians won't spot it.

They also told us that they tried to contact the aeroplane on the wireless last night, but without result. Either our wireless was out of order or the plane's one was. When the two trucks had loaded up we set off for Dalla which was about 30km away. We arrived at 1pm and set about getting lunch ready. When we had finished, our next item was to have a good wash. We went to where the water came out of the pipe and found that some enterprising people, presumably the Marmon-Herrington crowd, had made a beautiful bath there. So we stripped off and had a wonderful bathe. We then had our photos taken together with the prisoner, the machine-guns, the swords and the signpost. Altogether they should make a good photo.

The water pipe at Ain Dalla, turned into a cooling bath by building up the sides with empty four-gallon tins. Frank Jopling stands on the right.

We then set off on our rough journey home – the journey that I always dread. However, up to tonight the trip has been pretty good, as we travelled on a new track across the sand dunes. I must say we saw some wonderful country. Also today, one of our trucks burned out a clutch by backing down a hill with the clutch pushed in and then letting it out while travelling too fast. The fitter reckoned it would take half a day to fix, so the Captain decided to leave Dan Ormond's fitter's truck with the disabled vehicle and enough rations to get home. They will follow on when they are ready. We finished up the day by doing 215km.

◦**5 NOVEMBER 1940**◦ We again set off this morning at 7am across the rotten rough going. It seems to get rougher each time we cross it. The Captain has been driving the wireless truck since the V8 broke down, so he hasn't been travelling quite as fast as he did last time he came here. When we passed Mushroom Rock at 4pm, the roughest part of the journey was over, although the rest of the way is quite rough enough. The wireless truck which the

Captain was driving got a puncture on the way, so we had to stop and change the tyre. We are about 250km from Abbassia, so we will arrive back quite comfortably tomorrow afternoon. We have finished up today doing 271km.

We are all very worried whether we will be coming out on another trip or not. When Freyberg arrived back from England, he was as wild as anything when he had heard that we had left the NZ Division to come on this job. At the time we were under General Wavell and Freyberg had nothing to do with us at all. He went to General Wavell and all he heard from that quarter was that we were doing good work here and we would stay. So Freyberg sent a protest to the NZ Government. The Government said that all New Zealand soldiers came under the command of General Freyberg.

Mary said that three days before we left for this trip, all our officers were told we had done our last trip and we would not be going out again. However, we did! We then heard that Freyberg had said that we would eventually go back to our units, but not until we had trained the Tommies *[the British]*. However, the fight is still going on and all the officers in this outfit and General Wavell are fighting for us. Just what the outcome will be, we don't know. We would all be very sorry to go back to our units, as we have pioneered this job and we are making a name for New Zealand. The English officers here reckon they won't be able to carry on this job with just Tommies.

The new LRDG barracks were at Cairo's Citadel. (MacGibbon)

6 November 1940 We set off again this morning at 6.30am and travelled 240km by lunch time, when we came within sight of the pyramids. After lunch the prisoner was shifted on to another truck, as he would be leaving us when we got on the road. The Captain thought that as we were the ration truck, we had better carry straight on home. When we got to the turn-off, the Captain took the prisoner to an Arab battalion and Mary took over command.

After crossing the Kasr-el-Nil bridge, the driver of the front truck suddenly applied the brakes. The truck behind me crashed into the rear of my truck, damaging his mudguard and radiator, but was able to carry on. When we arrived back at the barracks there were letters and papers from Irene awaiting me. We got paid and had a good spruce-up. Our trip had covered 3,405 kilometres, which is just on 2,000 miles, an average of 1,000 miles per week.

7-22 November 1940 Trooper Jopling remained at base, maintaining his truck, writing letters and attending semaphore training. Vehicle and troop inspections were carried out by Major Bagnold.

23 November-4 December 1940 T Patrol transported benzine to foward dumps, which involved the usual difficult crossing of the Great Sand Sea, with vehicle break-downs and getting stuck. While in Libya they also laid mines on the roads and distributed thousands of pamphlets in Arabic inciting the Arabs to make trouble on Libya. On 5 December they returned to new barracks, as Jopling explained.

5-6 December 1940 We are changing barracks, this time to the Citadel in Cairo. They intend to make the LRDG bigger by including Tommies. We don't like the sound of it much, as we think that after we have trained all these Tommies we may be sent back to our units. We know that one officer and several of our NCOs are going back on the 14th. Some of them are going to their units and the others to some training depot. We have found out there will no longer be a W Patrol. They are going to be split up between R and T Patrols and the Tommies are taking over their trucks.

7-25 December 1940 A period of settling into their new base and driving into the sand dunes to train the newly-formed British G [Guards] Patrol. This patrol was made up of volunteers from the 3rd Battalion of the Coldstream and the 2nd Battalion. of the Scots Guards, under the command of Captain M D Crichton-Stuart. W Patrol was now disbanded and several of its men returned to their original units and were posted to Greece. The balance of the personnel were reassigned to R and T Patrols.

FEZZAN CAMPAIGN

The LRDG's next operation was to be in conjunction with the Free French Forces of the Chad Province. The plan was to undertake a series of raids on the Italian forts and garrisons of the Fezzan, in south west Libya. The main objective was Murzuk, the capital of the Fezzan. It was 2,150 kilometres from the Group's base in Cairo and 560 kilometres from the nearest French post in the Tibesti Mountains. On 26 December 1940, the newly-promoted Major P A Clayton led the 76 men of T and G Patrols in a column of 24 vehicles. They crossed the Egyptian and Kalansho sand seas and headed into unknown country to the north-west of Kufra. Trooper Jopling described the operation.

26 December 1940 This morning we packed up and placed what we didn't need in the store. Capt. Clayton has now been promoted to major, but I think he will still be known to the boys as 'the Skipper'. We left at 2.30pm and got within sight of the first dunes by tea time. After tea, the Skipper gave us his usual first-night talk on the object of our trip. This time we have the newly formed Guards Patrol *[G Patrol]* with us and we are going down into French territory to pick up French troops who want to have a go at 'Musso'. From there we head north and attack four places. Then we visit a few places back in French territory and head home.

The whole trip is scheduled to take us six weeks, but if the war is not over out here, and everything is going alright up north, we may take three months. This time we have two Arabs from the Arab army with us. One is sort of a prince among the Arabs. They will be used partly as interpreters and as an inducement for the Libyans to surrender.

It is now 7.30pm and three trucks of G Patrol were still missing, so the Skipper went looking for them and brought them back. Apparently one truck had carburettor trouble. The OC of G Patrol is Captain M D Crichton-Stuart and the 2IC is Lieutenant M A Gibbs, of Gibbs Dentrifice. We don't like either of them, but we don't have anything to do with them so it doesn't matter much. The Skipper is in charge of both patrols.

27 December 1940 We set off this morning at 7.30, and at 3.30 we had to wait for an hour for G Patrol. We stopped for lunch after doing 132km, started again after lunch and covered 230km until we camped at 5pm. It rained last night and we all thought it would be a downpour, but luckily there were only a few drops.

28 December 1940 Evidently the Skipper wants to reach Dalla tonight as he has been going flat out over very rough country since 1pm. At one stop we had to wait one hour for G Patrol, as they had more trouble. Now we have stopped for lunch. One of our trucks is left

A column of trucks spread out to avoid being stuck together in patches of soft sand.

behind with carburettor trouble and G Patrol's food truck hasn't turned up yet. I have never been missing at a meal time yet.

2.15pm The other trucks have just arrived and as soon as they have their lunch, we will be on our way again.

5.30pm We have now camped for the night just where the 'Whites' [*Heavy Section supply trucks*] made a dump before going down into the Dalla Basin, and we will now have tea.

29 December 1940 *10.00am* We have arrived at Dalla. When we set off this morning, each truck put on up to 32 cases of benzine and now we have to add four cases of water, as well as fill up our empty two-gallon tins. We have a huge load and my truck is easily carrying two and a half tons. We will be here until about 2.30pm as we have to fill all the water cases *[two 4-gallon tins per case]* and solder the caps on to stop them leaking. Also, a truck in G Patrol requires a new radiator. The Skipper thinks that we will travel about 8,000km before we reach home.

4.00pm We left at 2.30pm and had travelled about 20km when we saw a lot of trucks stuck. We got through alright and stopped on top of the hill to give them a hand. Fourteen trucks were stuck. My camera immediately went into action. We got them all through that and set off for 'Easy Ascent' where we expected to have some fun. I got slightly stuck owing to my truck being overloaded. We put a set of sand trays under it and it went straight out, in creeper gear. There are still a few on the hill, but they will be up here before long. We have now camped for the night, as it is 5.30pm and we have to prepare tea. We finished up the day by doing 63km.

30 December 1940 G Patrol is leading across the Sand Sea and we are bringing up the rear as it is harder going after 20-odd trucks have been over. We hadn't been going very long when we came across a long line of trucks that were stuck. I managed to get through without getting badly stuck. We were there for two and a half hours before we got the last truck through. We carried on and at every stop we had to wait for one or two trucks. It has been bitterly cold all day and we camped at 5pm after covering 92km. It is going to take us longer than 6 weeks to do the trip, travelling at this rate.

We heard Roosevelt's speech on the wireless tonight and it was as near to a declaration of war as anyone could get. We also heard that Germany tried to set London on fire and that the Guild Hall had been destroyed. More important still was a message from Cairo advising that W Patrol member Lt. Jim Sutherland *[Lt. J H Sutherland]* had been awarded the Military Cross and Bill Willcox *[Tpr. L A Willcox]* the Military Medal. This certainly surprised me, although I am glad they got the awards as both are great and know no fear. Those are the first decorations to be awarded to New Zealand soldiers in this war.

31 December 1940 New Year's Eve and here I am in the middle of the Sand Sea. Who would ever have thought twelve months ago that I would be spending New Year's Eve in the middle of the Egyptian Sand Sea. It is now 1.30pm and we have just had lunch. We have been in this spot since 9am. There was something wrong with the Skipper's V8 so they decided to fix it. In the meantime we have had some shooting practice.

5.30pm We left there at 2.15pm and for the last two hours have been travelling over lovely going. We finished up doing 129km and we are in sight of Big Cairn Dump.

10.00pm We had a sing-song around the old camp fire tonight, but we are not staying up to see the New Year in, which is the first time I haven't since I was about 7 years old. This trip the three of us on this truck, Eric Smith *[Tpr. E B Smith]* Pat Aislabie *[Tpr. W B Aislabie]* and myself won't do any picquet. Instead we do the cooking, which means that we have to get up at 5am every morning to get the breakfast ready.

1 JANUARY 1941 New Year's Day on the Egyptian Sand Sea. I suppose no white man has ever spent this day on the Egyptian Sand Sea before. It is now 1.30pm and after breakfast this morning some trucks went to Gravel Cairn and some to Two Hills dump. We stayed here and when the trucks came back from Two Hills, we had to sort out some rations they had brought back. After that, we got the New Year's dinner ready. You wouldn't believe that such a feed could be produced on the Sand Sea nearly 1,000 miles from Cairo. We made rissoles which were very good and plenty of them. Also we had fruit salad and iced Xmas cake with Merry Xmas on it, which were supplied by GHQ, plus three tangerines. Believe me, we felt full after all that.

This morning was the first time I ever believed there was such a thing as frost in the desert. When we got up this morning the trucks were quite white. There must have been 5 or 6 degrees of frost. We left again at 2.15pm, having almost emptied the dumps of benzine, water and rations, and set off for the Libyan Sand Sea, where we arrived at 5pm, having covered 172km of good going.

2 JANUARY 1941 There was another frost this morning, although not quite so heavy. We set off across the Libyan Sand Sea at 7.30am and hadn't been going long before one of the G Patrol trucks went over a dune too fast and took off. He burst both back tyres, broke two rails on the back of the truck and twisted the running board. In addition, the front axle was bent and a fair amount of damage was done to his load. The driver, incidentally, was the same man who drove my truck on the three-day training stint and I had warned him that he would have a smash when he got out here.

We are now camped right on the west side of the Libyan Sand Sea, about five kilometres from the Kufra-Jalo road. The Skipper is a bit worried as we have got to cross this road. We know it is watched every day by an air patrol but we don't know what time. However, we lit fires tonight, as we know they won't patrol it at night. We are going to have an early cup of tea in the morning, set off at dawn for about 100km and then have breakfast. We finished up today by doing 159km.

3 JANUARY 1941 We had a cup of tea and left at 6am just as dawn was breaking. From then until breakfast was about the coldest drive I have ever experienced. We stopped for breakfast at 8.30, having done 109km. After that we set off again, and by lunch time we found what appears to be another sand sea, or it may just be a row of dunes.

8.30pm It is a sand sea all right, and a very treacherous one too. Places which should be soft turn out hard, and places that should be hard turn out soft. We have now camped for the night, still on the sand sea and only about 70km from the first place we are going to attack. But this won't happen until the French have joined us. The Skipper says that the Italians had a go at getting through here from each end, but pronounced it impassable. However, since lunch we have travelled 85km, so we aren't doing to bad so far. We finished the day by doing 315km.

4 January 1941 The Skipper told us last night that reveille would be an half hour late this morning, so we didn't call the men until 6.30am. We were all ready to leave by 7.30am. The Skipper moved off, but had only gone about 200 yards before he was stuck. By the time he was out and we got away it was 8am. We travelled over good going for an hour when we struck the softest going we have had since we have been in the LRDG. It wasn't on the Sand Sea, as we left that after the first hour. It was more like Dalla: stony on top and soft dust underneath. I never had to use my sand trays, but nearly every other truck did.

Well, we have now arrived at a place miles from nowhere, approximately on the 18th longitude and 24th latitude, where some of us will have to wait for four or five days. Major Clayton is going on with four trucks to Kayugi to collect the French, and Lieut. Kennedy Shaw, with three trucks, is going to investigate Tereneghei Pass. The French say it is passable for trucks, but we want to find out for sure, in case we have to make a quick getaway. This truck is one of five in T Patrol which is staying here, as it is the ration truck. It is rather disappointing as I would have liked to have gone on one of the trips. However, it will be a nice rest. All G Patrol trucks are staying behind.

On our way here today, another G Patrol truck had a smash just in front of me. When I saw it I could have sworn it had turned over, but apparently it only nearly did. The man in the back was thrown out, but escaped with only a shaking. The front axle was bent and the tie rod was doubled up. However, it wasn't very long before they got it going again. We finished up by doing 234km.

5 January 1941 This morning we got up at the usual time and sorted out rations etc. for the two parties going away. They set off at 8am and are expected back January 7th or 8th. The rest of the day we just made ourselves comfortable and slept or read books and sunbathed in a warm afternoon sun.

6 January 1941 This morning we didn't get up until 8.15am and probably wouldn't have got up then, except for the fact that Capt. Crichton-Stuart had arranged to shoot the trench mortar. We wanted to be present, so we cooked a hurried breakfast and went to have a look. T Patrol shot with one gun and G with the other. Both of the first shots missed the target by quite a bit. So did G Patrol's second shot, but the T Patrol shot lanced right on the

Having just crossed the Great Sand Sea, the LRDG's medical officer, Captain F B Edmundson, leans against a Ford V8 15cwt. Though a New Zealander, during the Fezzan operations he was attached to the Guards patrol. Sitting in the vehicle is Sheikh Abd el Galil, leader of the Libyan resistance movement against the Italians. He proved useful as a guide and interpreter. Parked alongside is a Guards Chevrolet WB 30cwt mounting a .55 Boys anti-tank rifle and a .303 Lewis gun. Note the water condenser mounted on the front of the Ford. These condensers were used by all LRDG vehicles for recycling radiator steam into water.

target. After that there was a rifle competition of three shots. Five piastres in and winner take all. It as won by T Patrol and was worth 15 piastres.

In the afternoon I had a look at G Patrol's map, which explains the whole trip. While I was there, Capt. Crichton-Stuart came and explained things to me. The sand sea we came across was called the Rebiana Sand Sea and was reputed to be impassable. The four places we are supposed to attack are Wau el Kabir, Gatrun, Tejerri and Murzuk. The original intention was to attack the first-named place and then attack Murzuk, which we knew was pretty strong. But they got a long message on the wireless from Cairo the other night which explained the positions of eight field guns and a few other things, which showed that Murzuk was a lot more strongly fortified than we had at first thought.

It would be hard to take the other places without letting Murzuk know we were there, and thus we would lose the essence of surprise. So they have more or less decided to attack Murzuk before the smaller places. When we have done that, we go down to Tummo, which is on the border of French territory and Libya. From there we will go down to Faya, the largest town in Chad, and where Crichton-Stuart reckons we may have a party. Then we go south of Uweinat to Kharga, Assiut, and so to Cairo. It sounds as though it is going to be a great trip.

This evening I had a talk with Sheik Abd el Galil, who is travelling with us. He is a far more important man than I at first thought. He is a prince and his people are 'round

Major P A Clayton, the Fezzan operation commander, makes plans for the attack on Murzuk while conferring with Free French officers, at Kayugi in the foothills of the Tibesti mountains. From left to right: Lieutenant Eggenspiller, Lieutenant-Colonel d'Ornano (killed in action at Murzuk) Major Clayton and Captaine Massu. Note the petrol cases used as a map table.

Murzuk and Kufra etc. He is also a Bey which is a high sort of knighthood, conferred on him by King Farouk. He believes he would like to get to Murzuk before us and have a talk with the population. The Sheik reckons he could get the people to rise up against the Italians and then we come in. So we will see what happens.

7 JANUARY 1941 We heard this morning that the wireless truck had picked up a message from the Skipper saying that he had collected the French and would return today. They arrived at 12 noon and we set about making a cup of tea and lunch for them. During lunch the Skipper told us we were going to attack Murzuk first and that he didn't think the field guns were manned. There are three French officers *[Lt. Colonel J C d'Ornano, Captaine Massu, and Lieutenant Eggenspiller]*, 2 NCOs *[Sgts. Bloquet and Bourrat]* and 5 native troops. The Lt. Colonel is a count of some sort, but I don't quite know yet. The Lieutenant is adjutant of the French garrison at Fort Lamy. Lieut. Kennedy Shaw's party arrived back at 5pm this evening and reported that they had found the pass all right and that we could get through, though it is pretty rough in places. So now we will get ready to move off tomorrow morning. We are about 350km from Murzuk, so will probably attack it on 8 January. The Skipper told us that a French Camel Corps *[Captaine Sarazac's Groupe Nomade de Tibesti]* had already set off for Tejerri and would attack it on 14 January. That will save us some trouble.

This afternoon we showed the French our armaments and they seemed to pick things up very well, although they can't speak English. Our navigator Tony Browne can speak French fluently, as it is more or less his native language. He was brought up in Morocco and served in their army with this colonel, so he gets on very well.

8 January 1941 There was no lying in bed until after 8am this morning. Reveille was at 6am and we set off at 7.30am. We travelled over pretty good going for the first two hours but after that it was pretty soft. By lunchtime we had covered 107km. After lunch the country got rougher and rougher and in crossing one valley every truck got stuck. The surface was stony, but underneath there was a sort of fine dust. However, after a while we got through that and no-one was stuck again until we camped after doing 184km. We are still a good way from Murzuk, as we are going to the north and thus attacking from the main road. But this evening we had orders to clean all guns, so it seems as though we will strike something tomorrow. We listened to the wireless this evening and heard that Tobruk was now surrounded. Pretty fast work. And that our casualties at Bardia were less than 600. We are now practically due east of Murzuk and we have about 380km to go. When the Skipper

T Patrol members show the French how to operate .303 Vickers heavy machine-guns. Major Clayton is centre left in the white shirt and side cap. Colonel d'Ornano is behind the machine-gun.

collected the French he also collected sixty 12-gallon drums of benzine so we have got plenty of that for a while.

9 January 1941 *9.30am* We set off this morning at 7.15am over very wild sort of country with plenty of hills and rocks and at 9am after travelling only 17km we came across a basin with some trees in it, much the same as the Dalla Basin. We stopped about 4km away and inspected them through field glasses and could see a number of camels and at least two Arabs. So we were ordered to prepare our guns for action – not that we wanted to shoot the Arabs, but just in case there were any Italians there. So we carried on with our guns ready and again halted close to the trees. Old Abd was then sent out to talk with them and when he came back we set off once again. We are now on the road between Wau el Kebir and heading north. We have passed several feeding grounds for camels etc, but haven't met any Arabs so far. We have now halted again and the officers seem to be inspecting some tracks or something, but we will be off again in a minute.

12.30pm We have just had lunch among some scattered trees. We stopped here at 11am as the main bearing in one of the trucks was worn and the oil was just pouring through. They are now trying to fix it, although they haven't a spare main bearing. Most of us will

Jopling said this photo showed "...an interesting rock on the border of French West Africa and French Equatorial Africa."

probably go on shortly and let Lieut. Ballantyne and three trucks catch up when they have finished. The road we were on, which was more unlike a road than you would see anywhere, was between Wau el Kebir and El Fug'he. We are now in the most mountainous country we have been in yet and it is very rough. We only did 66km this morning.

The Arabs we saw were Tibbus, and they come from the border of Libya and French Equatorial Africa. Abd asked them if any Italians had been along here recently and they said, "Pooh! Italians come here!", as though it was the most unlikely thing they had ever heard.

Murzuk is about 300km due west of us at present and there are quite a few oases in between, which the Skipper wants to avoid if possible. We travelled very slowly yesterday and today, slower than the country warranted. I don't know if the Skipper is proceeding with caution or if he is looking after the trucks more carefully than usual.

4.00pm We set off again at 2pm over far better going. We have just come out of the mountains and onto a plain, but once again we have been travelling slower than we could have. We left Lieut. Ballantyne with four trucks to follow on and he will catch us up some time tonight. We have now halted – I suppose to find our position on the map.

4.45pm We have now stopped near another road and the Skipper has gone to see if there are any fresh tracks on it

5.15pm We retraced our tracks for about one and a half kilometres and have camped for the night. We're still allowed to have fires, so I had better get going with the tea.

10.00pm I have just got to bed. I'd been sitting up waiting for Bruce Ballantyne and his party to arrive and keeping their tea warm. They eventually arrived at 9.30pm. We were told by the Skipper that this road runs from Te Nesso to Hon, and that there are some fairly recent tracks on it, so tomorrow morning we will cross the road, travelling in each other's tracks. After that we will endeavour to cover our tracks in such a way that at least they won't look fresh.

When we arrived here this evening we could see two or three trees about 4 or 5km way, so the Colonel sent two of the natives to make sure there is no one underneath them. They returned after about two hours and reported that there no one was there. We only travelled 142km today.

Jopling's photograph of a Tibbu warror ready to go on a hunt.

10 JANUARY 1941 *8.30am* We set off this morning at 7.15am and have now crossed the road. The rear trucks are covering up our tracks. We have about 240km to go and should be just about there by tonight.

10.15am We have now travelled 45km and have halted near another road. It seems to have been one wide road all the way since the place where we covered our tracks. There were tracks crossing ours, but only one set was very new, and looked as though it had been done yesterday. The driver of that truck doesn't know how lucky he was, not being a day later.

11.30am When we set off from our last stop, we turned left (to the south). We saw a white escarpment and it just looked like waves breaking on the sea shore. It turned out to be a limestone ridge. We had a bit of rough going while crossing that, and just afterwards there was a soft patch which caught quite a few of our trucks.

We have now travelled 96km and have stopped to let the rest catch up. After waiting half an hour they decided to have lunch and fuse the hand grenades. I hope none of the pins come out in the truck. Apparently there is something wrong with Crichton-Stuart's V8 and they are now fixing it.

8.00pm We set off again at 1.30pm over pretty rough country. It was about the worst afternoon's drive I have had so far. We were driving straight into the sun and couldn't see where we were going. By the time we arrived here, after doing 223km, my eyes were pretty sore. To make matters worse, I scalded my leg when water splashed over while stirring rice. That is the second time on this trip – it is getting too much of a habit for my liking.

This afternoon we crossed many more tracks, both truck and camel. About ten km back we passed a palm-branch hut which one of our trucks went to investigate, but it turned out to be pretty old, apparently having belonged to a Tibbu once. We are now about 50km north of Murzuk, but are still allowed fires to cook with. Tomorrow we may attack the place, depending on circumstances.

ATTACK ON MURZUK

11 January 1941 *7.00am* This morning while getting breakfast ready, we broke our tin opener. While trying to open a tin without one, I cut my right thumb pretty deep. I got the medical orderly out of bed and he bandaged it up. He says he will have another look at it at lunch time and see if it needs stitching.

Well, now I am sitting in my truck with the engine warming up, waiting to head for Murzuk. So far we haven't been spotted and I imagine they will be very surprised when we open fire on them. The three V8s have gone ahead on a reconnaissance and we will follow in a few minutes, under Bruce Ballantyne. He told us that if we were spotted by planes we should stay on more or less the same course, but endeavour to dodge the bombs.

9.00am We are now near the road to Murzuk and the three V8s have gone to inspect it.

9.30am The wireless truck and myself are waiting in an ambush position a little further up the road, in case anything happens to come along. If they do, we will have two anti-tank rifles, two Lewis guns and two rifles firing all at once. The three V8s have gone down the road towards Murzuk on reconnaissance and the remainder of the trucks are hidden as much as possible about 2km away, within signal distance. We are staying like this until the Skipper comes back from his reconnaissance. The road is properly formed, but not bitumened. It is the first formed road we have seen in Libya so far.

10.00am The Skipper has just returned and has gone to the main body of trucks, so we may be recalled at any minute now.

10.30am We are now about a kilometre behind the rest of the party, who are just behind the last rise that leads to the fort. It seems we will stay out of the fighting as much as possible, although for the life of me I don't see why. We still have to guard the road.

When the attack comes off, we will need a good deal of luck as far as their wireless is concerned. They probably send messages every two hours or so and if we can get in just after a broadcast, that will be a great point in our favour. Well, I don't suppose it will be long until the attack comes off, so until then, I will close.

12 noon At 11.30am we were called up to the hill and got lunch ready. While we were eating, our look-out spotted an aeroplane taking off.

We have just been told we are to attack the aerodrome with six trucks, including the Bofors. To get there, we have to go straight past the fort for about 200 yards. The remainder of the trucks will attack the fort itself.

9.00pm Well it is all over now, and believe me it was pretty tough going while it lasted. Here is the story: We left our lunch place at 1pm and set off in line for the fort. On our way we picked an Italian postman in order to get some information out of him. We left his bike on the side of the road and Rex Beech *[Cpl. F R Beech]* picked it up and put it on his truck. We then carried on to the fort. As we drove up, they started to turn out the guard for us. They thought we were an Italian force and were going to give us a reception. We drove straight up the road to within 150 yards and then let them have it. Our six trucks went straight on past the fort and to the airfield.

We stopped about 700 yards from the hanger and saw quite a few soldiers running about and a number of scattered pillboxes. So we got behind a rise and opened fire on them. After a while, several had fallen and some Bofors shells had gone into the hangar. We then advanced to another rise, just in time to prevent some soldiers from entering an anti-aircraft pit. Soon the Skipper came past from the fort and went to circle the hangar. Just as he turned a corner, a machine-gun opened up at them from only 20 yards away. He jammed on his brakes and put his truck in reverse. How he and his crew – 'Wink' *Adams*

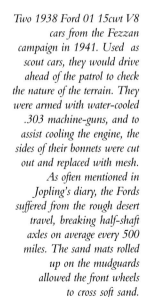

Two 1938 Ford 01 15cwt V8 cars from the Fezzan campaign in 1941. Used as scout cars, they would drive ahead of the patrol to check the nature of the terrain. They were armed with water-cooled .303 machine-guns, and to assist cooling the engine, the sides of their bonnets were cut out and replaced with mesh. As often mentioned in Jopling's diary, the Fords suffered from the rough desert travel, breaking half-shaft axles on average every 500 miles. The sand mats rolled up on the mudguards allowed the front wheels to cross soft sand.

[Tpr. W R Adams] and 'Clarrie' Roderick *[Lance Cpl. Loderick]* – escaped, goodness knows!

However, there was one sad story in the episode and that was the French colonel being shot through the throat. It was terrible, and the Skipper felt very bad about it. A prisoner (a sgt. operator) who the Skipper picked up somewhere, was also sitting in the back. He was hit and was in an awful mess. They just threw him overboard. One bullet went through the theodolite, which was on the running board just next to the Skipper. Another went through the truck at his back and one passed through the seat underneath him.

We were ordered to keep firing at the Italians and try to make them surrender. It was just after this that we turned round and saw the fort blazing fiercely. Ian McInnes *[Tpr. I H McInnes]* had sent a trench mortar bomb into the fort and it had hit a benzine dump or something. However, we kept up our fire on the hangar. Snipers were shooting at us all the time, but we couldn't see where the bullets were coming from.

There was the dickens of a noise going on all the time. We had 24 machine guns and 8 Boys anti-tank rifles and a good few service rifles going, as well as the two Bofors guns – without counting what the enemy was using. But one thing that was always more noticeable was the ping! of a sniper's bullet when he got one pretty close.

Well, after we had been shooting into the hangar for about two hours, a white flag was stuck out of the door. We ceased fire and sent one of our prisoners in to tell them to come out with their hands above their heads, which they did. I was surprised to see how many there were. About 20 came out, most wearing Italian Air Force blue uniforms.

We drove up and placed a guard over the prisoners, then had a look in the hangar. There were three beautiful Ghibli bombers, *[Caproni CA 309]* costing about £15,000 each. Also a magnificent sending and receiving wireless set and many bombs, parachutes and other valuable equipment. Of course all the boys were in for a bit of looting and while that was going on, the planes and building were soaked in benzine, the wireless set smashed, and we took thousands of rounds of .303 ammunition and many rifles. We left a trail of benzine and set a match to it. What a waste. But I suppose that is what war is, a war of destruction. For a long time there was thick black smoke rising and the thud of bombs going off.

Just before we set fire to the hangar, we heard that Cyril Hewson who had just been promoted to sergeant before this trip, had been killed at the fort, early in the proceedings. We

Getting out of town after the attack. Top: the Murzuk hanger burning. Above: the fort on fire.

were all very sorry to hear the news as he was very well liked by all and was a real good soldier. His Vickers had jammed and when he stood up to fix it, a bullet struck him in the chest. Mercifully he never knew what hit him; death was instantaneous.

Also sad was the death of the French colonel, but the saddest story comes from the other side. Soon after the firing started, the Italian commanding officer came from his private residence in a small car and headed for the fort. As he was going through the gate the Bofors gun opened fire, hitting the car amidships. It was also hit by a high concentration of machine-gun fire. It wasn't until later that they learned that his wife and two children had been in the vehicle with him. They must have been all killed. Everyone felt very bad about that, but all the same, they were certainly asking for trouble driving up to a fort while under attack like that.

To get back to the hanger – after we had set it on fire, the Skipper decided that he could only take two prisoners, as that was all we could feed. So he took the postman and the man who looked to be chief of the Air Force. He let the remainder go, as we could not shoot them in cold blood. We then had orders to rally where we had lunch and to leave the fort alone, as we had done all the damage we could and wouldn't gain much more even if we did capture it. So we headed along the road.

As we were travelling, we noticed a big cloud coming up from the north. At first we thought it was the smoke from the fires at the fort, but soon discovered it was blowing the other way. We then thought the cloud was caused by enemy trucks or something, but decided they couldn't make as much dust as that. The only other conclusion was that a dust

T Patrol and the Free French salute the combined grave of Lieutenant-Colonel J C d'Ornano, and Sergeant C D Hewson who were killed during the attack on Murzuk on 11 January 1941.

storm was coming up, although at the time there was hardly any wind at all. However, it arrived just before we got to the rally point, with a strong wind and plenty of dust.

We were very pleased to see the dust storm, strange as that might seem. It turned out to be a gift from heaven. Just when the dust storm came, our troops who were still at the fort made their retreat, and they became out of sight practically immediately. Another thing is that the day following a storm like that is always very hazy, so it will be very difficult for any plane to spot us tomorrow.

Well, after all that we managed to arrive at the rallying point without any trucks missing. We then set about the sad job of burying Lt.-Col. Jean d'Ornano and Sergeant Cyril Hewson of T Patrol. We dug a wide grave and, after wrapping each of them in their respective blankets, laid them side by side in the grave, NZ and Free French together in death. Major Clayton read the funeral service. When we finished there, the sun was setting and we travelled for about ten kilometres before camping for the night where we are at present. The enemy casualties must have been very high – 50 would be a conservative estimate. We lost two, with one wounded – although how we didn't have more I don't know.

There were some wonderful stories of narrow escapes. Tony Browne had a bullet through the back of his boot and yet it only just broke the skin. A Guardsman had a bullet just miss the back of his hand and it left a red mark where it passed over. One or two had bullets through their trousers that never touched their legs. There is the story of Captaine Massu who was hit in the leg by a bullet, burned the wound with his cigarette end and carried on as if nothing had happened. There is a man who was slightly cut in his leg by a bullet but is still walking around. Another got a bullet in the leg which broke a vein. Abd el Galil talked to a lot of the natives. They all knew him and were very pleased to meet him.

Well, it is late, so I must go to sleep.

The shared grave of Lieutenant-Colonel d'Ornano and Sergeant Hewson. The cross was made from petrol case wood, and marked with the Free French Cross of Lorraine and a New Zealand 'Onward' badge.

12 JANUARY 1941 *9.00am* I am afraid it took me a long time to go to sleep last night. This morning we set off at 7.30am and had been going for about an hour when we saw two camels coming towards us. So we got in line abreast and carried on. They turned out to be two Carabinieri – the Italian Military Police. They got the shock of their lives when they found out we weren't Italians. We took them prisoner and they told us where their fort was. So we are heading there.

11.00pm We are now at Traghen, the fort where the two prisoners came from. We drove up and got behind cover at about 1,000 yards away, then sent the prisoners in to tell the fort to surrender or else we would open up on them. They were away for about 20 minutes and we were beginning to think they were preparing to defend themselves, when they came out beating drums, singing and waving banners. It was a great sight and as they came up to us, we lined up the trucks. The Skipper then spoke to them. It was a complete surrender. Abd el Galil talked to a lot of the natives who came out and we were made friends. The Skipper then said we would fill our water tins at a well while he and the wireless truck went to the fort, so off we went with the Carabinieri in the leading truck showing the way. While filling the water tins, the Skipper sent word back by wireless asking for ten men and one truck, so off they went. I couldn't go as I had to stay with my truck.

11.45pm. The ten men, the Skipper and the wireless truck have returned. They had taken all the machine-guns and ammunition from the fort, put them in a heap and burned them. We are now just about ready to move off to another place called Umm el Arenab which has a wireless, so if a message was sent from Murzuk they will probably be expecting us.

1.00pm As we left Traghen we drove through the fort and all the population cheered us as we passed. The cheers the womenfolk made are very hard to describe.

Well, well! They certainly were expecting us at Umm el Arenab. We came down a road much the same as the one to Murzuk. It was a well spread-out fort and no cover in between. After stopping twice on our way down the slope and inspecting the place, we drove on and were just getting into the flat leading to the fort when the machine guns and rifles opened up on us. As we couldn't see them and we had no armour plating, we turned and headed for a rise about 2,000 yards from the fort. On the way one or two trucks got stuck in a soft patch. I bet they had an anxious time for a while. Even when we got up on the hill, the bullets were still whizzing past.

Once again, I'll say that how no-one got hit or any trucks damaged, I don't know. In the first burst the bullets were flying all around this truck and as we retreated up the hill they were hitting the sand all about us. When we got to the hill, the Skipper ordered the two Bofors to fire a few shells each into the fort. After that he decided it

Following the Murzuk raid, T Patrol cuts through an attractive palm grove as they turn back eastwards on the road to Traghen. "The trip from where we picked up the Carabinieri to the fort was very pretty sight – a road with palm trees on either side."

wasn't worth risking lives and trucks, as there wouldn't be anything worth having if we did capture it. The Skipper was quite satisfied that if we had stayed there for a day we would have taken it alright, but it wasn't worth the risk. So now we are going to move off, heading south for Gatrun

8.00pm After getting on top of a dune we saw a big flat plain ahead of us. It was a very welcome sight, as we have travelled over some very rough country in the last few days. While stopped on top of the dune we thought we heard planes coming. We went off again with guns ready for AA wide air formation, but we didn't see any planes. It had been very hazy all day, which has been a great streak of luck in our favour, as it would be practically impossible for an aeroplane to spy us unless they were flying very low and came right over the top of us. The trip from where we picked up the carabinieri to the fort was very pretty sight – a road with palm trees on either side. We now have four prisoners with us: the postman, the airforce man, and two from Traghen, one of whom is an officer. We camped about five kilometres from Umm el Araneb.

Major Clayton (in the sidecap) and T Patrol members meet with the tribal leaders who, with great ceremony, surrendered the fort at Traghen.

13 JANUARY 1941 *7.30am* We have finished breakfast and are waiting to move off. Seven of the G Patrol trucks are going to try to intercept the French before they attack Tejerri, to warn that the Italians are expecting them. The rest are going to Gatrun under the Skipper, the other party under Capt. Crichton-Stuart and Lieut. Kennedy Shaw.

12.00 noon We have just had lunch near the ruined Gatrun fort. We came down to the palms very cautiously and after a few stops to scan the countryside through the fieldglasses, we came within sight of this fort. It looked a very substantial place from a distance and we crept closer and closer expecting any minute to hear a machine-gun open up on us. We reckoned that even if the last place we were at didn't have a wireless, they were sure to have found some way of telling the Gatrun people that we were in the district. However, we finally made a dash only to find it was a ruined fort.

2.30pm After lunch we headed up a rise and came upon a landing ground. On the far side were oblong enclosures, each surrounded by a palm windbreak. After inspecting the landing ground we advanced cautiously and found four Arabs who came up and shook hands with the Skipper. Then Abd el Galil came along and had a chat with them. They told him that an aeroplane had been over here today. It circled twice and dropped a message saying that we had attacked Murzuk and also that Tejerri was presently being attacked. The Frenchmen must be attacking a day early and G Patrol will probably miss them.

Strange that we should hear the news from an Arab about five kilometres from the

65

township. However, he also told us there were about 30 soldiers down in the village, so the Skipper has sent the postman down to see if he can get them to surrender. The Skipper, the wireless truck and another truck are following him.

10.00pm Apparently the Skipper didn't send the postman in, but got him to write a message for one of the Arabs to take in. At about 3.30pm we got a signal from the Skipper to advance. As we got near the village we saw all the population getting out, and we took that to mean that they wouldn't surrender. The Skipper then told us to get as near to the fort as possible without exposing the trucks or men, as he didn't want to lose any of either. If he couldn't get it easily, he wouldn't bother getting it at all, as it wasn't worth it.

So off we went through the palms and took up our positions, but the nearest we could get under cover was 1,300 yards. The Bofors opened up and then we all followed with the machine guns, Boys and rifles. I happened to be just near the Bofors and the bullets were whining all around us. One hit the dust just in front of me. We saw several lumps of the fort fall down and also silenced a machine gun. One of our men reckons he saw a man fall out one of the machine gun posts. By this time the sun was getting pretty low and we wanted to be well away from here before we camped, so the order was given to cease fire and return to the rallying point.

A Chevrolet WB Bofors gun truck racing over a dune in the Fezzan. The horizon reflects the vast arid desert terrain the patrols operated in.

All the trucks had just gathered when the cry of, "aircraft!" went up. Then we saw a bomber approaching. In this outfit we don't mind how many machine-guns or rifles are firing at us, but one thing we don't like is bombers. We seem to be absolutely helpless against them, as they nearly always fly too high for machine-gun fire and when they pass straight overhead you wonder if they have let their bombs go. If so, will they land anywhere near you? Then you see them pass over and think, well, if they had let the bombs go they would have landed by now. But even then you are not sure and by the time you are, the plane is on its way back again.

To get back to the story – on the cry of, "aircraft!" closely followed by "Scatter!", we didn't need a second invitation as the drivers started up and got moving for cover as fast as possible. The gunners put on a drum or a belt of tracer bullets and as he came close, they opened up on him. Some of the shots looked pretty close. Meanwhile I was flat-out over soft going heading for a hillock, and the aeroplane went right overhead. I went through the sensations I have just described. However, he didn't drop that time and before he came back we had tucked ourself into this hillock and felt more secure. He circled around, came right over us again but made a very poor shot. After that it may have been too dark for him to see us, so off he went. We were pleased to see the last of him. As soon as he had gone we moved off. By this time it was quite dark and after travelling about five kilometres we removed our headlight covers and turned on the lights. After a further 40km from the fort we camped for the night.

14 January 1941 *9.00am* Reveille was half an hour early this morning and we were away as dawn was breaking, as we expected the plane over again this morning. We carried on for about 30km over rough hilly country, came down into a bit of a flat and saw G Patrol about 2km to our right. We joined up with them and they told us that they had not seen the Frenchmen. But they hadn't gone all the way to Tejerri as the Captain didn't want to interfere with the other party's campaign.

8.00pm We headed straight south for the Tummo Pass, through very rough mountainous country. We are now about 70km from Tummo. No vehicle has ever been through this pass, but to go through anywhere else we would have to travel an extra 800km and we don't have the benzine to do it. Actually we will be breaking international law as Tummo is in French West Africa which is under the Vichy Govt. It is more or less a neutral country and therefore we are not supposed to go through it. However, we hope not to be seen. Well, it is quite a relief to know we can take things easy without much fear of being attacked for a while by air or land. It is going to be somewhat of a Cook's Tour. We travelled 166km today.

Officers of the LRDG and Free French confer at Tummo. Left to right: Captain Edmundson, Lieutenant Ballantyne, Captaine Sarazac, Captaine Massu, Major Clayton, Lieutenant Kennedy Shaw.

15 January 1941 *3.00pm* We're now in French West Africa, whether we're allowed to be or not. We didn't go through the Tummo Pass, which we were told was impassable, but went round the mountain insead. We have had lunch and are now waiting for the doctor's V8. It has a broken back axle and hasn't arrived yet. We have done 101km so far today. This outfit is just about a League of Nations at present. We have NZ, Scots, English, French, Tibbus and Italians.

The Skipper and the wireless truck left us to go to Tummo, and at 4pm sent word back to say that he was in touch with a French soldier on a camel, and that everything was OK. So we set off too, even though the V8 hadn't arrived. However, we had gone about 6km when the Skipper sent a message that he didn't intend us to follow and to return to where we had been to camp for the night. That mistake cost us about 20 valuable gallons of benzine. In the meantime the doctor's V8 arrived, towed behind a 30 cwt. They brought the news that our spare axles did not fit the 1938 Ford V8. So they are sending a wireless message to Cairo to ask the Colonel to bring two or three 1938 axles with him on the plane that is going to meet us at Zouar. I suppose we will have to tow the Doctor's truck all the way there.

Just as I was going to bed, the advance party of the Tejerri troop arrived. They explained that they were fired on as they got in range of the fort. Apparently the Tejerri party had been warned that Murzuk had been attacked and told to be on alert. They fought for two hours, during which time one of the camel keepers deserted and went to the fort. There were no casualties, even though they were bombed.

16 JANUARY 1941 8.00am This morning the Skipper seems to be expecting an Italian plane. This well is the only one within hundreds of miles and the French party's camels haven't had a drink since they left here earlier. The Italians must know this is the place they will make for. One truck took all our empty 2 gallon tins to the well to fill them up. We scattered, covered our vehicles with hessian camouflage and are now waiting for the truck to return.

1.00pm The truck arrived back at 10am and shortly afterwards we got the signal to start up. After taking the camouflage off we all converged in the centre and lined the trucks up in order. Then the French came and had a look round them all. We left there about 11am and have now travelled 60km over good going, but we had to go slow because of having to tow the Ford V8. Yesterday afternoon we crossed into the Tropic of Cancer and now we are about 80km inside it and can certainly notice the difference in the temperature. Although a strong wind is blowing, I have had my shirt off nearly all day. Further north we had to wear underclothing, a shirt, one or two jerseys, with a sheepskin and overcoat on top, and even then we were cold. Since leaving this morning

Left, Captaine Massu of the Free French with members of T Patrol and Arab soldiers, in front of a Chevrolet WB 30cwt truck. They are dressed for the bitter desert cold, with the men on the right wearing coats fashioned from army blankets.

we have seen quite a few gazelle, but haven't been close enough to shoot.

This afternoon has been very rough – what we call 'Tiger Country', and we did only 45km in about three hours. This has never been crossed by a vehicle before and it is marked on the map as impassable. We have camped for the night on a nice sand dune.

17 January 1941 We set off this morning at 7am and again struck rough country interspersed with short stretches of sand. We have now stopped for lunch after doing 103km.

3.00pm We set off at 1.30pm and had some more rough country to cross, but all of a sudden it ended and we struck a lovely stretch of sand. When we got on to that stretch the trucks reminded me of a lot of calves let out into a paddock for the first time. They all more or less raced each other and we soon got so close to the Skipper's truck that he stopped and turned around, thinking we wanted him for something.

The weather is very hot as we must be getting near the Equator, but I would rather have it like this than as cold as it was a week or so ago. Just before lunch we went into a valley which we immediately called the Valley of Death. Sure enough practically every truck, including my own, got stuck. Eventually when we got out and caught up with the rest we found that they had shot a young gazelle and were skinning it. The Skipper said we would have lunch here. While that was happening we cut up the gazelle and started to cook it as they are much more tender if done straight away, so we will be having gazelle for tea tonight.

9.00pm We are now camped for the night after doing 194km over rough going once again. We mixed the gazelle in with the ordinary stew and it was very different from the last gazelle I tasted. This one was lovely and tender. There is at present a sing-song around the camp fire and there appears to be quite a bit of talent in the Guards Patrol. They got a message from Cairo tonight saying that the message we had sent requesting an axle for the V8 was indecipherable. Colonel Bagnold would have left by now, so we will probably leave the truck at Faya until we can get the replacement part.

18 January 1941 *10.30am* We set off this morning at 7.30am and so far the going has been very rough. We got into a basin it has been quite a job finding our way out. When we did find a way we had to lay a track of stones across a soft patch. There is no doubt we are going up and down some of the most impossible places this morning. We have just come down a cliff so steep that anyone would think you were mad if you had suggested going down it in a truck.

1.00pm We have just finished lunch in very wild and mountainous country. In the valley are a few trees and some scattered red sand dunes with shiny golden grass growing in tufts over them. This road, although not used very much, is the most clearly marked one we have seen yet. There are heaps of stones about every chain on both sides of the road. One set of tracks is very new – within the last couple of days – and we're wondering what they are. Tony Browne thinks it might be deserters from 'Vichy' West Africa to Free French Equatorial Africa, but I am inclined to think that they sent someone out to mark the road clearly when they heard we were coming out this way.

6.00pm We set off again at 1.30pm and struck rocky going interspersed with sand that was pretty soft in places. The 30 cwt truck towing the Ford V8 got stuck a few times, so we unhitched it and drove it out. Then all hands pushed the V8 out and we progressed very well. About 3.30pm we saw a gazelle, so quite a few rifles opened up and many rounds of ammunition were fired before Ian McInnes brought it down. We set about skinning it and having done that, we set off to catch up with the others.

We eventually stopped in a wadi with quite a lot of trees in it and were told that this was where we were to camp for the night. So after putting the gazelle on to cook after giving half to G Patrol, we opened up the bully beef. Then some of G Patrol came in and reported that they had two gazelles. Naturally they gave some to us, which meant we had opened up the bully beef unnecessarily. However, we decided we would cook the other gazelle tonight and have it for breakfast in the morning. Just after that when we heard that one of the French sergeants had shot something that was too big to carry home and they were taking a truck to cart it back here. They reckoned it was an antelope, but when they got it here it turned out to be an addax, which is very like a gazelle only about four times as big. Unlike the gazelle it drinks water, so now we have got plenty of meat.

I also got rather a shock this evening when I saw a hare run past. I never thought they were in the desert, but we must be getting close to a river or water of some kind. While were getting the tea ready, the Skipper went off to the left to look for a benzine dump which he believed to be there. He came back to say he couldn't locate it, but had found an unoccupied fort they called Dowso. Apparently when it rains, all this valley is beautifully green and when that happens, the French Camel Corps come out and leave their camels here to graze. We are now about five kilometres into French Equatorial Africa.

GUESTS OF THE FREE FRENCH

19 January 1941 For breakfast this morning we had soup and then steak. It was very nice. We opened a tin of NZ biscuits which were also very good. There are two ways into Zouar, where we are headed. However, one is just a camel track and it is marked on the map as impassable. Apparently it is a wadi and is very soft. That way is only 60km while the other way is 160km. The Skipper is taking five trucks along the camel track and the rest of us are going the long way. Some of us would have had to go the long way anyhow, because the truck towing the V8 wouldn't get through on the camel track.

Rough country on the road to Zouar. Note the sand channel hung on the side of the truck.

2.30pm We have now stopped for lunch after coming through a wadi where everyone got stuck – which is usual around here. There were many trees and a sort of prairie grass. So far this morning we have done about 106km, but I think there is more than 60km to go yet.

8.00pm Well I reckon I have just seen the 8th Wonder of the World and that was the road we have just come over. It is really beyond description. The country is just a mass of mountains of one solid piece of rock. We came along a road through these mountains for about 40km. It was very steep in places and had great corners on it, but the surface, considering the country it had to go through and with only a few trucks going through a year, was nothing short of marvellous. It was apparently done by prisoners who were thieves or murderers and chained together. However, we arrived at about 4pm and native soldiers on guard outside the fort. The trucks drove past and they presented arms and saluted.

There seem to be quite a few inhabitants here and they are as black as ink (Senegalese). The young boys run around stark naked, they look funny being all black with white dust on them. The party that went through the 'impassable' route arrived here at 11am, having had no trouble at all. They reckon it was a great sight, but were unable to see it until they were right at the entrance. Then it was just a narrow pass with high cliffs on each side.

Practically as soon as we had arrived we had to start getting tea ready. It was the usual stew with a bit of addax *[a large antelope]* in it. Nearly all those who had arrived earlier, at 11am, were half drunk by the time we got here, but it doesn't look as though we'll be able to get in that state. The locals have made as as welcome as they possibly could, considering that they only get stores from Faya once a month. The stores are carried by camels, which take 16 days to do the trip, so we can't expect much here.

Senegalese civilian prisoners drawing water from a well at Zouar in French Equatorial Africa. The prisoners were also used for hard labour tasks such as building roads.

⮞ 20 JANUARY 1941 ⮜ We didn't get out of bed until after the sun was up this morning and then set about getting breakfast ready. After that the three of us went to the well to get a wash. Everyone else had one last night, but we didn't get the time. We found the well situated in a beautiful vegetable garden with nearly every kind of vegetable imaginable, beautifully green and well kept. There were also carnations and pomegranates. There were some Senegalese soldiers and prisoners and they got the water out of the well and poured it in dishes for us. Then came the difficult job of getting the dirt off ourselves. We got the first coating off and then the soldiers emptied the water and filled the dishes again. After giving ourselves a good final soaping we got the prisoners to pour a watering can of water over us for a shower. It was great. After drying ourselves and getting into clean clothes we started to wash the dirty clothes, but just as we started, the soldiers took them off us and explained that they would do it. We didn't need any second invitation and left them to it, saying we would call back later. The clothes were filthy and believe me, I wasn't looking forward to cleaning them.

When we left we decided to have a look round the fort, but there wasn't much to see inside, except that it showed that it was useless to try to take a fort without high explosive guns. The outer walls are about 3 ft thick and you might as well shoot a Bofors in the air as aim it at the wall. There are dozens of holes to shoot from, a wireless room, a dynamo which is worked by hand, a medical room and sundry offices etc. Three flags are flying on the flag mast. At the top is the French flag, in the middle is the Free French Flag which is the same as the French, except it displays the Free French badge. When we got back to the truck we found a big pile of vegetables waiting, including lettuce, cabbage and onions. Some of the lettuce we are having for lunch, so we set about washing it and getting the meal ready.

Flags flying at Fort Zouar

4.00pm After lunch we had a bit of a spell and then changed the oil in my truck after which 'Fergy' *[Trooper I C Ferguson]* suggested we go for a walk down to the village. As we passed through, each native, whether he was sitting down or standing up, would immediately get up and salute as we passed. The huts are made mainly of matting made from rushes, but where they got the rushes from I don't know. The soldiers live in round mud huts with

Native Free French soldiers at Fort Zouar drying meat in the sun. This would be later used as field rations.

thatched roofs that look very nice. After that we went for our washing, and I got the surprise of my life. It was all folded up and looked as if it had been ironed although they hadn't. But they were spotlessly clean. How they managed to get them as clean as that in cold water I don't know.

We thanked them very much and set off back to the truck by a different route, passing a building where they kill a beast and cut it into strips and hang it out on a line to dry. They then have dried meat. It is very light to carry around and keeps practically indefinitely, but takes a long time to cook. When we arrived back at our trucks it was time to get tea ready. Col. Bagnold is due to arrive here at 5.35pm and we are hoping he has some mail and tobacco as nearly everyone is out of that.

8.00pm This morning we were told that we were going to be given some mutton and beef, so of course we thought of a nice leg of mutton. After breakfast they brought along a herd of bullocks and killed the biggest one for us just after that they brought our 'mutton', which turned out to be a herd of goats. They killed 14 of them and if we hadn't stopped them they would have killed the whole herd. They then set about skinning them and hung them on the fence. I don't like the idea of eating them much, as they have been hanging in the sun all day with flies around them and with either large crows or small ravens standing on them having a feed. However, we cooked some for stew with cabbage (we had lettuce for lunch) and cut up some steak for breakfast. The French made us bread which was very nice. I had some bread and cabbage, but no stew.

This morning I went down to the village and met Abd el Galil and he took us to a shack where there were about a dozen Libyans who had left Libya as soon as war was declared. We were made very welcome and they gave us two cups of the usual 'shay'. Then we returned

Foreground: the Guards Patrol truck, G2, broke the connecting rod in its engine, damaging it beyond repair. The vehicle was totally dismantled for spare parts. T Patrol Chevrolet WBs lined up in the background.

home and found an awful noise going on. Apparently some of the boys had helped themselves to some of our French rations of rum which had been placed in too handy a position.

21 JANUARY 1941 *10.00am* I forgot to mention that the day we arrived here, a truck in G Patrol broke the connecting rod in its engine which in turn smashed the whole engine, making the truck totally unrepairable. So they towed it in and have taken it totally to bits to use as spare parts. This morning the Colonel set off again in the plane, having brought no mail or tobacco. The boys are feeling a bit downhearted. Apparently he left Cairo about two weeks ago and forgot to bring any mail. He left the news that we are not going straight back to Cairo after Faya, but will attack Kufra in conjunction with a small land force.

He had received a cable requesting all films taken on the trip, for propaganda use. Until now this outfit has been very secret, but apparently it will now be made public. They guaranteed to take good care of the films and print them free, and they would be ready when we got back.

After that we drew our French rations. What a job it will be to make three meals a day out of them. We have olive oil, vinegar, unroasted coffee beans (it seems to take half a day to make a cup of coffee out of them), ordinary beans which take four hours to cook, some sugar in about ½ pound cones which are like concrete to break up, one tin of pressed meat per man per day and some flour. What a problem!!!!

1.00pm We have now finished lunch, of a bit of lettuce and half a slice of bread with a cup of tea. We are now ready to move off for Faya, and the sooner we get there the better. The French all have to buy their own cigarettes and they are provided with liquor, but they have

T Patrol rests for lunch. During these breaks, navigation, equipment and tyre pressures were always checked. Foreground right: Major Clayton's Ford 15cwt, Te Rangi.

75

managed to provide us with 20 cigarettes each which we all very much appreciate.

8.00pm We set off at 2pm and again the soldiers turned out and presented arms to us as we passed. Last night the women of the village turned on a bit of a dance for us. It was a great experience – the drums were beating and the women sang while they danced. Some of the women wore brightly coloured costumes and plenty of necklaces, bangles and anklets. Their hair was done in scores of little plaits. On the centre at the back was a big plait and on it were brooches etc. The poorer women just wore plain black dresses and had a few brooches on the biggest plait. The men wore headgear and their eyes were all we could see of their faces.

I always thought the gazelle was about the hardest animal to photograph, but I am beginning to think that these Tibbu women are harder still, as they turn their faces away as soon as they see the camera.

When we left we headed up that masterpiece of roads and about half way through we came upon five huge vultures eating a dead cow. I don't know what they are called, but they were enormous. The Skipper says that except for the condor of South America, they are the largest bird that flies. They stood about 2' 6" in height and had a wingspread of about 12 feet. We got to the end of the road after doing about 32km. We came across what appeared to be a dried-up river bed in which we all got stuck. But it didn't take long to get through and we laid sand channels down for the truck towing the V8 to drive over. Shortly after that we camped, after doing 53km.

We then set about trying to make a meal out of the French rations. When I was in Zouar, I asked one of the French how to make coffee out of what looked like green barley. He told me to boil it then break it up, then boil it again and I thought it was going to make a funny sort of coffee. However, this evening I did what he told me and the water went green, so I asked one or two to taste it. They reckoned that it didn't taste like coffee. I got one of the French officers to come and look at it and he said it was no good, as we had to roast it and then break it up and make coffee out of it. Which we did, after a good bit of work, and the coffee didn't taste too bad, except that there was no milk in it. However G Patrol beat me – they even put it in their stew.

We then cooked some of the beef into a stew with a few onions. I discovered there was also some rice in the French rations, so I used some for a pudding. The French had made us a small bread roll each before we left Zouar, but other than that, we only had flour to make what we could out of.

After tea, the Skipper suggested making bread of sorts, so we mixed flour, water and salt into a dough and tried cooking it in several different ways. We cooked it in the ashes, in a frying pan with just enough oil to keep it from sticking to the pan, and fried it in oil. We decided that the second way was best, but it was a big job to do enough for the whole patrol. So for tomorrow we decided to mix enough dough for each truck to their own the way they liked it.

22 January 1941 We had tripe and onions for breakfast this morning. Very nice, but it took a lot of cooking. We left at 7.30am and before long we struck another of those dried-up river beds. We had quite a job getting all the trucks across including the doctor's V8. We stopped for lunch after 60km of rough going. We had French tinned meat, lettuce and an onion for lunch and two bottles of lime juice left over from our own rations. We set off again after lunch and again struck one of the dried-up river beds, but it wasn't quite such a job getting through as the one in the morning. We carried on for another 60km before camping for the night. We then mixed dough and gave some to each truck to do what they liked with it. For tea we had stew made from rice mixed with the French tinned meat, which was very stringy. The first drink at night we had was tea from our original rations, the second coffee. We have done 122km today and have 235 to do. If the going improves we may get there tomorrow. We saw plenty of gazelle and camels and in one place we passed two huts where the men who look after the camels lived.

23 January 1941 The going today has been very rough except for a few patches. We have done 262km and we are still 60km from Faya. The French map turned out to be all wrong. However, we will definitely arrive there tomorrow morning.

24 January 1941 *9.30am* We set off this morning at 7.30pm and after travelling for two hours we have done 32km. We struck a very long soft patch where practically everyone, including two V8s, got stuck. We had to push the doctor's V8 a lot. In one place we had to push it for ¼ mile. It has been a new kind of soft stuff to us and about the worst. On top is ordinary sand with huge ripples in places and underneath is fine powdery stuff which is thrown up in thick clouds of dust.

10.30am We are now in a wadi the like of which we have never seen before. There are big mounds of tussock with soft sand in between, and bits of rock here and there. We have now come 38km in three hours and only 6km in the last hour. The biggest job is towing the truck. They are at present getting it out of a 'stick' and we will be moving on again soon.

3.30pm Well we arrived here eventually, at 1.30pm. The last 10 or 15km was on a road through palm trees, and quite a lot of natives saluted us as we passed. It isn't quite what we expected. It is the biggest town in French Equatorial Africa, but unfortunately there are no shops or anything, and I wanted to get more films for my camera. We arrived in the main square of the fort without ceremony and lined up the trucks in two rows, T Patrol in front. The French colonel came round and had a look at us. We must have looked a dirty lot of troops.

We were then taken to a sort of barracks which turned out to be a mud building with sand floor, but was very cool inside. While we were having a wash, the French brought our lunch of tinned meat, biscuits, dried bananas and a quarter bottle of red wine each. We saw our first ostrich while we were having a wash. It just roams around here and I think it is more or less tame. After lunch we had to go down and draw rations for tea and it was nearly 6pm before we eventually got them. We made tea and then decided to go and have a look at the sights, but I'm afraid we didn't see many as we hadn't gone far before some French took us in hand and gave us a party.

You could hardly call this a town. It is more of a big military outpost among thousands of acres of palms. The total population is about 5,000 and there are about 50 Europeans – all officers or sergeants.

⌁ 25 January 1941 ⌁ *10.00pm* I went down at 8am to draw the day's rations and, after doing a bit to the truck, the rest of the day was free, as two other men are cooking today. This afternoon I went into the village and found that there are a few shops after all – such as they are and what there is in them. There is also a sort of market place where seated women sell mostly different kinds of herbs. There are also firewood and baskets etc. for sale. From there we went to the wireless station and after the French had given us some beautiful coffee and wine, they showed us round the whole place. We then left them and after we had gone about 20 yards, some more sergeants invited us in and gave us a six-course dinner and some wine, zibit etc. When we set out to return to the barracks, Rex Beech fell into a well. Luckily it wasn't very deep, but he yelled out that he had broken his leg, so I brought the other two who were with me and we pulled him out. He had hurt his knee, but no fracture.

They managed to get an axle for the doctor's V8 here and today I saw the driver driving around in it. We believe that truck had one of the longest tows on record. We towed it for 1,293km (771 miles) over all types of country and it took us seven days to do it.

⌁ 26 January 1941 ⌁ This morning we had to get up and cook the breakfast at 6.30am. Then we went and got the rations, cut up the meat for tea and prepared lunch. We roasted some coffee beans and got some native soldiers to grind them up in a bowl and stick. There were three of them on duty all day to do anything we needed done and believe me, they came in handy. In the afternoon I had to take everything off my truck and then reloaded it with the new benzine and water etc. At 3.30pm I collected three day's rations and then of course we had to get tea ready.

While we were having a rest, Major Clayton explained our job at Kufra and he said they were going to try and make it a purely French affair if possible. We will attack at night and next day we'll see what damage has been done and guard the roads to and from Kufra. There will be ten bombers from Fort Lamy *[a Free French base]* and two hospital planes currently at Sarra wells. There are about 650 white Frenchmen and 300 natives, while we are the only British representatives. It is going to be a two to five day campaign. One thing that is going to be hard on us is that no cigarettes are available. We are going to have to go without them.

I am not as badly off as some of men, as I was given four packets of 20 by the French, who have been very good to us. We are nearly ready to leave tomorrow morning for Ounianga.

27 January 1941 We were up at 5am and had breakfast ready by 6.15am. A dog had apparently been prowling around during the night and pinched the meat that we were to have for breakfast. So we had to have tinned meat and rice, and as the tinned meat goes tough and stringy in stew, we ate it cold.

We were all lined up on the road outside the barracks by 7.30am, but had to wait about half an hour for G Patrol. We eventually got moving shortly after 8am and the Skipper stopped near the fort, only to find that two of G Patrol trucks had carburettor trouble, so we had to wait for them to get fixed. During this time, hundreds of natives gathered near the trucks. Someone happened to take out his false teeth and the natives couldn't stand that at all. However, they were kept amused during the rest of our wait there.

We eventually got away at 10am and set off along the road to Ounianga. We stopped for lunch after covering 40km and found that two G Patrol trucks were missing. We had our lunch and had been sitting down for about half an hour when one of the trucks came in and reported that the other truck had gone the same way as the one near Zouar – it was a total wreck. So the Skipper decided to leave G Patrol behind to strip the vehicle and catch up with us later. Two of our trucks had punctures this morning. We set off again and the road became formed, but very rough and over some very rugged country. There were two more punctures before we eventually camped for the night at 5.30pm, after doing 110km.

28 January 1941 It was cold and breezy when we got up this morning and after breakfast we set off at 7am. The Skipper reckons we were about 5,000 feet up last night. We had only been going about two kilometres before we passed more French trucks which hadn't set off yet. Then the wind became very strong and we experienced our first real sand storm. Believe me it was very unpleasant. The wind was travelling across the road and the sand beat straight at us from the side.

I can quite understand why the Arabs have the headdress they do. I happened to have a scarf and it didn't take me long to wrap it round my head the way the Arabs do. Practically all other drivers found something to wrap round their faces so that only their goggles could be seen.

We had to keep very close to the truck in front or else lose sight of it altogether. Twice the sand was so thick that the Skipper got off the road and then had to search for it again. However, we arrived at Ounianga at 1pm and found a fairly sheltered place to have lunch. It was decided to stay on for the night. After having a wash, I picked some watercress to take back to camp. There were frogs and tadpoles in the springs. On my way back to camp, I saw a camel train of about 100 camels come in. By this time the wind had dropped to a breeze and there wasn't much dust flying. We got tea ready and then listened to the wireless and so to bed As we did so, we heard the natives beating the drums.

29 January 1941 *1.00pm* We set off about 7.30am this morning. G Patrol arrived last night and they are staying behind to pick up mail, rations and cigarettes which are coming out by plane tomorrow. They will catch us up later – hopefully soon. We arrived at Tekro at 10.30 after a more or less uneventful run. The wind has dropped to normal now.

When we arrived at Tekro, a soldier stopped us at the point of the bayonet. The Skipper got a bit worried when he found that the fitter's truck with the French officer on board was not with us. It was back with another truck which had a slipping clutch. However when it didn't arrive after a while, the Skipper walked up to the fort with the soldier keeping his distance and pointing the bayonet at him all the way. He eventually found the officer in charge, explained who we were and then we were made welcome.

The last time we were here there were only three Tibbu soldiers, but this time there were about twelve soldiers and the officer. It was rather a coincidence that the three Tibbus who were here last year and get relieved every month, should be on duty again this time. We filled our two-gallon water tins and the French officer gave us two packets of cigs to be divided among the whole patrol. We then set off again for Sarra wells and have now stopped for lunch about 20km from Tekro. From here on seems more like home, as we all know this country and we are looking forward to some good going between here and Sarra.

8.00pm We camped for the night at 4pm after travelling about 100km from Tekro. All guns had to be cleaned and tested before tea. The going this afternoon has been the best for weeks. At Faya our four prisoners were put behind bars for their own safety, as the natives would love to cut their throats. But while they were behind bars they wouldn't eat anything, so they were let out for meals. To show how much the natives wanted to cut their throats, one night when I had left my shirt and contents in the cookhouse, a native brought it back to me. In repayment, he wanted me to hand over the prisoners so their throats could be slit.

30 January 1941 We set off this morning at 7.30am and had a bit of rough going for a while. Soon got into the good going that we remembered from our last trip here. We had just got within 5km of Sarra wells when we saw a truck racing off to our left. The Skipper told us to wait here while he investigated, but we could see that if he were to catch up with it he would have to travel a long way. However, he stopped at the point where we first saw the truck and apparently examined the tracks. He came back and told us that he reckoned it was one of the French vehicles that was ahead of us, so he decided to carry on to the well. It was apparently a prearranged place where French would leave a note, and sure enough there was a note which solved the problem beyond doubt. So we also left a note, for when they returned.

We then looked at the well and found it had been knocked in and was dry. I dropped a stone down and it took eight seconds to hit the bottom. When it did, it was a thud instead of a splash. If the Italians did that, I suppose Bishara will be in the same condition. We are now about one kilometre north of Sarra having lunch and waiting to see if the French come back. If Bishara is also dry it will make things pretty awkward for the French, especially the Camel Corps, if they don't take Kufra. However, it will probably make them even more determined than they already are.

It is five weeks today since we left Cairo. Most of us are quite satisfied here and will be more so when we get our mail.

8.00pm We didn't leave after lunch until 4pm and the French still hadn't returned. We travelled over what we expected to be rough going, but we kept to the west of our previous tracks and struck some good going. We have now stopped for the night after doing 240km for the day. It is the most we have done in a single day for weeks.

ATTACK AT GEBEL SHERIF

31 January 1941 *10.00am* We left his morning at 7am and travelled 85km over good going to arrive at Bishara at 10am.

10.15am Just as the Skipper had got out of his truck to look at the well there was a call of "aircraft!", so we have all scattered and made for hills. A plane came over us and then swerved away. He must have spotted us and gone back to Kufra to make his report. We will probably have a visit from them this afternoon.

11.30am We have arrived at our rendezvous, 25km north of Bishara in some hills called Gebel Sherif. We have camouflaged the trucks and are getting ready for lunch. There is a picquet on top of the hill and if he sees aircraft he will fire a single shot and we will all take cover and not move. If the picquet sees land forces he will fire three shots and we'll get our trucks ready for action. We are almost certain to hear one shot this afternoon. The well at Bishara was also blown in and the soldiers had arrived by plane, as we could see where it had landed and the footprints to and from.

2.00pm The plane has arrived again and is circling around us. Every minute we expect a bomb to drop, but so far he just seems to be looking for us.

Well, I'm writing this at 8pm Feb. 1st which is the first opportunity I have had since I saw the enemy trucks. I will carry on from where I left off. As soon as I saw the trucks I rushed down to my rifle and fired three shots, whereupon everyone threw everything they had on the truck ready to move, all the time watching the plane. When it came overhead we rushed for cover, but he didn't drop any bombs. We were then in a proper fix – we didn't know whether to concentrate our attention on the plane or the trucks. Apparently the trucks, which were armed diesels, *[Fiat 637s, mounting 20mm Breda guns]* had been waiting for us and the plane had been their spotter. They were the Italian Auto-Saharan Company and the Skipper had always warned us to regard them as equal to the best British soldiers.

The trucks went behind the hill and there we were, taking cover from the plane while wondering if the troops from the trucks were going to come over the hill at us or what. However, after about half an hour the Skipper gave the order to start up, so we did and we went over to him. He told me to go to one of the entrances of the wadi, back up to it and see if anyone was there. He would follow on with all the rest. So I went over and was just backing up, when they opened fire only about a chain away with Breda machine-guns. Talk about the 'Valley of Death'. We had walked right into a death trap and if the Italians had worked out their attack a bit better none of us would have come out alive.

As it was, these Beda guns opened up with high explosive, shrapnel and armour piercing shells. They are 20 mm shells, but fired from an automatic gun. Well, I for one never expected to be writing this now and how my truck got missed I don't know. As soon as they opened up, we retreated to the other exit, naturally expecting to receive the same treatment there. Strange as it may seem, we were able to drive out of the wadi with only the shells from the first Breda guns chasing us.

Well, when we got out and counted the trucks, we found that three were missing. The plane was still circling overhead and now that we were out of the wadi we expected it to drop bombs, but couldn't see any. While milling around, we saw three men running out of the valley, so a truck rushed over and picked them up. The we saw smoke rising and knew a truck had gone up in flames. We still milled around and after about ten minutes another man ran out. The Skipper sent me and two other trucks to give them covering fire, so off we went. When Tommy McNeil *[Tpr. T B McNeil]* clambered aboard one of the trucks, we headed back, with shells bursting all round us.

The first three to run out were the two McInnes boys *[Tpr. I H McInnes, Pte. D J McInnes]* and Jock Bruce *[Pte. J Bruce, RAMC]*, our medical orderly. Their benzine tank had been leaking before they arrived at the valley and it had apparently drained right out, as the truck would not start. As usual, there is always a humorous side of everything and this time was when they arrived in the valley.

McInnes *[I H McInnes]* suggested that they mend the tank straight away but the Skipper, expecting bombers over during the afternoon said, "No, never mind, it will probably have some more holes in it by night."

When Tommy McNeil came in, he told the story of Rex Beach the corporal on his truck. As soon as the Italian guns opened up, Rex returned fire with his Vickers and only stopped when a high explosive shell hit him dead centre. McInnes's truck was the first to go up in smoke and then Tommy's. When he saw his go up, he decided there were three things he could do: surrender, take to the hills, or make a run down the gully towards our trucks. All except the first option were practically suicide. Yet he chose the last, and if he hadn't have been so small he would probably have been hit. As it was, he had a piece of shrapnel in his arm which turned out to be a bit of copper from a driving band.

He told us that Skin Moore *[Tpr. R J Moore]* and his crew Jack Winchester, *[Guardsman A Winchester]* who had been through Dunkirk, and John Easton, *[Guardsman J Easton]* another Scotsman, and two of our prisoners had taken to the hills. They must be either prisoners or killed. He also told us that when he decided to make a run for it, he told 'Snowy' the Tommy fitter *[Private A Tighe]* who was riding on his truck to follow. He doesn't know whether Snowy did follow and was killed or whether he took to the hills. Two of our prisoners were in McInnes' truck when it was hit by a shell, exploded and caught fire, so they must be dead.

About 4pm we circled round the two trucks in case any men came running out on that side. When we got to the other side we saw the third column of smoke rising and heard the bangs of munitions going up, but we couldn't see any more and we didn't locate a target for the Bofors to open up on.

In the meantime, a second bomber arrived overhead and was circling round the hills. While we were stopped, the two trucks we had left on the other side of the hill came racing in and told us that they were being chased. So the Skipper ordered us to run to a prearranged rendezvous and told Bruce Ballantyne that if (the Skipper) didn't turn up there, to carry on and join the French.

Off we went and immediately the bombers attacked. By this time, a third bomber had arrived on the scene. Luckily the going was good except for a few scattered boulders. There we were, trying to dodge the boulders and the bombs, all at the same time. The first plane came across us from the right and, by judging the speed of the truck and that of the plane, I reckoned I would pass the bombs by the time they landed. So I gave 'Tirau' *[Jopling's truck]* all she had and she went like a champion. Then we heard, 'Boom! Boom! Boom!' and saw

T Patrol truck Te Paki, one of three destroyed in the ambush at Gebel Sherif. In front of the vehicle lies an Italian prisoner killed in the crossfire. Note the large quantity of burnt out four-gallon tins that had contained fuel and water.
(LRDG (NZ) Association.)

the line of bombs drop about a chain behind us. We saw them go closer still to Bruce Ballantyne's truck, yet it kept going OK. Then we saw another plane coming from the right and reckoned that if I kept going ahead I would run straight into the bombs. So I turned left and soon after saw another line of bombs bursting just to our right.

Well we dodged like this for about half an hour. These two planes were Ghiblis *[Caproni Ca 309]*. After a while we saw the third plane coming towards us. This was a Savoia plane *[Savoia-Marchetti SM 79]* – a bigger and better plane than the Ghibli. He dived down, heading straight for our truck. Well, I thought this was the end, as except for our speed we never had a chance of dodging. I thought he was going to drop his bombs when he came over and that they must either hit or go so close that they would wreck the truck. However, as he came within about a hundred yards 'Smithy' *[Trooper E B Smith]*, my gunner, opened up with the Lewis gun and emptied a whole drum into him. Some of his shots obviously hit when the plane passed over our truck, as it was only about 14 feet above us. I waited for the crash as the bomb burst on the truck, but it didn't happen. All we saw was a line of machine-gun bullets, which missed the tail of the truck by inches.

From then on, the planes concentrated on other vehicles and we headed flat-out for the rendezvous. It wasn't long before we were in the lead. Three of us arrived at the rendezvous, followed later by another three, making a total of six. Besides the three which we knew had

Destroyed T Patrol trucks at Gebel Sherif after an attack by the Italian Auto-Saharan Company in 31 January 1941. In the foreground is the Chevrolet WB in which Corporal Rex Beech was killed while delaying the enemy with his Vickers machine-gun. At the rear is Te Aroha, Trooper Ron Moore's truck. It was from this point that he and his crew set out on their remarkable 10-day trek to Allied lines.
(LRDG (NZ) Association.)

been destroyed, the Skipper's truck and the wireless truck were still missing.

We decided to make a cup of tea and have some rum and hoped they would arrive soon. Just as the tea was boiling, I yelled out, "Trucks coming!" We all got up on a sand dune and saw the wireless truck come into sight. Afterwards they explained that they had been machine-gunned by a dive bomber for about 20 minutes and the truck had been hit several times. As they left the truck and took cover, Tony Browne had been grazed in the foot and Vince Spain *[Trooper V C Spain]* had been grazed three times in the leg and foot. The plane apparently thought their truck was finished, so then concentrated on the Skipper's V8. When the aircraft left, the others hopped back on board and they headed for the rendezvous. They reckon that the last time they saw the Skipper's truck, a burst of machine-gun fire went right across its front seat. They didn't know what happened after that. 'Wink' Adams was driving and the Skipper was sitting beside him in the front seat. 'Clarrie' Roderick was in the back, manning the Vickers.

Bruce Ballantyne had his orders, which were to warn the French that the Italians were waiting for them, so we decided to head for the French positions. At about 8pm we camped for the night 120km from Gebel Sherif. There we had another cup of tea and some biscuits. The three of us on my truck will do picquet tonight and we have to be up at about 4pm for breakfast. I was on picquet from 11pm to 12pm and it was the longest hour I have ever spent. I jumped at the slightest sound, no matter what it was, and the next morning the others said the same. While we were boiling the tea, someone said they saw a light on the horizon. Out went the fires, but it was only a setting star.

1 FEBRUARY 1941 We were up at 4am this morning to boil the billy for a cup of tea at 5am. We put a few biscuits in our pockets and just as we were packing up, someone yelled, "Trucks on the horizon!" We all rushed to our vehicles while Bruce looked through his glasses – only to find they were just a couple of rocks. Well, we set off at 5.45am, expecting the bombers would be over at about 8am. We were anxious to get to the other side of Sarra before they came, and it was close to 8am when we got there.

Just before we arrived at Sarra, we saw G Patrol minus Lieutenant Gibbs' troop, which is collecting our mail, and we explained everything to them. They started to load their trucks and seemed to us to be very slow. I suppose it was the nervous state we were in – expecting a plane over any minute. We carried on and left them to follow, and, just as we were beginning to feel more or less safe and had stopped to let the rest catch up, the yell "aircraft!" went up. We hopped into the trucks and were off before you could say "Knife!" But as at Bishara, as soon as the plane spotted us it turned around and headed back. Nonetheless, that didn't stop us and we kept on until we met Gibbs' troop with our mail etc on board. We explained the situation to them and Gibbs said that the French had taken a course to our right as his troop went to intercept them.

We carried on until 1pm when we had a bit of lunch. Moving on again, we soon saw French trucks ahead. Joining up with them was going to be a rather delicate matter, as they could think we were Italians and open up on us. We waited on top of a hill while one truck went ahead to explain who we were. Then we followed on. We arrived at the border where we are now camped, at 4pm. We have travelled about 500km since 5pm last night and everyone is tired out. You have only to look at them to see what a strain they have been through during the last 24 hours. All we need now is a good night's sleep.

2 FEBRUARY 1941 Apparently Colonel Leclerc of the Free French had decided to call the Kufra operation off for now, but their bombers are still going to attack it, starting today. I hope they spot the Auto-Saharan patrol and give them a taste of what they gave us. Last night we received our mail. It was wonderful. I had a telegram from Irene and one from her mother. I also received four letters from Irene and a parcel. Bruce has gone to meet Colonel Leclerc, who was supposed to be about 50km up the road, but apparently is now at Sarra. We have to wait for his return, which probably won't be tonight.

Lately I have been getting a fair bit of toothache, especially at night, and with this sitting round all day it has come back. We have had some great news from Cairo tonight. They sent over a message in plain English that the Skipper, 'Wink' Adams and 'Clarrie' Roderick are prisoners of war. Also that the Air Force mechanic from Murzuk is now free. We were all very pleased to hear it, as we had expected the worst.

I am afraid the rest must have been killed.

3 FEBRUARY 1941 I hardly slept at all last night and decided I had to get the tooth out somehow. So I went to the doctor and he wouldn't take it out as it was a back tooth and he had no pincers to get hold of it, He said he would give me dope. I have had toothache all day today and have been very miserable. If it is going to be like this for the ten days until we get to Cairo, I shall probably be crazy by then.

Bruce arrived back at about 1.30 this morning and at breakfast he told us the story. First of all, at Colonel Leclerc's request, Bruce thanked the patrol for all they had done and especially T Patrol for what they had found the other day. 'Manuka' which is the truck that stopped behind at Tekro to navigate for the French, is going to make a sort of reconnaissance of Kufra. We are picking up some benzine here and are taking two French trucks with us to see if there are still any Italians at Uweinat. If so, the French will return and the whole force will take it. We will then carry on to Cairo via Wadi Halfa, a place I want to see. I believe it is a beautiful drive from there to Cairo.

When Bruce was coming home last night, Crichton-Stuart was with him in his V8 and about 60km from here, he knocked a hole in his sump with a boulder. Because of that we won't leave here now until tomorrow morning.

◈ **4 February 1941** ◈ We set off at last for Cairo at 7.30 this morning and have now stopped for lunch after doing 150km over lovely sandy going. More or less another sand sea. We have one 15cwt Dodge and one 30 cwt Bedford *[the French trucks]* with us. They get stuck more often than we do, but are keeping up pretty well.

8.00pm We have camped for the night after doing 272km, which is a lot further than we expected to do. It has been good going all the way, but we still haven't crossed our tracks of last September. I am on picquet again tonight, as we are short handed.

This evening our wireless operator was trying to get Cairo when an Italian station came in on the same frequency and repeated, "Moore is here" several times. It seems as though Moore is not dead, but a prisoner.

◈ **5 February 1941** ◈ *9.00am* I was on picquet from 4am to 5am and as breakfast wasn't until 6am, I made fish cakes to fill in the time. They turned out very nice. We left this morning at 6am and we have now done 75km. The doctor's truck has broken another axle. So the two French trucks and three of ours, including Crichton-Stuart, have gone on to Uweinat to find out if anyone is there. They are going to try to not be seen, so neither of the heavier Bofors trucks have gone with them. We are going straight on to Kharga and then Cairo, but the others will probably catch up before we get there. Unfortunately we are not going through Wadi Halfa, as we have enough benzine to take us straight to Cairo. The reason we were going to Wadi Halfa in the first place was to pick up benzine.

1.00pm We have just finished lunch and we can see Kissu and Uweinat just on our left. Two G Patrol trucks haven't arrived here yet, so our fitter's truck has gone back to find out what is the matter. They only took one and a half hours to fix the doctor's truck, which was pretty good going.

8.00pm We have now camped for the night after doing 240km for the day, which is pretty good considering we had to wait one and a half hours for the doctor's V8, and there were delays from 7 tyres having to be changed due to punctures.

We are camped in the Sudan, about 14km south of Kissu. Uweinat is plainly visible about 35km away.

◈ **6 February 1941** ◈ We set off at 6.30 this morning, but at 8am we had to wait for one of G Patrol to change a tyre owing to a puncture. We set off again at 10am. Then we had to wait for our Bofors truck to change a tyre. I was driving along behind the doctor's truck when I saw a wheel take off in one direction and the V8 in another. Needless to say it was another broken axle. So Bruce decided to have lunch and we are waiting for the fitters to finish the V8. So far we have travelled 159km.

8 00pm Just before we moved off, the yell of "Trucks coming!" went up and we all stood to our trucks ready for any emergency. They turned out to be Crichton-Stuart with the two trucks. They went close to Uweinat, but left everything else for the French. They say there are some very recent Auto-Saharan tracks here. Probably if we hadn't stayed a few days on the French border we might have found them waiting for us. After they had shown the French where Ain Dua and Ain Zouar were, they left to catch us up.

We set off again at 2.30pm and the doctor's V8 broke another axle at 4.30pm, so Bruce decided to camp here for the the night. We had travelled 220km. It has been very warm all day and cloudy. At 7pm I was listening to the wireless without a shirt on when a wall of wind hit us and the dust blew. It is still blowing and is very cold now. I had to put on my shirt, jersey and overcoat. I hope the wind drops by the morning, although I don't give it much hope.

7 FEBRUARY 1941 We set off this morning at 7am and travelled over the beautiful going, although a bit soft. By lunch time we had covered 202km. After lunch the country gradually got rougher and wilder, until now it is just a mass of hills and we have to make our way through valleys and over the hills.

The doctor's Ford 15 cwt sunk up to its rear axle. To make it easier to push out, the men unloaded the stores, including the medical kit contained in the wicker basket.

The wind has been blowing strongly all day and it has been very cold. This morning the sand was blowing so bad that it hurt us as it hit our faces. We have finished up by doing 355km, which I think is our record normal daily mileage. We are about 90km from Kharga and it is still about 600 from there to Cairo. We will be travelling all night and tomorrow night, as there is nowhere to sleep along that road.

This evening there were a lot of smiling faces when we heard over the air that Benghazi had fallen. We consider our war here practically over now.

◈ **8 February 1941** ◈ *12 noon* Well, we have set off on our more or less a non-stop run to Cairo of approximately 819km. We are now at Kharga after covering 164km. Here we are to pick up benzine and cigarettes and then set off for Cairo. The water for tea is on the fire now and we will be having lunch shortly.

Dick Croucher, *[Lt. C H B Croucher]* who just before we left Cairo was a lance corporal and was promoted to lieutenant in one jump into the Tommy army, came here a while ago and told us that the NZ Division didn't want us back and that if we weren't back by February 16th we would go into the 4th Reinforcements.

◈ **9 February 1941** ◈ We arrived back at the Citadel at 11am, after travelling about 800km non stop except for meals etc. Our eyes are sore and look bloodshot, and we are all pretty tired. As soon as we arrived, Colonel Bagnold inspected us and what trucks we had left, and had a look at our bullet holes. The British sgt. major then told us to take our trucks round to the store and forget about them, as he would get someone else to unload them. The next job was to get our mail and pay – which we got at 3pm. After reading our mail we went into Cairo to get a haircut and shave.

Back at base the trucks were unloaded and given the usual post-operational maintenance. Jopling was given four days leave which included an appointment with the army dentist. By chance he met a correspondent who planned to visit the LRDG, as its existence was now to be revealed to the public. Due to the impact of the Fezzan campaign, GHQ was not longer in a position to regard the Group as a secret unit, so all its activities and deeds could now be published. Frank explains in his diary:

◈ **11 February 1941** ◈ He told me he was a correspondent and that in a few days our escapades would be made public and published all over the world. I told him that I had a long diary and plenty of photos and he said that that was just what he wanted. He came back to the barracks with me and I was allowed to show him my diary and photos. I agreed to lend them to him for a few days.

This publicity went further and radio broadcasts were recorded, as follows:

13 FEBRUARY 1941 Today we were told that at 9am tomorrow morning some of us were going to do some broadcasting, describing everything about this LRDG. They wanted me to give a talk on French rations. So today we prepared our speeches.

14 FEBRUARY 1941 We went out to Maadi at 9am and finished making the records by 2pm. The announcer told me he had read my diary and he would like to record me reading it. I said I would do it, but it would have to go through the censor first.

15-24 FEBRUARY: Jopling also went to the office of the 'Parade' magazine where they went through his photos looking for those suitable for publication and wrote the captions. In addition, his comrades wanted copies of his photos, so he spent a day sorting out negatives for processing. One day while on leave in Cairo he witnessed a boy being run over by a tram. He wrote briefly about the incident: "It was a sight I would not want to see again, the boy was in an awful mess, but death must have been instantaneous."

The men were pleased to hear that Major Clayton, though now a POW, had been awarded the Distinguished Service Order. Also, that after a ten-day trek, Ron Moore, Jack Winchester and Alf Tighe had been picked up by the French in an exhausted state near Sarra. But they were saddened to learn that Jack Easton had died.

Bruce Ballantyne was promoted to captain and made commander of T Patrol. His 2 I/C was Lieutenant E W (Walter) Ellingham, who had joined the LRDG with 23 other men from the 4th Reinforcements. These troops replaced those who had to return to their units and would later fight in Greece and Crete. The patrol's next mission would be to relieve R Patrol, which for the previous two months had helped Australian troops lay siege against the Italian-occupied town of Giarabub, about 260 kilometres south of Bardia.

SIEGE OF GIARABUB

25 FEBRUARY 1941 I heard this morning that we were moving out again tomorrow morning to relieve R Patrol who have been patrolling around Giarabub. They are trying to starve the town into surrender, as they don't want to shell it because it is a holy city. R Patrol has been there two months making sure no food gets in or troops get out. Now we are to relieve them. It is very short notice and was very unexpected, as all our Chevs are at Universal Motors getting fixed up and we expected to be here another two weeks. However, it appears that we are taking four new V8s *[Ford F30 4x4 30cwt trucks.]* So today was naturally busy getting them loaded up for the trip.

26-28 FEBRUARY: On their way to Giarabub the patrol suffered very bad weather with strong winds and rain. On 1 March they met up with Captain D G Steele, commander of R Patrol.

1 MARCH 1941 The weather is still bitterly cold and we left Siwa at 11am after taking on water and benzine. We met Captain Steele with a few of his patrol in their wireless truck. He had heard that we were on our way, so came to meet us. They had just brought in four American D4 tractors captured from an Italian convoy that had been machine-gunned by our planes. R Patrol had been sent out to pick up anything worthwhile and burn the rest. They said they had heard about our escapades over the wireless, but that the Murzuk affair had been credited to the French.

2 MARCH 1941 3.00pm We set off again this morning at 7am, as cold as ever. Arrived at the Aussie camp at 9am. There were about 200 camped there, but they were nearly all away on patrol. They too were making sure no convoys went in or out of Giarabub. Apparently all the Libyan soldiers in Giarabub have surrendered themselves to the Aussies, some of them coming in the middle of the night and waking the troops up. We left there at 9.30am, leaving Bruce Ballantyne and Capt. Steele behind to see some Aussie officer.

We were led by one of R Patrol who knew the road but after we had covered about 70km, they decided that they were on the wrong road and started hunting for the right one, without success. We were about to set off along another road when McInnes asked if they took the tractors in from the camp yesterday. They said "yes", so Mac suggested that they retrace their tracks until they came to the tractor marks and follow them. It was just as well we did, as that other road would have taken us well away from the camp.

We eventually arrived at the camp at 12.30pm. They were very glad to see us, as they are tired of staying out here doing nothing. They reckoned they'd never seen anything, yet we had only been there about an hour when the yell of "aircraft!" went up. There to the north-east of us were two Italian bombers heading west and about half an hour later they came back to the west side of us.

Three trucks have gone out to show our NCOs where the minefields are and I don't suppose it will be long before they arrive back.

8.00pm The trucks arrived back at 4pm and we set about getting tea ready. R Patrol are all very keen to get away tomorrow, as they have been here nearly 10 weeks.

An R Patrol Chevrolet WB with her crew wrapped up against the cold. R Patrol vehicles featured a tiki symbol on the bonnet, whereas a kiwi identified T Patrol vehicles. Tthe headlights and windscreen are covered in cloth to prevent sun reflection giving away the patrols position. A .303 Lewis gun is mounted on the left.

⌐**3 March 1941**⌐ We got R Patrol away at 7.30am this morning and I had a look at what rations they left us. The LRDG has had Aussie rations and they certainly seem to give plenty, as R Patrol left cases of food untouched. We are supposed to collect next week's rations tomorrow or the next day. It has turned out a lovely day today and I am just thinking that this life will do me quite well for a while. I made rissoles for lunch today and they were very much appreciated. This evening we heard over the wireless that the French had taken Kufra. Good for them and I hope they got the Saharan Company too.

At 1.30pm Lieut. Ellingham took a party to look around the minefields and at 3pm Bruce Ballantyne and Tony Browne went to look for a new camp site. This one has been used long enough, so we are moving out tomorrow.

⌐**4 March 1941**⌐ Another party went out to relieve the men that went to Abbots Gulch, which is a place the Italians would have to go through if they decided to make a run for it. If they do so, we would wireless an aerodrome which would send out bombers. The watch stays at Abbots Gulch 24 hours and is then relieved by another party. This afternoon at 1.15pm I was lying down having a smoke when the expected call of "aircraft!" went up along with "Take cover and don't move." I grudgingly got up and, not forgetting my tin hat, found some cover where I am now sitting. The two enemy planes took the same course as they did the other day, but so far have not returned. It is a lovely warm day and I only have my shorts on.

8.00pm The planes haven't come back yet, so they must have gone well round. This afternoon we had a game of bridge.

5-7 MARCH: *The watch continued uneventfully.*

8 MARCH 1941 Today was warm again and this morning Bruce Ballantyne took another truck to the Aussie camp for water and benzine. He also wanted to see the Aussie colonel. At about 10am we saw three planes do the same circle as before. There is no doubt they have got something up their sleeve. They wouldn't hang on at Giarabub as they are if they knew that they would have to surrender in the end. The sooner we get a fighter or two up there, the sooner we will put a stop to these bombers coming over.

Bruce arrived back at 5pm with a gazelle and then we heard about a stunt we are going to do the day after tomorrow. Apparently the idea is to get within two or three thousand yards and then get our Bofors truck to tempt the mobile Italian gun to come and chase us. If it works, Aussie guns will open up and try to put him it of action. We heard on the wireless tonight from Berlin that the attack on Giarabub had been repulsed. I don't know what attack they are talking about, as no attack has yet been made.

9 MARCH 1941 This morning I went for a trip down to the mines that are laid on the south road, but saw nothing there. On our way back we saw two men standing on a hill, so we got our guns ready and approached stealthily, but they turned out to be Bruce Ballantyne and Sergeant Jack Sheppard. When we drew alongside them they asked us if we had fired any flares or seen anything, when we replied in the negative they told us that one of the boys had seen a red flare go up in our direction, so came to investigate.

We returned to camp and another two trucks went out to look all round, but they returned without seeing anything. This afternoon at 2.30pm we saw five bombers coming from Giarabub closer to us than any so far. We are wondering how we didn't hear them going there. No doubt that there is something fishy going on there. If they were certain that they would have to surrender shortly, they wouldn't be sending all these bombers over. *[It was later revealed the the town was being supplied by parachute drop.]* This evening Bruce told me that I wouldn't be going on this stunt tomorrow, but would be in charge of base. Two trucks and five men are staying behind. We heard a NZ News Bulletin on the wireless tonight which was very good. I had to prepare 28 lunches today for the men going out tomorrow.

T Patrol's flag. The fabric was green and the letter white. Thy were usually flown on the commander and 2 IC vehicles.

10 MARCH 1941 *10.00am* Well, we had reveille at 6am, and the nine trucks left at 8am. Bruce told me that they expected to be back at 4.30pm and said I should have plenty of water boiling, as two troops of Aussies as well as a few Tommy Royal Artillery would be coming back with them. He also told me that if he didn't turn up tonight, to go down to the Aussie camp at 8am tomorrow. So far we have not heard any shooting, but I suppose it will start any time now.

4.30pam We had just made morning tea when we heard trucks approaching and I got up on top of a hill with the glasses and saw three trucks coming. I could see that they were our trucks and the leading one was flying the green flag – the recognition signal. I wondered why the three trucks were coming back, but soon found out when they joined us. Yesterday the Aussie colonel got hit by some shrapnel and was badly wounded, so they postponed the stunt. However, when they arrived at their meeting place they saw some men on a hill not far away. At first they thought they were Aussies, so they went to investigate. They turned out to be eight Libyan soldiers who escaped from Giarabub to surrender. We heard the Italian guns last night and apparently they were shooting at these Libyans as they made their escape. They told us that the aeroplanes are only dropping food, but the Italians get it all and the Libyans practically starve.

A campsite during the siege at Giarabub, March 1941. This semi-permanent camp uses the truck for comfort and shade. Note the range of supplies and cooking arrangements like pots and primus stoves. The men would rest under the shelter during the midday heat. The weapons have been covered to prevent windblown dust and sand jamming the mechanisms.

At 11am we heard planes and got on top of a rise and scanned the horizon with glasses. Sure enough two planes were coming down the same track as usual and I followed them through the glasses all the time. They were below the horizon at Giarabub for 12 minutes, then came up over the sand sea and then went out of sight again, in the direction of Jalo. Sgt. Shepherd's truck and another are over on the south road which the planes follow after leaving the town. But the planes didn't waver in their flight so I presume they never spotted Shepherd. His party arrived back at 5pm and said that the planes had passed right overhead. Either they weren't seen, or no notice was taken of them.

Bruce Ballantyne and his crew stayed at the Aussie camp tonight and five trucks, including the wireless truck, are setting out tomorrow to look at Jalo.

11-13 MARCH *The Giarabub watch continued and the weather deteriorated.*

14 MARCH 1941 *2.00pm* Today is a proper miserable day. Last night the wind blew our shelter down and today the wind is still blowing strong. So is the sand. The sand got so bad that we had to shift our truck to a better position, but even now the sand is very bad. As far as our food is concerned, everything that is opened gets full of sand and it is hard to boil the billy. In fact it is uncomfortable to do anything. After lunch two trucks went to see the Aussies at Abbots Gulch.

15-17 MARCH *The routine continued, only broken by small local reconnaissance patrols and the excitement of receiving mail.*

18 MARCH 1941 At 11.30am we heard trucks and it turned out to be the Jalo party. They reckoned they had been looking for us for the last half hour, so they went back to

T Patrol Ford F30 trucks cross a gap in the the Wire. Built by the Italians along the Egypt/Libya border, this tangled barbed-wire fence ran for 320 kilometres from Bardia to Giarabub. (Craw)

A White truck of the LRDG's Heavy Section. These trucks hauled supplies to bases and forward dumps to ensure the patrols were always well provisioned.

direct the others while I prepared lunch for 33 men. The others arrived at 12.30pm and brought our mail. I received two from Irene and three from mother. It was wonderful, and I am afraid I missed my lunch in my excitement to read them.

The men said Jalo was unoccupied, but they found 14 burnt-out trucks there. They must have been short of benzine and rather than leave them, they set them on fire. White flags were flying from every mast at Jalo fort. They hoisted one of T Patrol's green flags above one of them. No one was there except some native civilians who were apparently short of food. They gave them some biscuits and tea and in return the natives gave them some eggs. The next morning the men had scrambled eggs for breakfast.

Apparently we are to take our battle position on Thursday and on that night the Aussie infantry will attack. Only one battalion and a *[12 gun]* battery of artillery are coming. Tomorrow we are all going down near the Aussie camp. At 4pm we got a nasty shock when the cry of "aircraft!" went up and six planes came right overhead. We expected bombs to burst all around us, but much to our relief they passed without dropping any. They must have seen us all the same. Perhaps it is just as well we are leaving here tomorrow. I think they must know about the impending attack on Giarabub.

19 MARCH 1941 *9.00am* I got up at 5am and had breakfast ready by 5.45am. After that we packed up and were away by 7am. Just after we set off, the Bofors truck had carburettor trouble. We waited for a while then decided to go on slowly, but it didn't catch up with us until 9.15. We stopped in some hills about 9 miles from the barbed wire fence *[known to the patrols as 'the wire']* which runs from Giarabub to the coast, and decided to make our home here for a while. We are camped about 12 miles from the town. We boiled up and then Bruce asked if I would like to go and have a yarn with the Aussies, as he had to visit them. When we arrived there I wanted to find out as much as possible about the forthcoming attack on Giarabub. I found out that the infantry are in their positions, but are expecting to wait for three days before the main attack. They are very well armed, as they have Tommy guns as well as 3 inch mortars, which are very effective. They have air support by way of three Lysanders that are used as artillery spotters and one Vickers Valentia employed as a hospital plane.

20 March 1941 Last night we saw what appeared to be a thunder and lightning display, but actually it was the *[Royal Artillery]* 25 pounders in action all night and this morning. Today there is another of those blinking sand storms, which makes things very unpleasant. Before lunch we were told we'd move before tea, so I cooked a hot lunch, thinking that we might not be allowed fires tonight, and also that we might get into a sandier spot than this. We had just had a cup of tea and were all loaded up to go, but Bruce has just got a wireless message from the Aussies and is deciphering it. We will be on the move shortly.

8.00pm We arrived here at 5.30pm – between Abbots Gulch and the south road, and about five kilometres from Giarabub. As soon as we arrived we had to find a suitable place, hidden as much as possible from aircraft, and then get tea ready. We found a great spot to hide the truck, but tea wasn't too easy as the wind and sand were still blowing. However, we managed to get tea ready by 6.15pm, after which we built a sort of shelter at the back of the truck. Just as we finished it, it started to rain. We saw the best display of forked lightning we had ever seen. Fortunately, we only got the edge of the storm or we would have been flooded out. We are about 11km from Giarabub.

21 March 1941 At about 2am the wind dropped altogether for two hours and at 4am it got up again in exactly the opposite direction, making our tent useless. Reveille was at 6am, so at 5am we had to try and get breakfast. It was a rotten job in this sort of weather, but somehow we eventually got it ready. After breakfast we moved about a kilometre to try and get some better shelter, but it is just as bad where we are now. At 9am, one troop went up and looked at the south road and came back to say they had seen nothing. They went again this afternoon and at the same time another troop went to Abbots Gulch. Both returned without seeing anything.

It seems strange that we should be fighting Giarabub and yet we have to tune into the Rome radio to find out how we are getting on. They said that the heavy artillery and infantry attack on the town had been successfully repulsed. But of course, coming from

Rome that could mean anything. They also said that Giarabub was going to fight to the last man. If so, there is certainly going to be some slaughter before it is taken. The sand storm has been a lot worse today and they say that a sand storm either lasts one day or three days, so I suppose we will have another day of it tomorrow. Needless to say, no planes came over today or yesterday. I am on picquet tonight.

22 March 1941 *10.00am* The wind blew very strongly during the night, so we put three trucks together and made a house. But whatever you do, it is impossible to keep out the sand. At 5am the wind calmed down, only to start up again at 9am, but so far it has not reached the severity of yesterday. Our wireless truck received a message from the Aussies: "We are at the Villa, the bubble has burst." Well, that could mean anything, so Bruce has gone to the Aussies to find out. If Giarabub has fallen, he will wireless instructions to pick up our mines and proceed to the town via the south road. If not, he will tell us what to do.

Official T Patrol photograph taken just outside Cairo in March 1941, after the the siege of Giarabub. Back row, left to right: F W Jopling, R T Porter, R A Simpson, W D S Forbes, J P L Macassey, L A McIver, V J Heard, E C Stutterd, A J Job, R W N Lewis, I G McCulloch, T E Ritchie, G T Smith, (obscured). In front: M H Craw, L Payne, O W Wright. (Craw)

1.45pm I was sitting in my truck reading when I heard a rumble and I yelled out that I had heard either gunfire or bombs dropping. No one seemed to believe me and shortly afterwards I asked, "Are those our trucks coming?" Someone replied, "What trucks?" Then another pointed out four planes almost above us. They sounded just like trucks. Then we heard a terrific bang and saw clouds of dust rise up about 3km away. I don't know whether they were aiming at us or Giarabub, but it was a pretty rotten shot. They must have been at least 8,000 feet up. They were bigger bombs than the ones they had previously dropped.

3.30pm No more planes have been over yet, but we happened to switch on to Daventry radio for the news and there we heard that Giarabub had fallen and 800 prisoners taken. Here we are fighting Giarabub, and we had to find out when it had fallen from Daventry in England.

8.00pm Bruce arrived back at 5pm, having been to Giarabub. He says that we all we have to do now is pick up our mines and go home. His V8 broke an axle today, so that will have to be fixed tomorrow. He says the Aussies killed 180 Italians, wounded about 300 and captured 600, making a total of over 1,000 altogether. The Aussies had 28 killed and 87 wounded. Those four planes we saw flying at about 8,000 ft were Heinkels and they had dive-bombed Giarabub, but without doing any damage. They must have had one or two bombs left, so let them go near us on the way home. Well, that is the last oasis in Libya to be captured. Our next jobs will be in Tripoli and the Fezzan.

Trooper Ron 'Skin' Moore of T Patrol. Moore led an epic ten-day desert trek on foot, which saved all his crew other than one soldier who later died of exhaustion and wounds. For this effort, Moore was the first member of 2NZEF to receive a Distinguished Conduct Medal. Moore wears a keffiyeh, the mustard coloured official LRDG headdress issued in 1941. It gave good protection from sandstorms and the sun.

23-24 MARCH 1941 *The patrol lifted all the mines they had laid, packed up and set out for Cairo. They had received a message from GHQ, saying they had to stop about ten miles outside Cairo, so official photographers could take their pictures.*

25 MARCH 1941 We set off this morning at 7am and had lunch 50 miles from Alexandria. I had a puncture and another truck is being towed because it has worn out a big end. We set off again and stopped at Halfway House at 3.20pm for refreshments, then carried on to where we are now, 58km from Cairo. We could have gone straight in, but have to wait for our photos to be taken. We had just lit the fires etc. when G Patrol joined us and camped alongside us for the night. They are apparently heading for Benghazi, and are sure to see some action there. Y Patrol *[Yeomanry]* are also leaving in the morning.

We heard a bit about the adventures of Skin Moore, Winchester, Tighe and Easton. They walked from Gebel Sherif to past Sarra, a distance of 220 miles with only two gallons of water between them all. Easton had been wounded in the throat and Moore was shot in the foot and the whole trip took 10 days. When the French found them they made some tea. Easton drank his and when he had finished, he said in a weak voice, "I don't take sugar in my tea," and died shortly after. At Sarra, Tighe found a match in one of the buildings, and they collected anything that could burn and lit a fire. This warmed them up and probably enabled them to keep going for a while longer. They are all still in hospital, suffering mostly from exhaustion. *[See Appendix 1 – Frank's letter to Irene regarding a misleading newspaper account of Easton's death.]*

26 March 1941 9.00am We set off this morning shortly after 7am and we are now waiting for the photographer to turn up. There was a thick fog this morning, but it has now cleared.

8.00am The photographer duly turned up and took a lot of photos for official records. We eventually left there at 11.15am and arrived at the Citadel at 12 noon. We were paid one pound and we went to Cairo to get cleaned up and have a bath. I was very surprised to see how they have increased the ARP *[air raid precautions]* in Cairo. There are new shelters all over the place.

27 March-8 April 1941: *The original Chevrolet WB 30s were being replaced by four wheel drive Ford F30s and these vehicles were prepared for desert use. Trooper Ron Moore had returned to the patrol after recovering from his great trek and had been awarded the Distinguished Conduct Medal. He and Jopling were ordered to Maadi camp to record their experiences for a radio broadcast. The patrol was told to prepare for its next trip, which was to establish a base at Tazerbo near Kufra. Meanwhile, no news had been heard from G and Y Patrols for some time, and it was feared that they had run into serious trouble, as the Germans were advancing on Benghazi and had taken Jalo. It was not until the wounded patrol commander arrived by plane that the situation was revealed.*

8 April 1941 The OC of Y Patrol arrived by plane today. He was wounded and had signalled the RAF who landed and took him on board, leaving his driver and a third man behind. This is a terrible thing for a patrol OC to do and there may yet be a court martial over it. It appears that his patrol were chasing an enemy unit when his truck ran over a mine. How the remainder of his patrol is or where they are, he doesn't know. We also heard news from G Patrol today. From what we can gather there are 16 men alive, all on one truck. Apparently enemy bombers came over and dropped mines, and then chased the patrol into them.

TO KUFRA

9-11 APRIL 1941: *Final preparations were made for the trip to Kufra.*

12 APRIL 1941 *1.30pm* We left here this morning with some of the HQ trucks. We have a captured Italian truck *[Fiat Spa. AS 37]* and it was very slow, so when we got past the pyramids they unloaded it and distributed the load among the other vehicles. After that it was a bit better until one of the HQ trucks got stuck and held us up for quite a bit. Well, we have now finished lunch and HQ has gone on, so we will follow shortly. Colonel Bagnold is with us, but for some reason or other, Capt. Ballantyne is staying in Cairo until Monday

8.00pm Apparently Colonel Bagnold wanted to reach Big Dunes before he camped, but as something went wrong with the Spa, we have camped about ten miles from the dunes. None of us were looking forward to the trip with the V8s, *[Ford 4x4 F30s]* but so far I think they are as good as the Chevs. They are not nearly so comfortable in the front seat, but they go alright and they seem to ride the bumps better than the Chevs. However, the fun will start when something goes wrong, as the engines are very hard to get at. We heard today that R Patrol had been bombed at Kufra. We all reckoned it was a mad idea making a base at Kufra when the Germans were advancing. However I suppose the 'Heads' know what they are doing. We finished up the day by doing 122 miles.

This trip I have at last managed to get off the ration truck. I am now driving the Bofors truck which is called the 'Hare'. It was great just to sit down until someone else called, "Come and get it!" This time Denis Bassett *[Tpr. D M Bassett]*, Tom Ritchie *[Tpr. T E Ritchie]* and Merlyn Craw *[Tpr. M H Craw]* are on the ration truck. On my truck I have Tom Walsh *[Gnr. T E Walsh]* and 'Sandy' Sanders *[Gnr. E Sanders]*.

13 APRIL 1941 *8.00am Easter Day* We left this morning at 6am and had pretty good going up to now. Colonel Bagnold's V8 broke down and we are now waiting for him, after covering 42 miles.

5.00pm Colonel Bagnold didn't arrive back until 9am and when he did, we set off again along the Baharia Road. At 10am the Spa broke a big end, so they decided to leave it behind. While they were taking everything they needed off it, Shaw told me to follow him to Baharia to get some oranges. So off we went, driving pretty fast considering the going, and we eventually arrived there at 1pm. There is a population of 6,000, all natives. Just before we left, a sand storm sprung up, which made things a bit uncomfortable in places. There are a few Arab Legion in the town who look after the place. When we arrived, our job was to endeavour to buy some oranges. By 3pm we had got to 220, so we decided it was time we got moving as Bagnold seemed to be in a hurry. When we got back to the Arab Legion post, we found all the other trucks waiting for us and we immediately set off again, heading for Ain Dalla. We are now at a bad spot. I was lucky enough to try a new track and got over without getting stuck, but most of the other trucks got stuck and we are now waiting for the last few to come over.

10.00pm We stopped for the night at 6.15pm after travelling 128 miles. My battery wasn't charging, so the first job was to try to repair it. We changed the dynamo, but found it still wouldn't work. After examining the voltage regulator we discovered that the cutout would stay cut out instead of going in. We were still none the wiser, as we couldn't understand why

Ford F30 trucks lined up outside the Citadel in Cairo before their first trip. By mid 1941 the F30s had replaced the well-worn Chevrolet WBs. The metal canopy frames were later removed. (Craw)

it wouldn't cut in. We have been messing round with it ever since we stopped, but we have decided to give it a spell until the morning. Two Libyan prisoners are travelling with us to be mess orderlies for the officers when we get to Kufra.

14 -18 APRIL 1941 *The journey to Kufra continued with the usual stop at Ain Dalla to fill water tins and take on supplies left from a dump set up there. On the 15th, while camping in the Egyptian Sand Sea, Jopling celebrated his second birthday in the Middle East.*

19 APRIL 1941 *10.00am* Well, here we are at Kufra. At present we are under palm trees which surround the Salt Lake. The lake is more salt than lake and it is snow white, which makes a great contrast to the green palms and sandy desert. The Colonel and Lieut. Kennedy Shaw have gone up to the fort to talk with the Free French, and are looking for a camp site for us.

1.00pm We set off shortly after 10am and passed the hangar, which had been badly damaged by Free French bombs when they took the place. Inside was a Savoia SM79 plane, also damaged by bombs. Outside was a Ghibli which had crashed. The French have two Lysanders, but one of them is out of commission as it made a forced landing and was damaged. We are now on our camp site among palms and other trees. For a tent we are using the overhead framework of a truck and putting the tarpaulin over the tops. The flies here are worse than we have seen anywhere so far, and cause us a lot of discomfort. Although we haven't seen any yet, we are told that there are a lot of snakes and scorpions here.

A Ford F30 4x4 30cwt truck that had fallen into a well. While their four-wheel drive was an advantage in soft sand, these vehicles used more fuel than the Chevs. Another disadvantage was that the engine was underneath the cab and the heat it generated created much discomfort for the driver and his passenger. The radiator grill and bonnet were permanently removed to help cool the V8 engine.

7.00pm Things seem as if they are going to be fairly regimented while we are here. Reveille 5.15, parade 6am, breakfast 6.15 and work 7 to 12, followed by afternoon siesta. There is to be a guard at night and a picquet during the day and I am on tonight for 24 hours doing two on and four off.

20 APRIL 1941 The strongest wind we have had in the desert so far sprung up last night. Unfortunately the guards had no cover over them and the dust was terrific. It is still blowing today, but not so bad as last night. It has been very uncomfortable all day. This morning the flies were beyond description and until then I had never appreciated the value of a fly net. As a rule they are too hot, but this morning being underneath one was like living in a palace. At night when the flies vanish, the mosquitos take their place. We did not hear from Dick Croucher last night and they can't get in touch with him tonight, so tomorrow they are going to send the Lysander out to look for them.

21 April 1941 *11.00am* This morning the wind had dropped and we were told that Col. Leclerc was arriving here by plane and that the old hands of T Patrol were going to put on a guard of honour for him when he arrived. This is in return for the compliment he paid us at Zouar and Faya. So this morning we did a bit of practicing, as we've done no rifle drill for ages. We were all down at the aerodrome waiting for Col. Leclerc, but they didn't see any sign of him, so they may send us out again this afternoon. There is a pay parade at 12 noon when we will receive 25 francs (12½ piastres). What we are going to use it for, I don't know.

8.00pm Col. Leclerc did not arrive this afternoon, but the plane went out again to look for Dick Croucher. They arrived back at 5.30pm to say they had only found Dick and said he was still coming, but apparently slowly. Two trucks left this afternoon for Wadi Halfa to bring back some Sudanese for here. Another truck left to meet Dick to pick up rations and benzine, as we are now getting low. At 3.00pm this afternoon I went for a swim in a round concrete swimming pool about 5 ft deep. It was great and I will go there every day if possible.

22 April 1941 *2.00pm* At 9.00am we were told to rush down to the aerodrome with rifle and bayonet, web belt, slacks and boots, as Col. Leclerc was due to arrive in about 20 minutes. So we rushed down there, but he didn't turn up until 12.30pm. There to meet him were ourselves, some Senegalese and some Libyan troops who are now fighting for us, as well as hundreds of natives from the village. It was quite impressive as some of the dress was very bright in colour and the Senegalese were very good at the rifle drill. The Colonel arrived in a Valentia plane with another one as escort. Well, there is a swim on now, so I am off.

8.00pm The swim was great. While at the swimming bath I saw a big scorpion and took a photo of it. It was the biggest I have seen so far. We hear that Bruce should arrive here tomorrow with some mail and also Prendergast *[Major G L Prendergast, LRDG's 2 IC; also a pilot]* is arriving tomorrow with some mail in his plane *[the Waco, one of the two liaison aircraft used by the LRDG]*. There was no news on the wireless about Tobruk and Sollum, but the Anzacs are fighting a great rearguard in Greece.

23-27 April 1941 *Time was spent building slit trenches in case of air attack and digging other trenches*

Top: Salt Lake, Kufra Oasis. (Ellis)

Above: Kufra airfield after the Free French captured the town from the Italians in March 1941. In the foreground are the remains of a Caprioni Ca 309 Ghibli light bomber. Kufra would become an important LRDG base.

to lay telephone cables. Life at Kufra was becoming very regimented, with inspections and punishments; something the LRDG had not encountered for a long time. As Jopling recorded in his diary:

The men are very discontented today, firstly because reveille from now on will be half hour earlier (4.45am) which is ridiculous out here. In addition, there is a parade at 5.45am and another at 6.30am. We work from then until 11.30am, which means that there are over six hours between breakfast and lunch, which is too long. Then we have to work again from 4.30pm till dark. After lunch it is too hot to do anything except swim in the pools.

On top of all that, the men who arrived on the 'Whites' *[Heavy Section trucks]* yesterday, are all 'on the mat' this morning for not having shaved before breakfast. They are to get 30 minutes rifle drill. That doesn't go down well, when you could almost say we are behind the German lines and at any minute we might be surrounded and have to fight for our lives. If the 'Heads' keep it up, there will be riots in the camp.

28 APRIL 1941 4.00pm Today I was on guard, so I did no other work. This morning the guard had to fall in to have the sentence passed on a corporal who was among those who had not shaved. He was charged and the sentence was that he had to be reduced to the ranks. This afternoon I went for a swim, although the guard was not supposed to leave the guard tent. The Col. left this morning in the Waco plane via Tazerbo where R and S are, then via Big Cairn and Siwa where, if it hasn't already been taken by the Huns, he will refuel. He is taking quite a risk, as there are no guns or parachutes on board the plane.

French native troops line up on parade at Kufra airfield in honour of a visit by Colonel Leclerc of the Free French. Jopling had climbed the radio mast on the left to photograph the town.

29 APRIL-3 MAY *Heavy Section trucks were arriving at Kufra carrying quartermaster stores, officers' mess gear, orderly room papers, canteen supplies and other equipment. This all had to be sorted to establish a long-term base. In their spare time the men organized basketball games.*

4 MAY 1941 Last night I was on guard. At 10.15pm I was awakened to fall out. I looked at my watch and saw that it wasn't time for me to go on yet and said so. I was told to be quiet as the orderly officer was there. Then I said, "that doesn't make any difference as it isn't time to go on yet!" Then I realised they wanted me to fall out for inspection by the orderly officer, who said, "Put that man on the mat!" Today I have been told what the charge is: 'Hesitating to obey an order'. What is the army coming to? I suppose I will know what my sentence is shortly.

This evening the two basketball teams that drew yesterday played again and, as one member of the team was missing, I substituted. We won 2-0. After that we had to play the winner of the other match. Well, after playing one match a man has had enough, but two matches on end was too much for us, especially against two fresh teams. We were leading 2-0 at half time, but it the second half the strain began to tell and we lost 3-2. It was a very hot and strenuous activity.

5 May 1941 This morning I went up on my charge and got two extra guard duties, so tonight I am on guard again. Today we have been tidying the place up a bit.

6 May 1941 Tony Browne, who went to Wadi Halfa to bring back a Sudanese convoy, arrived this afternoon. The remainder of the convoy of 40 trucks are not due until tomorrow morning.

7 May 1941 Last night we heard that Major General Freyberg is now in command of the Allied troops in Crete, so I suppose that is where the NZers are. The convoy arrived this morning and we had to unload the trucks.

Today has been the hottest day this year. I don't know what the temperature was, but it must easily have been 120 degrees or maybe 125 degrees. This afternoon I went for a swim, but alas the pool was empty. There was about half an inch in the bottom, so we got undressed and wallowed in it. At least it was wet. Every now and then the windmill would turn slowly and a pump full of water would come out of the pipe. There was always someone waiting for it when it came out, as it was cool water, whereas in the bath it was like hot water. A convoy left this morning to pick up all the stray trucks that have been left in the desert, take them to Cairo to get fixed and then bring them back. They will probably spend about two weeks in Cairo.

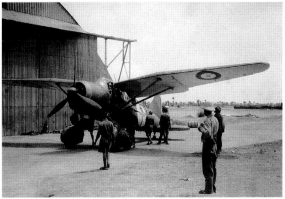

T Patrol members examine a French Westland Lysander reconnaissance aircraft at Kufra airfield.

8-15 May 1941 *Life at Kufra continued with the added discomfort of frequent dust storms. With increasing hot weather, a number of men were falling sick.*

16 May 1941 The dust storm is still blowing, which makes the weather a lot cooler. Today I shifted my benzine pipe. Apparently, when you are travelling along in the hot weather the engine suddenly stops. The benzine gets so hot that it turns to gas before it gets to the pump and therefore doesn't pump. Sometimes you have to wait a long time before you can get it started again, which would be just too bad if a Hun patrol was chasing you, so today I brought the pipe up through the floor board and let it through into the engine at the shortest distance from the pump.

17-20 May 1941 *The wind continued to blow while the men tried to complete their daily tasks. Jopling climbed a 200 ft radio mast, intending to take photos of Kufra, but found the camera wouldn't work as sand had jammed the mechanism.*

21 May 1941 Today we did some shooting. This afternoon we cleaned our rifles and then had a game of rounders played with a rolled-up sock. It was a failure, although T Patrol won by one round to nil. The Valentia set off this morning for the Sudanese patrol, to pick up a man who got burned when a primus stove blew up.

The Adjutant has altered the timetable again, so it is now reveille 4.30am, breakfast 5.00, parade 6.00 and finish the morning's work at 10.30am. At 10.00pm this evening I was just going to bed when I heard my name called out. I was told that I had to go on guard. I was informed that one of the guards was under close arrest for sleeping at his post, and I had to take his place. Another man is also on the mat for being absent from the guard tent.

22 May 1941 On guard all day. This morning I was escort for the two prisoners when they went before Bruce Ballantyne. He remanded them both to the Colonel. This afternoon I was escort when they went before the Colonel. The man who slept on sentry is very lucky, he had a bad ankle and is on light duties. He reckoned that his ankle got sore and when he sat down to rest it he fell asleep. The penalty was ten extra guards. The other man who was absent for half an hour from the guard tent was sentenced to 14 days field punishment, which is a pretty stiff sentence. The timetable has again been altered: Reveille 4.00am, morning tea 4.30, work from 5 to 7.15, breakfast 7.30, work from 8.30 to 10.30am.

23 May-5 June 1941 *Because one of the base cooks was leaving, Jopling was offered the job for an extra 2/6 a day. Though he agreed to do it, the special allowance only applied while he was at base. Later, while sick with the flu, he had to continue preparing meals because the other cook had cut his finger and could do little work. Another supply convoy of 30 trucks arrived, bringing more base and canteen stores. Especially welcome were cigarettes, which were running short.*

6 June 1941 Today a letter from Major Clayton to his sister in Cairo was posted up on the notice board. It was dated February 12th and said that when he was leaving Gebel Sherif, one of the planes machine-gunned them and burst two of their tyres and punctured the radiator and benzine tank. One bullet hit Major Clayton on the head, but luckily he had his tin hat on, which prevented a wound. They changed the tyres, filled the radiator and set off again, but after covering about half a mile they ran out of benzine. By this time the plane was still machine-gunning them while the Itie patrol was arriving on the scene. Major Clayton received a wound in the arm and, seeing that further resistance was useless, he told Wink and Clarrie to surrender. The plane that was attacking them received 22 bullet holes and its navigator was wounded. Major Clayton says they have been well treated, but at the time of writing he was not with Wink and Clarrie as they had been sent on ahead.

7-9 JUNE 1941 *Orders came through that T Patrol was to relieve R Patrol at Tazerbo. Jopling had to give up his cooking job with its extra 2/6 a day and was reassigned from the Bofors truck to another vehicle as a Boys anti-tank gunner. On 9 June the patrol left Kufra for Tazerbo, via Zighen.*

Frank Jopling's photograph of a scorpion, which he described as "the biggest I had seen so far." Scorpions were treated with respect. Though their sting was not fatal, it could incapacitate a person for up to 36 hours. The arachnid, which struck suddenly with deadly effect, was an appropriate symbol adopted by the LRDG for their cap badge.

TAZERBO

10 June 1941 *11.30am* We are now at Zighen. S Patrol, who are the Rhodesians, have made this into a wonderful place. There is no population and only one or two palm trees. All you have to do is to scrape a hole with your hands and you can get a nice cool drink of water. It is marvelous to see nothing but sandy waste all around you and yet there is an abundance of water only about one foot underground. The Rhodesians have made full use of this and have dug a swimming pool which is very cold, far colder than the one in Kufra.

The 'lookout' site is on top of a palm tree and they are going to put a swivel chair up there. What next?

The cookhouse is really a wonderful bit of work. They got some timber from the landing

T Patrol visits the S Patrol camp at Zighen. Despite their harsh surroundings the Rhodesians had established a reasonably comfortable base. (Craw)

ground we passed, which by the way is where W Patrol captured the trucks on the LRP's first trip. But to get back to the cookhouse and mess room. It is built around a palm tree and has a better kitchen than you see on some farms in NZ. They have made a stove out of a benzine drum filled with sand. *[This was known as a Benghazi Burner. The sand was soaked with petrol and set alight.]* Also a small refrigerator made from a small biscuit tin inside a large one. The big one has lots of holes in it and in between the two tins is filled with charcoal. The charcoal is kept wet and the evaporation keeps the inside tin as cool as a refrigerator. They have a wine, or I should say a rum cellar underground and they have built a big oven at the back. They tell me that they use dry biscuits as fuel for it.

Captain D G Steele, R Patrol, sitting in his Ford F8 8 cwt commander's vehicle. He later commanded A (NZ) Squadron, with the rank of major, and received the OBE in recognition of his services while based at Siwa and Jalo. (Pittaway/Fourie collection)

8.00pm We left Zighen at 4pm and arrived here at Tazerbo at 6pm after travelling 65 miles over good going all the way. When we arrived we expected to see a lot of dirty bearded men, but instead they were all clean shaven. One or two had grown moustaches whose ends had been waxed. They looked characters. Captain Steele had given orders that every man must be shaven by 6pm this evening. R Patrol reckon Steele has got a disease which I have been trying to find a name for some time. They call it 'sand happy'. I know one or two who have it. They do a lot of childish sort of things. All R Patrol are looking forward to going back, as I think they are going to Cairo. A lot of them have desert sores, but so have we, including myself.

11 JUNE 1941 This morning Steele took Bruce Ballantyne and one or two others into Tazerbo and introduced them to Ally, who is the chief of the village. Ally gave them 'shay' in the usual manner. The first one they had was very sweet and very strong. Then they passed round a bowl of water to wash it down. Then they had another cup not quite as strong, with some mint in it and still very sweet, after which another bowl of water went around around. Then they had another cup which was the last and the best. It wasn't too strong – just a bit of mint in it and it tasted quite good. Ally saw Major Clayton and Wink and Clarrie when they were captured. He said that the Major had a bandage on his arm.

R Patrol left at 11am. We took up positions against mounds which are scattered around here. The vegetation looks like a bush with all stalks and no leaves. We are about ten miles from Tazerbo, the reason being to get away from the flies. R Patrol had to dig their own well here. They dug down about 20 feet and then put in a pump. Today was about the hottest day we have had this year. R Patrol have two thermometers and yesterday it was 117 degrees in the shade, but today is far hotter.

12-13 June *T Patrol settled into their new camp on the outskirts of Tazerbo.*

14 June 1941 *8.00pm* Last night Tony Browne was bitten in two places by a snake. While he was listening to the wireless, the snake apparently got into his bed and when he got in he sat on it. That is the first time any of us have been bitten. The medical orderly *[Private Jock Bruce, RAMC, attached to T Patrol]* came running over and put iodine on the bites and then gave him some pills to make him sick. He gave him two more pills to take in two hours, if he was awake. "If ye dinna wake ye'll be dead!" he said. A cheerful thing to tell a man. However, after suffering agony for about six hours Tony seems alright now.

The three of us from my truck were sitting under our tarpaulin when I saw what I took to be a lizard and said, "Look at that lizard!" It was a new one on me. It had gone under the front wheel of the truck, but when we looked we couldn't see it. So I got a shovel and dug down and sure enough it came up and Harley *[Trooper H H Cleaver]* yelled, "That's not a lizard, it's an asp!" I have heard a lot about asps and how poisonous they are, but I have never seen one before. This was a yellow green, the same color as the vegetation around here. It was a lot thicker than a lizard and had a big snake's head on it. Its tail looked as if it had been cut off at some time or other. Whether it had been or was natural I don't know. Anyhow we tried to kill it, but it moved so fast and buried itself in the sand several times that in the end we lost it.

Just before tea Harley decided he would sleep in the truck in future, as he didn't like sleeping with asps. He rolled up his bedding and chucked it up on the truck, then as he came back for some more of his belongings from where his bed had been, he let out a yell and shouted, "Its got me, its got me, the bastard!" I saw that a scorpion had stung him. The sting is very painful for about half an hour, after which it soon gets better. Yet we had to laugh, although Harley didn't think it was any laughing matter at the time. After that both George Garven *[Trooper G C Garven]* and myself decided that asps and scorpions were too much for us also, so we took our bedding out and we are going to sleep away from any vegetation.

15 June 1941 When I got up this morning I was glad I had slept out there, as where I usually slept were the tracks of what must have been a very long snake. Each mark being about three inches from tip to tip, but this one was about 16 inches from tip to tip and we could see the rough pattern of the snake's skin on the tracks. It may be just a different type of snake, but nevertheless I was glad I wasn't sleeping in my usual place.

8.00pm When I told everyone about these new tracks and said it was a snake track, they all said I was 'sand happy' and I should keep my hat on during the day. They reckoned it was certainly not a snake and was probably done by a snake rolling over. However, I know better and I will find that snake even if I have to follow it to Benghazi.

17 June 1941 *10.00am* This morning I again went to where I knew the snake was and found its tracks heading away from the tamarisk, so I followed. It had travelled 3 or 4,000 yards last night, eventually finishing up in other tamarisk hill. I looked around where its tracks entered and then I saw a movement. It was a snake, so I yelled to a nearby truck to bring a shovel, which they did. They made a swipe at it, cutting its tail off. Then they scooped it out into the open and we saw that it was not much longer than the tracks it made. It was fairly thick for its length and had a big flat head. The general opinion is that it is a sand viper, which is about the most deadly poisonous reptile in Africa. I don't know whether a man would be safer fighting the Italians or waiting here for something to bite him.

Bruce and two other trucks went out to the aerodrome this morning to meet the Waco. At 8.00am two Lysanders flew overhead, but Bruce had not arrived back yet.

Campsite at Tazerbo, set up next to a Ford F30 truck. L-R: Troopers Harley Cleaver and Frank Jopling. Sometimes the men preferred to sleep in their trucks rather than on the ground, because of the scorpions and snakes.

Corporal G C Garven of T Patrol with his .303 EY grenade-launching rifle. These weapons were effective at lobbing M36 hand grenades into enemy forts and positions, and were used with good results on a number of occasions.

Trooper I H McInnes practicing with his two-inch mortar. It had a range of 500 yards and fired high explosive or smoke bombs. Using this weapon, he earned the Military Medal for setting fire to the fort at Murzuk in January 1941.

18 June-28 July 1941 During this time the patrol shifted camp twice, and each time they had to spend several days digging new wells. The water had a brackish taste that spoilt the tea. Meanwhile the flies, heat and dust storms continued to plague the men. As Jopling recorded, among other things:

8 July 1941 The wind and sand are blowing hard today and we were going to look for another place to dig a well, but it is too windy. This evening McInnes and Garven fired the mortar and grenade rifle and during the proceedings nearly blew us all up. Garven put a mortar bomb down the barrel and as he did so it went off. If it had caught his hand it would have exploded and killed us all.

9 July 1941 This morning we went looking for another place to dig a well and after striking rock at 6 ft down, we left it. After our next effort at 8 ft down we struck water, so we are moving camp tomorrow morning. This afternoon we heard from Cairo that McInnes *[Tpr. I H McInnes]* had been awarded the MM, Tony Browne *[Cpl. L H Browne]* the DCM, and Lieut. Kennedy Shaw and Colonel Bagnold the OBE. All of those were for the battle at Murzuk. I also believe that Major Mitford was awarded the MC.

Various supply, reconnaissance and liaison duties were carried out during their time at Tazerbo. To help break the monotony, sports matches were organised versus S Patrol, followed by concerts and parties. The patrol was pleased to return to Kufra on 28 July. Jopling wrote about what was coming up for them:

26 July 1941 Today we were told that on no account were we to mention anything about going on our next trip. When we eventually get back to Cairo we are not allowed to say anything about it to our friends, because if the trip is successful and we get there and back without being spotted, which sounds a bit unlikely, it will be secret for two or three months. The doctor is coming with us and so is Captain Kennedy Shaw.

No diary notes are to be kept and no letters if they give any information as regards the unit. No papers such as cigarette packets, match boxes, or anything with English writing on can be thrown away on the trip – it must be well buried. There are to be three wireless trucks and we are being split up into three parties. I am in C party which will not go as far as the others. I will be cooking for them as usual.

RECONNAISSANCE AND CHARTING

27- 29 JULY 1941 *Three days after arriving in Kufra, T Patrol set off on what was to be a reconnaissance, mapping and road watching mission, far behind enemy lines. GHQ in Cairo were anticipating a British advance into Tripolitania, so they wanted information about the 'going' for wheeled and tracked vehicles, sites for landing grounds and the local supplies of water. Jopling outlined the mission, about which he had obvious concerns:*

◆ **30 JULY 1941** ◆ We were told what our main jobs were on this trip. In my opinion it will be almost a miracle if everyone comes back. We are to head north until we come to broken country about 15 miles south of the Marada-Kufra road and about 30 miles south of the

One of the primary tasks of the LRDG was reconnaissance and mapping to determine the 'going' for future Eighth Army operations – such as the famous 'left hooks'. Here a T Patrol Ford F30 motors towards uncharted mountainous territory.

Marada-Jalo road. The party I am in will stay there, together with all the old hands except one. The remainder will be split into two: one party, with Bruce in charge, is to go to the Hon-Sirte road and find out if it would be practicable to send a large force there and, if so, to watch the traffic on the road. The other, with Lieutenant Ellingham and Captain Kennedy Shaw, will go between Sirte and Tripoli, about 1,000 miles behind the enemy lines. They will watch the coast road to find out how much traffic is travelling between Tripoli and Cyrenaica. Also to establish if it would be possible for a force to sit on the edge of the road and bag a few convoys as they came along. In addition, they have to try to find some suitable landing grounds for the RAF.

It will be more or less a 'war of nerves' for us in the rear party, as we have to stay here until the others come back. If the tracks of the two forward parties are spotted, planes are certain to follow them down to us. They are almost sure to be seen as they have to cross the Marada-Jalo road, which is patrolled by air.

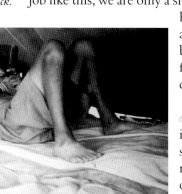

After a long day, Lieutenant Walter Ellingham, 2 IC, T Patrol, relaxes with a book in a cosy shelter erected beside his truck.

31 July 1941 Well, here we are at our rendezvous, and to give it its dues, it is a great place for cover from aircraft. There are 18 of us here and we have a picquet on for 24 hours per day. Each man will do one hour every 18 hours. To give an example of what war is on a job like this, we are only a small patrol and are like one big family. Now half of the patrol have gone north and are on a very dangerous job. Our orders are to wait here for 12 days and if our mates have not returned by then we are to dump all our spare benzine and head straight for Kufra, not knowing whether they have been killed or captured and powerless to give them any help.

1 August 1941 I was on picquet between 12.30 and 1.30pm in a temperature that must have been well over 120 in the shade. We stand on the highest rise in the blazing sun with a rifle and a pair of binoculars. We scan the horizon for any signs of ground forces, scan the sky for aircraft and at the same time listen for any engine. During the middle of the day there is a heavy mirage which makes the horizon fairly close, sometimes only a few hundred yards away. Early in the morning or late afternoon the horizon is many miles away, and for that reason, we don't expect to spot any aircraft during the middle of the day, as they would be very hard to see. If we see aircraft we are to fire one shot and if we see ground forces, we fire two shots and rush to our trucks.

2 August 1941 Today I was on picquet between 4.30 and 5.30pm. When I started, the horizon was only two or three miles away. But by 5.30pm it was about 12 miles away. The weather is very hot here, far hotter than at Tazerbo. Luckily our water ration is one and a half gallons per day per man, which is higher than we have ever had before.

3-10 August 1941 *The wait at base camp passed without incident. Kennedy Shaw's party returned on 7 August and Bruce Ballantyne's party returned on 10 August. The reconnaissance mission was successful and much valuable information was gathered for future operations. Several weeks later, S Patrol made a similar reconnaissance farther to the east, between Jalo and Agedabia. All these tasks were completed without discovery by the enemy.*

10 August 1941 Bruce arrived at 11.30am with only three of his four trucks. One was being towed and looked a total wreck. He went over a dune in his 15 cwt, took off at the top and did a 51ft jump. The fan broke off, damaging the radiator and coil. They managed to get it going again, but found it used too much water which they couldn't afford to lose, so they unloaded the vehicle and took it in tow.

The patrol didn't get as far as the road they were aiming for, as the going was too rough, but they discovered that it would definitely not be practicable to send a large force that way. They didn't see a thing on the trip except for a large camel train which didn't spot them. This means that both jobs have been completed without our patrols being seen by the enemy, which is nothing short of marvellous. This afternoon the fitter got to work on the 15 cwt and by 2pm had got it going again, which is a great piece of work. At 3.30 we set out for Kufra.

This Ford F30 30cwt drove over a small sand dune at speed, took off and landed heavily, resulting in a collapsed front suspension. This was one of the many dangers of desert travel.

11-20 August 1941 *The patrol was back at base for a week before returning to Cairo to go on leave. In the meantime Kufra presented the usual problems with flies, but this time the men also had to contend with an infestation of ants. As Jopling wrote, "The ants drove me out of my hut last night and I slept on the truck where I got bitten by mosquitos, but I think they were lesser of the two evils." Also at Kufra the base ran an LRDG newspaper called Tracks, and Jopling wrote an article for them titled, 'The Fortunes and Misfortunes of T Patrol'. On the 19th the patrol began their journey to Cairo, but along the way were plagued by rough going, punctures and vehicle breakdowns.*

21 August 1941 This morning there was one of the prettiest sunrises I have seen and it brought with it a day of misfortunes. Firstly the HQ truck's generator seized up. We had no spare generators so we had to tow the truck. Up to lunchtime we were dropping a 40 gal. drum of water and a tin containing bully and biscuits every 15 miles in case anybody got lost along the way. The towed truck arrived in just as lunch was ready and they took some on board with them and went straight on. We set off about 15 minutes later, and hadn't gone more than half a mile when our truck didn't seem to be getting the benzine properly. We stopped and the fitter came alongside and I told him about our problem. He then pressed down hard on the accelerator and there was a crash in the engine as if a grenade had gone off. We found that the generator pulley had broken off, the fan had flown off and hit the radiator and the water just poured out of it. Having no spare generators, radiators or fans, we also had to be towed.

Steering a towed truck over the desert is one of the worst jobs I know. We set off with one truck towing us, but as it was all third gear work, the towing truck started to boil. So we decided to try two trucks towing which proved better, but not as good as we expected. However, it stopped the boiling. About an hour later, at 6.15pm, we caught up with the rest of the patrol to find that the 15cwt had been towed for the previous 15 miles with a broken axle. The fitters are busy fixing it now. We have done 192 miles today, which is not bad under the circumstances. We passed S Patrol going back to Kufra having had their leave. Apparently all the kit bags that they had left behind had been well gone through and anything worth pinching had been taken.

A Heavy Section truck tows the damaged Ford away for repair.

⌐**22 August 1941**⌐ The two towed trucks set off at 4.45 this morning and arrived at Kharga at 9am after covering 75 miles, only to find that there were no spare parts there at all. So having managed to get some benzine, we set off for Assyut at 11am. After climbing the escarpment for which the towing trucks had to go into auxiliary low gear, we stopped for lunch. I drove the towed truck to Assyut and believe me it was a dirty job on a dusty road. We arrived there at 6pm, had tea, then set off on the last hop of about 250

miles to Cairo. We put on our lights and kept travelling until 10pm when we had a cup of tea. From there on I drove the towed truck until 7am when the 15 cwt broke another axle, so we had breakfast. After breakfast we put the 15 cwt on the back of one of the 30 cwts and arrived at the Citadel at 1pm after travelling about 530 miles in 32 hours while towing two trucks. It was the longest and fastest tow for 30 cwt trucks in the world.

23 AUGUST-11 SEPTEMBER *T Patrol was back in Cairo on leave, having been replaced by S Patrol who returned to Kufra. At the Citadel the trucks were overhauled and the usual base duties and inspections undertaken. In between these activities, Jopling went to the movies, bought a new camera and experienced several minor air raids. Major Guy Prendergast had now taken over command of the LRDG and Lt.Col. Ralph Bagnold was promoted to full Colonel, and Inspector of Desert Troops, GHQ Middle East. Prendergast, like Bagnold, was another pre-war desert explorer. He was a skilled pilot, and he had done much of his exploration by air. He flew one of the two Waco liaison aircraft used by the LRDG. On 12 September Jopling was told he had to return to his original unit.*

☞ 12 SEPTEMBER 1941 ☜ Bruce Ballantyne came along this morning to tell us that five men had to go back to the Division. He said he was sorry he had to do it, but all the original members except the NCOs, the Bofors gunners and the batmen would have to go back. There were only three of us, so two of the new hands had to return also. Three are to go back

Members of T Patrol (back two rows) relax at the NZ Forces Club in Cairo, 1941. In the foreground are Australian troops. After a long patrol most of the men looked forward to a shave, a bath, a good meal and beer.

every month from now on, so Bruce says that if we want to come back to the LRDG we should volunteer after a month and he will come and pick us out again, so in that case it will be a bit of a holiday. It will probably mean that while the push is on up on the coast we will be stuck in base at Maadi, where we are going on 15 September.

13-16 SEPTEMBER **1941** *Jopling said goodbye to his patrol and had to undergo medical and kit inspections before rejoining the NZ Division camp at Maadi.*

17 SEPTEMBER **1941** We were told this morning that we would be marching out at 10.30am. and we had to do about a five mile route march with full web, haversack, respirator, tin hat and rifle, to get to the Composite Regiment. Believe me, we were glad when we arrived at our destination. Then after calling at three orderly rooms – the Composite Orderly

Left to right: General Claude Auchinleck (C in C Middle East), Captain Bruce Ballantyne (T Patrol Commander), Lt. Colonel Ralph Bagnold (Commander LRDG), attend an inspection at the Citadel in Cairo, 1941. In the foreground is a 37 mm Bofors anti-tank gun on the back of a Ford F 30 truck. These weapons were mainly used against enemy forts. (Craw)

A parade at Maadi Camp photographed by Gunner Struan MacGibbon (6th Brigade parade, 12 February 1942).

Room, the Div. Cav. Orderly Room and the Squadron Orderly Room – we were shown a tent where we could dump our gear. The rest of the day was our own.

The morning's paper reported that in last night's air raid a number of explosive and incendiary bombs were dropped in and around Cairo. 39 people were killed and 93 injured. I wonder if Rome will be bombed now. Abbassia and Heliopolis were the main places to be attacked. That was the first air raid actually in Cairo itself.

18 September 1941 Today we had a Regimental parade and did nothing else all day.

19 September - 2 October 1941 Was just a monotonous nothing. All we did was fatigue after fatigue, so I was determined to get back to the LRDG. I saw Bruce and he said he would do all he could to get me back right away. I also saw the Army Public Relations Service and they made me official diarist for the LRDG and they reckoned they would certainly get me back.

23 September 1941 General Auchinleck inspected the LRDG and commenced his speech with "Gentlemen!" which is very unusual in the Army. He went on to say, "I have heard a lot about you, and since coming here, I have seen and heard a lot more. Your information in the past has been most valuable, in fact, we couldn't have done it without you and I know that in future you will bring back the information we require as you have always done in the past. I know that your job is a hard job, a lonely job and a dangerous job, but if I was a young man that is just the sort of job I would want." He also said that we would not be back in Cairo until all Libya was captured.

In August 1941, Major Guy Prendergast replaced the newly-promoted Colonel Ralph Bagnold who had founded the LRDG. Prendergast was a pre-war desert explorer and a skilled pilot. Here he stands in front of the Waco, one of two Waco aircraft used by the unit for liaison work, evacuating sick or wounded and delivering spare parts to the patrols.
(Ellis)

3 October 1941 I again went up to the Public Relations Service and Captain Halstead showed me a letter that had been sent to the Camp Commandant which said I should be relieved for special work for the LRDG, so that I could be at the Citadel by Sunday 5 October. He also told me that I had been made official correspondent and photographer to the LRDG for the NZ War Office, Middle East War Office, and the London War Office. Also that Col. Prendergast was trying to get me a £75 Contax camera with a telephoto lens. I hope he succeeds.

4 October 1941 Today I had official confirmation that I am to return to the LRDG by tomorrow.

5 October 1941 At 11.00am this morning a truck arrived to take me to the Citadel and I got there just in time for lunch. It is great to be back again. Lt. Ellingham has gone to the hospital and our 2 I/C is now Lieutenant Costello *[2nd Lt. P Costello]* who seems to be quite a linguist and a good man. We also have with us Lieutenant Paul Freyberg, who is General Freyberg's son. The General said he was sending him out with us to toughen him up a bit and he looks as though he can do with it. However, he gets on well with the boys. We are taking him to Siwa with us, but what he will do there I don't know yet.

6 October 1941 I went down to M.E. HQ *[Middle East HQ]* this morning to see Col. Bagnold about the £75 camera and he told me that for the time being he had given up the idea. Because if I took it on, he would want the films developed and printed out on the job, which would entail a special truck as well as ice boxes etc. to keep the stuff cool. The job was complicated enough without making it any worse. "However, later on we may give it a go," he said. "And I am pleased to see you back in the patrol again Jopling." I told him he wasn't half as pleased as I was.

TO SIWA

7-22 OCTOBER *On 11 October, T Patrol set out from Cairo to Siwa and met with R Patrol which had already arrived. These patrols had taken over from G and Y Patrols which had been in Siwa since August. The large patrols were now split in half, with T and R becoming, respectively, T1 and T2; and R1 and R2. These patrols became smaller, more effective units of five to six vehicles with three men assigned to each truck and two in the commander's Ford 15 cwt or jeep.*

Siwa served as a stepping-off point for many LRDG operations, including combined operations with Lieutenant Colonel David Stirling's Special Air Service against enemy airfields and convoys. Though T Patrol went out on various missions, Jopling remained at base during this time looking after supplies and other routine duties. The men also built AA gun pits and trenches after an Italian spotter plane the men christened 'Siwa Bill' began regular flights over the base. However Siwa Bill never caused any trouble.

23 OCTOBER 1941 This morning we had a rifle shoot and I was very pleased with my effort. Sergeant Barker *[Sgt. R F T Barker Div. Cav., an LRDG pilot]* flew in this morning in his Waco and told us that all S Patrol had arrived back in Kufra, safe and sound after a long reconnaissance like the one we had been on. He was taking the information they had gathered back to Cairo. This afternoon we heard planes and thought it was Siwa Bill, but it turned out to be two of our own. The boys seemed quite disappointed. They are quite anxious to have a go at him now they are all prepared. Later on I went for a swim. I also have one before breakfast every morning. The natives seem full of business today. Ramadan ended yesterday, which was a feast day. Today seems to be the start of the harvest season, as they are all busy taking the dates from the trees.

10.00pm T Patrol brings back the goods once again. Sergeant McInnes heard that Bruce had telephoned here from Giarabub to say that Lt. Freyberg was on his way to Siwa with two captured trucks and four German prisoners and that if they didn't arrive by 9am tomorrow, to send someone out to look for them. Well, they arrived at 7.30pm this evening and have some great stories to tell. They have been to within 30km of Benghazi and watched the town being bombed three nights in succession and also during the daytime. Their job

Date palms, Siwa oasis. This town was famous for its dates, said to be the best in Egypt. It also served as an LRDG base.

The first Afrika Korps POWs taken by the LRDG. In the background are the British Bedford trucks which they were travelling in when captured. (Craw)

was apparently to find out if tanks could travel around there without meeting too much opposition or rough going.

The boys reckon they are thinking of landing tanks up there from the sea, but that remains to be seen. However, they had done their job up there and seen many destroyed tanks, trucks and planes from the last push. When they were coming home they saw a lot of .303, .50 and .55 ammunition scattered around, so decided to pick some of it up. While doing this, they saw two trucks and a motor bike about a mile away. Bruce said, "After them!" and off they went. Bruce and a RAF officer, *[Pilot Officer Rawnsley]* who was attached to the patrol as an observer, were first to catch up with them. They fired a few bursts of machine gun fire in front of their vehicles, whereupon the Germans pulled up and surrendered. They captured an officer and six NCOs, who became the LRDG's first Afrika Korps prisoners. The trucks were British Bedfords which must have been captured from us in the withdrawal from Benghazi. The motor bike and side car was a German make, a BMW. They also had a Schmeisser submachine-gun which is far superior to ours, a Mauser rifle and several pistols.

For some reason or other Bruce sent Lt. Freyberg ahead with the five NCOs while he and the RAF officer, with the captured German officer, stayed behind to give Lt. Freyberg some practice at navigation. He said that he would catch them up later. Well, they set off and had gone a fair way when Freyberg began to wonder where Bruce had got to. Looking back, they saw smoke rising, so the fitter's truck went back to find out what had gone wrong.

From here the story carries on to 24 October when Bruce and the RAF officer arrived back on the fitter's truck, minus the prisoner. A member of the fitter's truck told us that when they got back to where they had left Bruce, at an old fort right against the wire, they saw a cloud of smoke rising from the building. They saw someone wave something, so they advanced cautiously and eventually recognised Bruce. They drove up and Bruce told them that after the rest of the trucks had left, he and the RAF officer decided to have a wash and took off their revolvers. The RAF officer left his on the seat of the truck and Bruce put his on the side of the truck.

While washing, they suddenly heard, "Put them up!" They turned around and saw the German officer with a revolver in his hand. He told them to walk away and they had no option but to obey. The German then hopped behind the steering wheel and drove off back across Libya. The RAF officer then headed down the wire to try to get in touch with a patrol and Bruce went to the fort and lit a fire with some old tyres that were lying around. From there they headed down the wire, picked up the RAF officer and headed for Giarabub. By the time they arrived and had sent messages to the RAF etc, they reckoned the prisoner had got about six hours start. Up to the time of writing, no further news has come through, so I imagine he has got safely back to his lines.

Bruce admits it was his fault for sending the other trucks ahead, although it was Rawnsley's

An Italian Camionetta Desertica SPA TL-37 beside an abandoned gun position. The LRDG often came across the debris of battle, and recovered useful arms, ammunition and equipment.

Bottom: the LRDG Waco prepares for take off. These versatile light aircraft were skilfully flown and navigated and could land almost anywhere.

Below: the Waco being re-fuelled. Note the Kiwi in a shield insignia behind the engine cowling. This aircraft was flown by Sergeant F T Barker, a New Zealander in the LRDG who held a private pilot's licence.

revolver that was left so handy and was used against them. Personally it puzzles me. I can't understand why they were both washing at the same time, with their backs turned toward the prisoner, and had left their revolvers on the truck. It certainly was a bad show. However, it is done and we will have to make the best of it. It will probably make our trips even more dangerous than they are now, as the Germans are sure to have air and land patrols all along the north from now on. We have also lost one of our main assets: 'the essence of surprise'.

As usual there was a humorous side to it. When the German officer surprised them, Rawnsley was stark naked and he had to put up his hands and walk out in the desert in his birthday suit. Rawnsley, although he made a mess of things there, is very much liked by the boys and is a great help to the morale of the troops. He knows no fear and is always wanting to go to the most impossible places. He said he has never enjoyed himself so much in all his life as on that trip. On the other hand, the boys haven't got much time for Lt. Freyberg. They reckon he was 'jittery' from start to finish and he gave everyone else the jitters. They are not looking forward to the day when he takes out a patrol out on his own.

25 OCTOBER 1941 The R1 Patrol party which went out the day we arrived in Siwa, arrived back today with two prisoners – one Italian, one Libyan. Their job was to get prisoners, so with one truck they attacked what they thought to be the last truck of the convoy and got a shock when 16 more followed up. Their Vickers jammed, so the R Patrol commander, Captain Jake Easonsmith, grabbed a tommy gun and held up the driver, who took it out of his hand and headed off across the desert. He was dealt with accordingly. When the shooting became a bit too heavy they made off in their truck with machine gun and rifle fire following them, but escaped without casualties. Last night the German prisoners were questioned and they got quite bit of information out of them.

Today they called for three volunteers to be navigators, so I volunteered as I am keen to learn how to 'shoot the stars'. This afternoon we went on a short trip to get in some practice at plotting our course on the map.

26 OCTOBER 1941 This morning we plotted our course on the map and didn't do bad for our first effort. While up at the orderly room, Sgt. Barker arrived in the Waco from Cairo on his way back to Kufra. Just after he landed, old 'Siwa Bill' came over, but he was at a higher altitude that he had ever been before.

And now we come to the best news of the lot. The German officer who escaped has been recaptured. Apparently the truck broke down and a South African patrol picked him up and is now at Melfa. Two of our trucks have gone to pick him up and bring him here. You have no idea how relieved everyone is to know that all the information he had will not get back to the enemy.

Last night we heard on the wireless that our "armoured patrols were active around Sollum and one patrol penetrated deep into enemy territory and brought back five German prisoners." From that description you would think we were an 'armoured patrol'. This evening the wireless mentioned how important Siwa and Giarabub were to us and how it was like a dagger in the back of the enemy. I wonder why they go to the trouble of attracting the enemy's attention to us.

Lieutenant Paul Freyberg standing beside a captured Italian Lancia truck. The son of Major General Freyberg, he served with T Patrol for a time to gain field command experience. He was later wounded during an air attack. (Craw)

This afternoon we went on another trip. This time it was on the Sand Sea and we plotted our course on the map when we arrived back.

27-31 October *Jopling continued his navigation training. He learned how to plot for 'dead reckoning', operate a theodolite, and in the evenings endeavoured to pick out the stars with the aid of the Star Chart navigation guide.*

1 November 1941 This morning we did more theodolite work and were just setting off for camp when one of our trucks came out and picked us up. I was told that we were going out this afternoon, not in one of our trucks, but with R Patrol. Well, we set off at 2pm over the same bumpy road on which we travelled to Giarabub earlier, and arrived at Williams Pass at 5pm. We were surprised when Captain Hunter *[Capt. A D N Hunter]* said we would carry on to Giarabub tonight.

We carrived in Giarabub at 8.30pm. Although the going had been very rough, the road had improved 100% since the last time I came along. I am Vickers gunner on Capt. Hunter's truck and riding in the back, I once landed in the front seat after the car hit a series of bumps between William's Pass and here. This patrol is under command of Capt. Hunter who is the new 2 I/C of T Patrol. He only joined us the other day, so we have yet to see what he is like. The Brigadier's car has arrived and Capt. Hunter and Lt. Croucher have gone up there to talk things over.

2 NOVEMBER 1941 Capt. Hunter told us this morning what our job is to be. Apparently the RAF reported that they spotted a large force at Bir El Hacheim. It was three columns and miles long. Our job is to discover what sort of vehicles they are and what armaments they have. It sounds a bit cheeky for two trucks to do though. At present we have four trucks and when we come to a crossroad on the route to El Hacheim, we are going to split up. Capt. Hunter's and another truck are going to Bir El Hacheim while Dick Croucher and the remaining truck are going to Bir El Gubba. Well, we are all ready to move off now, so we won't be long.

At 11am we came to a well named Ad Addaf. It seems to be very deep and has no water in it. We left and hadn't been going very long before we saw that only one truck was following us. We pulled up, and when the other trucks eventually caught us up we discovered that one had sustained a broken centre bolt in the back spring. Capt. Hunter decided that he would have to send that truck back as it wasn't safe to take it with us. They sent one old hand and one new hand back with it, as they want all the experienced men on this job. We have now stopped for lunch, after covering 46 miles. The going was very rough for a start, but it is a lot better now.

It always strikes me as strange when the CO should apologize when he has to send anyone back from a job like this one. People left behind are always very disappointed they cannot go on these trips and yet when we see a patrol go out, we quite expect it will be the last time we will ever see them – for the duration, anyhow. I suppose we won't be splitting into two parties now there are only three trucks.

10.00pm We have camped for the night after covering 83 miles. We stopped early this afternoon near a dump which the LRDG made some time ago. I was up until late this evening, shooting stars with Dick Croucher to find our exact position.

3 NOVEMBER 1941 *7.00am* We are just about to move off again. I will be quite surprised if we do not see a plane or other signs of enemy activity today, but that remains to be seen.

12 noon Here we are, 15 miles SW of Bir El Hacheim. We are about to have lunch, prime some grenades and get all guns ready for action. So far we have seen no sign of enemy planes. This is not surprising, as there is a fairly heavy haze in our favour. We hope it stays with us.

1.00pm We were just having lunch when we heard engines. For a while we thought it was a ground force approaching. We rushed to our trucks and I got behind my Vickers, when we saw six Savoia *[Italian Savoia Marchetti SM79]* bombers droning straight overhead at about 8,000 feet and apparently heading towards Giarabub or Siwa. They travelled straight on, which is just as well. Six are a few too many to have on our tails. We are going to wait here until 4pm, so that if we get spotted around El Hacheim, it will be too dark to send planes after us.

3.00pm We are setting off again, at 3.20pm. At present everyone is just lying around as though it were a Sunday afternoon siesta. Although some of them look as though they are sleeping, you can bet your life they will be on their feet at the slightest sound of an engine.

3.20pm We are just about to move off. Well, as is usual in a stunt like this, I am a little behind with my diary. However, here is the story: We left at 3.20 and headed towards Bir El Hacheim from the SW. The first thing we saw looked initially like a tower with a red flag flying from it. We saw no sign of life, so decided to go and investigate. It turned out to be a large cairn. The flag was red on one side, white on the other. We saw three more forming a square, so came to the conclusion it was an aerodrome, so we then headed south. On our way we crossed a number of fresh vehicle tracks which appeared to be from some type of very small tank.

We carried on for about three miles and still saw no sign of Bir El Hacheim which is marked on the map as being a town of over 25,000 inhabitants. Later, we crossed some very new motorbike tracks. By this time the sun had set, so we decided to head west for about 30 miles and camp for the night. We set off at right angles to the motorcycle tracks, but hadn't gone very far before we crossed more tracks. We carried on and crossed a third set, which we followed. I considered this was very risky, considering it was nearly dark and we could not know whether it led into an Italian camp or not. However, we set off along them and hadn't been going long when I saw three heads sticking up above a bush.

I yelled to Capt. Hunter, "On your feet, Sir! On your left!" I still didn't know what we were running into, but it was too late to worry about that and we stopped the trucks just past that point. I trained my Vickers onto the area mentioned, but held my fire as it would have been just slaughter to have opened fire. There were four in that group and one on the other side of the truck. When they realised that we weren't Ities and meant business, they came out with their hands up. We then saw that they had motor bikes hidden in the bushes. We searched the prisoners and then set about smashing the bikes as we did not have room on

The Bagnold sun compass. Because the desert had few identifiable navigation landmarks, the LRDG relied on this compass to help find their way. The horizontal circle, divided into 360 degrees, had a central needle which cast a shadow across the graduations. By rotating the circle every 30 minutes throughout the day to correspond with the sun's movement across the sky, the shadow was made to indicate the true bearing on which the car was travelling. (Gillingham)

the trucks to take them back. After putting the prisoners' blankets and clothing etc. on board, we set off west at full speed in the dark. Believe me we hit a few bumps.

We had picked up a wireless from the prisoners and were in a hurry to get away. Heading about ten miles west, we turned south and after almost crashing over an escarpment decided to move more carefully. I sat on the back of the truck with a prismatic compass in my hand, directing the driver. We eventually arrived at our previous night's camping place and decided it was safe to make a cup of tea and a feed. We set off again at 2.30am and passed three armoured cars about 50 yards on our left, without a challenge or shot being fired! Needless to say, we did not stop to investigate whether they were enemy or our own, as we were told that none of our patrols were working west of grid 42 and at that time we were well west of grid 42. From there we carried on until 4.30am when we stopped for breakfast and a bit of a spell.

4 November 1941 We set off again at 6.30am and travelled along the track for Giarabub, keeping a good lookout for enemy planes, which we expected to be looking for us. However, we saw none and just as we were entering Giarabub we passed a party of T Patrol going out on another trip. We stopped for a yarn and saw they had a Lt. Col. with them and also an Air Force officer who was looking for a suitable landing ground for the RAF. Kennedy Shaw was in charge.

We left them and arrived in Giarabub at 11am and went straight to the Brigadier Major. They took two prisoners for questioning and decided to send one to Mersa Matruh by plane. The rest would come with us to Siwa and from there to Mersa, later on. We set off for Siwa at 3.30pm and decided to keep on travelling until we arrived there. On arrival we handed the prisoners to HQ to look after and then headed for our camp where we talked the trip over with the rest of T Patrol, and then to bed.

I can truly say that it is a miracle the LRDG gets away with it the way they have done up until now. If GHQ want information, they tell us to do the job, whereupon we set off in unarmoured and practically unarmed trucks, against armoured cars or planes, which are the two most likely things we would strike. We bring back the information required or prisoners who can provide it, and generally a lot more besides. It seems to me the LRDG are doing the impossible and getting away with it.

We were surprised to see that Bruce's party were back when we arrived. They apparently ran into a large enemy force and had returned. This morning I had to learn how to find my position on a map after having 'shot' the stars with a theodolite. It was all very interesting.

6-21 November *Jopling's navigation course continued both at Siwa base and in the desert. Later they undertook reconnaissance duties around El Hacheim, observing enemy movements.*

◦ **22 November 1941** ◦ *9.30am* Bruce Ballantyne arrived by air this morning at 8am. He has been promoted to Major. Our party was the only one that has reported any movements so far, and back at Siwa they are very pleased with what we have done. Bruce brought our mail back. I received two letters. We intend to leave here in about an hour's time, as soon as we have sent a message back. This time we are going to the east of Hacheim. One LRDG party got shot up by our own Hurricanes, and although no one was hurt, every vehicle was hit and the wireless truck burnt out.

12 noon We started at 10.30am and headed due north. We stopped for lunch after covering 22 miles. We had just halted when we heard planes. Two came almost overhead, flying very high. Shortly afterwards, we heard more and saw one heading NW and then bank round and head SE.

1.00pm We were about to move off when three planes showed up on our left. However it turned out to be eight planes and we were very relieved when we saw our markings on them. Well, we are about to move off again now.

3.00pm We have just spotted a plane on the ground to our left, but we can't see what markings. However, we are going to charge up to it and find out.

We did this, and met no opposition. It was a big troop-carrying Savoia plane [*Savoia-*

Remains of a burned-out Ford F30 truck after an air attack. Because the patrols mainly operated behind the lines, they were vulnerable to attacks from both enemy and allied air forces. With much fuel and ammunition on board, these trucks could be easily set on fire.

Marchetti SM82] which had apparently made a forced landing. There was one grave alongside the plane, and a dead man or what was left of him, under the left wing.

4.30pm We left the plane at 3.45pm and were travelling north when we saw some dust on the horizon. One cloud of dust soon grew to several clouds of dust, which turned out to be three armoured cars. We fired a red Very light, but received no answer. Bruce looked through his telescope and saw pennants flying from the center of the wireless mast, when they should have been at the top. So things didn't look too rosy. We gazed at each other through binoculars, neither side knowing whether the other side was friend or foe.

Then Bruce made up his mind. He would go and find out. If there was any excitement, we were to head south until we met some of our troops and could inform them. So off he went, and there we stood, waiting for a shot to be fired from the other side. Bruce stopped a couple of times in his journey, but eventually arrived without any shots being fired. He then came back and told us to follow him. It was a South African armoured car patrol. Bruce then called me over and we compared maps. The SA officer showed us the area he was patrolling, which was the area we were supposed to watch. He said he hadn't been told anything about recognition signals for ground troops, but he recognised the flag out to the right of our vehicle because they once used it. We asked him what their aircraft recognition signal was, and he told us a white 'T' on a black background. We had been going to use the white flares, but I think perhaps the T is better now.

A crashed Italian Savoia-Marchetti SM82 found by T Patrol beside a mangled body and a grave. The LRDG often came across downed aircraft and sometimes took weapons and ammunition from them to use in their own trucks. (Craw)

Captain Bruce Ballantyne, T Patrol commander, standing beside his pilot vehicle, a Ford F8 8cwt named Te Rangi III. *It was also known as the 'baby Ford' or 'Stinker'. These vehicles were only used by the LRDG for a short period.*

9.00pm Well, we said our 'adieus' and headed back south again for about 12 miles and camped for the night. I had to shoot the stars tonight as there was hardly any sun all day and my direction finding (D/R) was mainly guesswork. I am on picquet from 9pm till 10pm.

23 NOVEMBER 1941 *11.00am* We set off this morning at 7am – southward, and stopped at 8am to hear the news from Daventry. In it we heard that the New Zealanders had captured Capuzzo. We also heard that we have almost undisputed air superiority and that when they hear a plane up there they hardly bother to look up. The announcer had barely got the words out of his mouth before we heard aircraft and six planes loomed up upon us. We looked up and saw one Heinkel with a Messerschmitt fighter escort, followed by four Stukas. We watched for a while and saw them bank round and head straight for us. We thought, "Here goes for a lively half hour or so," but as LRDG luck would have it, they must have decided we were not worth the trouble of bombing and they banked 'round onto their original course again. After they had gone we headed south again and are now in a little wadi four miles from Etla. Last night we sent a message saying that armoured cars are patrolling our area. So today I suppose we will get a message to go west of El Hacheim. Five lots of planes passed over us last night. Everyone woke up each time.

4.30pm We have just seen three more armoured cars about three miles to our north and we presume they are South Africans. Bruce is sending a message about this to Siwa.

9.00pm On the wireless this evening we heard that Bardia is in our hands. Big tank battles are still raging and the British admit that our losses are heavy, but that the enemy losses are greater. In this diary I have not written down every plane we have seen or heard, but only those that gave us the biggest frights. We are right on the aeroplane sky lanes and there is almost a continual stream of aircraft going each way the whole day. There are as many, if not more, enemy aircraft as our own.

24 November 1941 We sent in a message to say we have three broken springs and one man down with malaria and they signalled back for us to return to Siwa. So we are dumping the benzine and just taking enough to get us back to Siwa where we will fit new springs, take on more rations and come out again.

8.00pm We dumped the benzine, set off at 2.15pm and camped just on the Egyptian side of the wire at Quara. The baby Ford V8 *[Ford F8, 8cwt]* got a puncture, so Bruce told me to take the lead and he would catch us up, which he did just before we hit the wire. On the wireless this evening we heard that the New Zealanders had captured Gambut.

Frank Jopling enjoyed his photography. Here he takes a photo of camels at Siwa.

◈ **25 November 1941** ◈   We set off again at 7.30am and arrived in Siwa at 3pm.   On arriving back we were told that four men from other half of T Patrol (T2) had been taken prisoner. They are Capt. Hunter, Cpl. F Kendall, L/Cpl. R T Porter and Tpr. L A McIver. We haven't heard any details yet, but the remainder of the patrol should be in either tomorrow night or the following morning.

The 8cwt 'baby' Ford V8, from a wartime Italian identification manual

◈ **26 November 1941** ◈   Today I made a map of the trip, after which I had a swim and a shave. Apparently our next job is going to be fairly lively, as Bruce has ordered extra Bofors shells. We are also making camouflage nets for each vehicle.

◈ **27 November 1941** ◈   This morning we made camouflage nets and this afternoon covered two trucks with a different patterned net. Colonel Prendergast inspected them from a long way off and said they were very good, so we are now going to make one for each truck.

◈ **28 November 1941** ◈   Bruce told me this morning that he and I may be going away for a few days on loan to someone else. He says he will know more about it tonight. Today we carried on making camouflage nets. Last night the remainder of T2 Patrol arrived in, and their story goes something like this:

   They were watching three roads north west of Mechili and were about five miles apart. Ray Porter was on watch on the most northerly of the three roads and when a truck went to pick him up, there was no sign of him or his bedding. All they found was a diary he had been keeping, stuck in some stones close by. They came back and reported it to Capt. Hunter and the following morning two trucks went up and were attacked by two Italian trucks, one of which had a Breda gun. The Bofors truck turned around and headed back to their camp and the last they saw of Capt. Hunter's truck, they were shooting it out.

   When they arrived back in camp, the Bofors crew told the others they were being chased and to pack up and get going. They did this in double quick time and so came back to Siwa. Well, I suppose I have no right to comment on the proceedings, but it seems to me there must have been some bad management somewhere. Firstly, when a man just vanishes off picquet leaving nothing except his diary hidden among some stones, I would approach that spot very cautiously. Secondly, it doesn't seem to me to be right that only one man should be watching that road, five miles from his nearest mate. Thirdly, if there were only two enemy trucks one of which had a Breda on it, and two of our trucks, one with a Bofors, they ought to have been able to put up a bit of a fight. However, it is all over and done now and the fact remains that Porter is almost certainly a prisoner of war. As for the other three, anything may have happened. 'Bing' Morris *[Lt. C S Morris]* who was our sergeant major in the Div. Cav. and now a lieutenant, is to be our new 2 IC.

WITH THE EIGHTH ARMY

◈ **29 November 1941** ◈ Today we got benzine and rations. From now on our base is to be at Jalo, and half of our patrol *[T2]* and HQ are leaving for that place on December 1st. Bruce's half of the patrol are going up top to do 'Army co-operation' – whatever that is. However, rumours get around and the story at present is that we are going to navigate artillery to some spot or other. Bruce told me today that from now on I am No. 1 navigator of the patrol, so it seems as though it rests with me to get this artillery in the correct spot. However, we are apparently not leaving for a week or so.

◈ **30 November 1941** ◈ Today we were busy getting Bing Morris's half of the patrol *[T1]* ready to move off tomorrow. My job was to see that they had all the maps and navigation equipment necessary. Several of the trucks have had new engines put in since arriving back from the last patrol, but the biggest job seems to be to get springs. Apparently they are unprocurable and so we have to weld them. It is hard to imagine how welded springs will stand up to the work and I don't feel very optimistic about the idea. This evening we heard on the wireless that the Russians have the Huns on the run from Rostov. That is good news – I hope they keep it up.

◈ **1 December 1941** ◈ Bing Morris's half of the patrol set out this morning for Jalo with some HQ. The wireless has been giving Jalo a lot of publicity lately and they say that in future, operations from Jalo will be numerous and important. Broadcasting that isn't going to help us any by, and even now the Huns are bombing it every day.

◈ **2 December 1941** ◈ *12.30pm* I was woken this morning by Bruce telling Sergeant McInnes that we are leaving as soon as we can get ready. This morning I went to Kennedy Shaw to get a theodolite and in my travels heard that Dick Croucher had picked up Capt. Hunter. This is great news and he will probably be able to tell us what happened to the rest of the party. Apparently two lots of troops are to be navigated to two separate places, so an R Patrol navigator is coming with us also. We set off at 3pm but had only just got away from

Siwa, when one of the trucks broke the bracket of its air cleaner. The fitters looked through their spare parts and found that they had no spare brackets, so a truck returned to Siwa to get two. We carried on for five miles and camped the night only 16 miles from Siwa. Was it cold! There was a very cold wind, and to make matters worse, it rained.

◆ **3 December 1941** ◆ *12 noon* We set off this morning at 7am and have travelled 80 miles along a good track. We are now having lunch at a well called Bir Bayly.

2.00pm We have travelled ten miles since lunch and have now stopped within sight of the wire and are watching the Jerries bombing Maddalena aerodrome. We have just seen 22 of our own planes fly over.

9.00pm We have camped for the night 16 miles west of the wire, having travelled 135 miles. Between the wire and here was very rough going and a continual stream of ambulances passed us heading for the wire. Just as we came through the wire, which was about 12 miles north of Fort Maddalena, the sky became literally black with our planes, bombers and fighters. I am writing this in bed by moonlight and there is a continual rumble of guns etc. to the NW. What our job is this time, is still rather indefinite. We are heading for some HQ or other, I don't know whose yet. From there we are to take a brigade of Guards and some artillery to a place near Benghazi. I don't know if that is correct, but that is all we can gather so far. However, we only have about 20 miles to go to get to this HQ, so we will probably know all about it tomorrow morning.

Captain C S 'Bing' Morris, commander T2 Patrol. In December 1941 he earned the Military Cross after a joint action with the SAS. In 1942 he replaced Major Steele as Officer in Command of A (NZ) Squadron. Note the bronze LRDG badge on his cap. (Pittaway/Fourie collection)

◆ **4 December 1941** ◆ We set off at 7.30am this morning, found the crowd we wanted at 9.45 and camped near them. We have seen two lots of British planes, 22 in each. We also saw one Savoia bomber. Some Bofors opened up on him from just alongside us and very quickly chased him away. It is very different being here with a lot of other troops close at hand, compared with being out on our own. Here when a plane comes over, it does not worry us at all. The chances of enemy aircraft concentrating on us are very remote and hearing those Bofors AA guns makes us feel as safe as a church.

◆ **5 December 1941** ◆ This morning we heard much noise of bombs and gunfire to the north. We saw several planes, so thought there must be some bombing going on. Later we saw four fighters heading straight for us with their guns firing at intervals and travelling at a height of about 50 feet. We then heard a shout, "Take cover!" – which we promptly did. The leading plane was a Hurricane and the other three were ME 109s. After they had passed us we saw the Hurricane crash.

The Guards are moving about 12 miles north this afternoon and we will be going with them.

8.00pm We have just seen the sight we have been waiting for, but I am getting ahead of myself. We left our last camping place at 1.30 and travelled 12 miles in over two hours. We are 12 miles north of our last camp and are staying here for the night. Now the exciting part. Just as the sun was getting low we heard gunfire and realised that a 'dog fight' was taking place. There were 30 fighters. They came right over the top of us and we all enjoyed it very much, but rather to our disappointment no planes burst into flames and fell to the earth. However, I took a couple of photos which I hope will come out all right.

6 December 1941 *12 noon* Well, we are still in the same place, awaiting further news and orders. The number of aircraft about is almost incredible. Most of them are ours. Just before lunch we heard a lot of aircraft and saw about 40 Tomahawks. Away above them were a lot more. With the help of a telescope we saw that they had crosses on them and were flying in the opposite direction. Then we spotted another 40 of our planes – bombers and fighters – and neither side took any notice of the other.

9.00pm From all accounts the Hun seems to be advancing a bit. Odd enemy planes come over here, but do not drop any bombs. Our AA opens up sometimes and gets pretty close. This afternoon we saw a ME 109 crash with a Hurricane on his tail. The number of trucks moving around here has to be seen to be believed. As far as the eye can see is just one mass of trucks. We are about 12 miles from Bir el Gubi, where most of the fighting is at present.

12 Midnight I am on picquet and writing this by moonlight. We were talking to some Tommy artillery who are attached to the Indians, and according to them, it was the Indians who got surrounded this morning, but the artillery gave them covering fire. They put up smoke screens which we could see from here and they all escaped. However, these artillery men reckon the Hun is properly on the run up here and it was the Huns retreating from around Tobruk Hills who surrounded the Indians. This evening Bruce told me we had to close in on the Brigadier's tent and asked me what bearing it was to Fort Maddalena. I told him it was approximately 110. He said to set my prismatic for that bearing just in case we had to move off that night.

7 December 1941 *8.00pm* We have just had 40 enemy planes over us, mostly Stukas. They dive bombed someone about two miles to our SW and believe me, they were not light bombs. The AA opened up on them, but none came down. Everyone is busy digging slit trenches for themselves now. So far today we have only seen one of ours, but about 50 enemy planes. We heard a rumour this morning that the Maori Battalion made a bayonet charge and recaptured 700 New Zealanders, took 100 prisoners and only lost two of their own men. Not bad! If true.

12 noon About 11am the same lot of Stukas came over and dive bombed exactly the same spot. We have hardly seen any of our own aircraft so far today. There seems to be a big tank battle raging somewhere, as we can hear the two pounders making a terrific noise.

2.00pm The Stukas again came over and dive bombed someone to the NW of us this time. We quite expect to see them over again before sunset. There are 24 of our fighters in the air at present circling round, and the engineers have just set off three unexploded bombs. The fighters were over in no time. They are just waiting for the Stukas to come over again. Let's hope they do. It would be a great battle.

9.00pm Just after the fighters went back, the Stukas turned up for the fourth time today and bombed to the NW. They returned without meeting any opposition. We heard on the news that Japan had declared war on America and Gt. Britain as from dawn this morning. Japan has attacked dozens of places, hundreds of miles apart, which proves that she had made up her mind to attack America long before she declared war. Just how that will affect the war remains to be seen. America has already lost a lot of soldiers and her navy has also suffered heavily.

An Me110 fighter-bomber, shot down by T patrol. (Craw)

8 December 1941 *12 noon* I was standing by my truck a while ago when I suddenly saw some planes coming over the horizon very low. I said, "Hell, look at this!" and there was a rush for guns etc. They turned out to be 12 ME 110s. One of them crashed about a mile or so further on. We have since learned from the prisoners captured from that plane, that our fighters shot down two of them before they got to us and another further on, making a total of four out of the one lot – not bad. We are moving up about four miles so it seems as though things are going to be OK up top.

9.00pm We travelled nearly four miles NW and have now camped for the night.

9 December 1941 *9.00am* We have just seen two of our fighters shoot down a German bomber. It had apparently made a fairly good landing, so our fighters kept at it until it burst into flames.

11.00am This seems to be a good day for our fighters. We have just seen six of them shoot down another German bomber. Apparently this bomber had not let his bombs go, because when it landed we heard the loud explosions of bombs bursting. One survivor out of the two in the first plane shot down is now under guard about 200 yards from us. He is unhurt.

2.00pm We heard this morning that the Germans are still retreating and we are going to move further forward this afternoon.

5.00pm They have changed their minds. We are staying here tonight. At present large bombs being dropped further north. Our planes are over intermittently all day in groups of 20, 30 and 40. There is no doubt about our having air superiority out here at present.

11 December 1941 We set off at 7.30am and have travelled 30 miles NW. We have just crossed the Trigh el Abd.

Hello – here are some enemy aircraft approaching. 12 bombers and 12 fighters. They are not Stukas. They have dropped their bombs just behind the tail end of our column. They are apparently oil bombs, as a cloud of black smoke is rising. I do not know yet what damage has been done.

1.30pm We have now stopped at a cairn marked on the map as 169. Just in front of us are flashes and bangs like artillery shells exploding. However, Bruce and the CO have gone on in front to investigate. We have about 700 vehicles with us in convoy and the LRDG are supposed to tell them where they are. As far as I can gather, the bombs did not hit anyone in our column, but hit a couple of other trucks and caused a few casualties.

2.15pm Bruce has just come back to say that the engineers are exploding land mines etc and that it is quite safe for us to go across.

3.00pm We have now camped and can see El Adem about seven miles east of us. Along the trip we saw crashed planes all over the desert and they weren't all German either.

9.00pm I learned that those bombers hit four trucks at the tail end of our convoy, killing two men and injuring others. It just shows the luck of the LRDG once again. We have always travelled at the rear of the column until today, when we took the lead, and the tail end 'got it.'

12 December 1941 El Adem is apparently being used as an aerodrome for our fighters and it is just like a huge beehive. Planes going in and coming out just like a lot of bees in a hive. If Jerry comes over today it will be just too bad for them. There are ten fighters that do nothing but circle round and round all morning, protecting the aerodrome.

12.30pm Well, well, well!! Just before lunch we saw three Jerry bombers coming straight for us. As they got close, down went their noses, so we knew we were in for something. We donned our tin hats and lay on the ground by the trucks, then – bang, bang, bang! – two enormous bombs were dropped by each plane. Four of them dropped all around our five trucks. Two dropped before they got to us. When they had passed we were certain that some of us must have been killed, as we had no slit trenches. However, when we eventually got up we found that Lt. Freyberg was the only one injured. Although several of us, including myself, were hit by bits of shrapnel, they didn't do any harm. Lt. Freyberg got a small fragment in his back, but nothing serious. He now has to go to a dressing station to get it extracted and won't be back for a while. One man got his leg blown off by a bomb that fell short of us. I don't know if there were any other casualties.

A piece of metal punctured one of our tyres, going right through one side and sticking out the other. Our truck was hit in several places including the aerial, which snapped. T4 was also hit several times, but the truck didn't sustain any real damage. We picked up a piece of shrapnel weighing about 15 lbs which had travelled 100 yards through the air. The amazing part of the whole thing was, that although our planes were like bees all morning, not one was to be seen when those bombers came over.

2.00pm Once again the sky is just a mass of our fighters, but I suppose if Jerry bombers

T Patrol members examine a crashed Italian Ju87 Stuka. These dive bombers encountered the patrols on a number of occasions, sometimes with devastating results. (Craw)

come over again this afternoon none of our planes will be seen. We are going to move further west and are now all packed up ready to move.

9.00pm We have now camped for the night about 17 miles due north of Bir El Hacheim. In that bombing today, one landed in a slit trench and killed a Guardsman. Altogether three were killed and several injured in the raid. The poor Guardsmen can't understand how we get away with it. We fired at the planes from the trucks and had no slit trenches and four 500 lb. bombs dropped all around us, yet only one man received a slight injury. They have slit trenches and don't fire from trucks and yet three got killed and several injured by two bombs.

13 December 1941 *10.00am* Bruce received a message last night to ask the Brigadier if we can go back, as it is silly staying here doing nothing and getting people bombed and injured. He has now gone to see him.

11.00am A Jerry bomber has just been over and dropped a few more bombs, which landed about 200 yards away. Four of our fighters spotted him and set off after him, but he rose into the clouds and they have lost him.

Hello! Here comes another one – I can see three bombs falling, but this time they are going to drop about ¼ mile away from us. Bang! – there they go, and up into the clouds again.

Gosh! Here comes another one! There are about 40 fighters flying around here and yet they don't seem to be taking the slightest bit of notice of these Jerry planes. They are our own fighters, too!

Bang! There go some more bombs about ½ mile away this time and up he goes into the clouds again. "Here he comes!" someone shouts. I don't see him yet and I can see three more bombs falling. Bang! they go, about a ¼ mile away again. This is getting a bit sickening. It is not so bad when you can see them coming, but when they just come down through the clouds, drop their bombs, and back off into the clouds again, it isn't too good for the nerves.

Here comes another one – passing almost straight over the top of us. He has not dropped any bombs thank goodness!

1.30pm We just heard a crowd of planes and then saw what appeared to be about 20 fighters going into a vertical dive, one after the other. We suddenly realised they were not fighters, but Stukas. They bombed about a mile and a half from us and sure dropped a few eggs. I'll bet someone got killed or injured. The bombers have been over again, but dropped their load a long way away from here. Bruce has come back from General Marriott, who suggested that we return to Siwa until the force is ready to concentrate at Maddalena. So we have sent a message to Siwa, asking Col. Prendergast to wire Army HQ for permission for us to return to base until required. The bombs that dropped close to us this morning injured four men, but none were killed.

An Italian Lancia Ro 3 truck mounting a heavy gun, burned out in a desert battlefield. At El Duda, Jopling wrote, "The whole desert, as far as you can see on either side of the road, is just littered with derelict tanks and trucks."

14 December 1941 We have seen two single Jerry bombers, but neither of them dropped any bombs. About four miles away, Stukas had another go at someone. Last night we saw one Stuka come crashing to the ground, though the pilot came down by parachute. This morning we received a message to say that Col. Prendergast was flying to Army HQ today, and would find out what they wanted to do with us.

Bruce has just come back from HQ and this afternoon we are going about 9½ miles east, where the Brigade is going to concentrate. I don't suppose we will be returning to Siwa now. Perhaps we will go back to Maddalena when the Brigade has concentrated.

9.00pm A nice little surprise. At 1.00pm the green troop set off, together with one of the Brigade officers, to the crossroads of the Trigh Capuzzo and Bir Hacheim-Acroma roads. I thought that was as far as we were going to go, but Bruce said, "Are you ready Jop?" I replied in the affirmative and off we went. I did not know where we were supposed to be heading. However, we headed east along the Trigh Capuzzo. We passed the camp where we were bombed and which is now occupied by a large number of tanks, presumably heading for Derna. We carried on until we came to El Adem and then turned left, until we came to a turn off with a signpost which said, "To Cairo".

El Adem is just a mass of ruined buildings. The RAF sure seem to have been at work there. We carried on and eventually came to El Duda where a big tank battle had taken place. What we saw there has to be seen to be believed. Gosh! It must have been some battle. The whole desert, as far as you can see on either side of the road, is just littered with derelict tanks and trucks. To be honest, there are a lot more of ours than Jerries.

We carried on passing wrecked tanks and trucks all the way until we came to the main road, where another officer met us. There is an aerodrome here called Sidi Amud. We then turned right along a bitumen road and hadn't gone far before we met a 'Red Cap' *[military policeman]* It's been quite a while since we have seen one of those. We travelled about 1½ miles, turned left off the road and discovered we were at advanced Army HQ. Bruce and a few more officers are to have a conference about our big trip. We can see the sea from here, but it is far too cold to go for a swim.

We seem to have jumped out of the frying pan into the fire, as we hadn't been here half an hour before the Jerry bombers came over and dropped bombs. That lot hadn't been gone more than fifteen minutes, before another lot came over. They didn't harm us, though they may have hurt someone else.

15-18 DECEMBER 1941 *The LRDG remained at the advanced Army HQ waiting orders for the column to advance. The reason for this large scale operation was that in mid December, Rommel had disengaged his forces from the battle in Cyrenaica and began to withdraw towards Agedabia. In an*

Crew of a Marmon Herrington armoured car of the King's Dragoon Guards pose for a photo after a desert meeting with T2 Patrol. The LRDG patrols occasionally encountered both Axis and Allied armoured cars undertaking forward reconnaissance work. Where possible, the LRDG would avoid contact with enemy armour, and relied on speed to escape from these vehicles, which were better protected and heavily armed. (Ellis)

attempt to prevent the enemy's escape from Benghazi, the Eighth Army despatched columns, including the 22nd Guards Brigade, across the desert south of Gebel Akhdar to the Benghazi-Agedabia road. Frank Jopling's duty as a navigator was to guide the main column westwards towards Antelat. In addition, R1 and R2 patrols acted as flanking scouts for the Brigade. R Patrol navigator, Corporal Ron Tinker, with two trucks, navigated the Scots Guards through Msus towards Sceleidima, 50 kilometres to the north of Antelat.

19 December 1941 This morning Bruce rushed up to Army HQ and met General Ritchie, who said that the work of the LRDG had been a decisive factor in the success of this push. Bruce says we are starting on our big trip tomorrow and that the Jerries will be retreating for their lives. I will be feeling quite important navigating the whole show. There will be about 6,000 front line troops in this force of ours and the idea seems to be to cut off the enemy south of Benghazi. We will have to travel fairly quickly to get there before the Huns escape.

20 December 1941 *9.00am* We had breakfast at 6.00am and two of our trucks with an R Patrol navigator *[Cpl. R A Tinker]* left at 7.30 to lead about 2,000 Scots Guards. Meanwhile, we are waiting to lead the Coldstream Guards, Brigade HQ and some artillery and tanks, totalling about 4,000 men.

12 noon Well, we have started on our big trip.

We have now stopped for half an hour, after having travelled 30 miles. Being with a large convoy like this, we have to travel much slower than if we were by ourselves. We average about 12 miles an hour. Well, a cup of tea is on, so I had better go and get it.

9.00pm We set off again at 12.15pm and at 2.00pm we saw three trucks travelling fast on our left. They stopped in some scrub, so a scout car was sent to investigate. They turned out to be Scots Guards' trucks which had previously broken down and were catching up with their party.

We have now camped for the night after covering 73 miles. I have already 'shot' the stars and fixed our position. We still have about 120 miles to do before we reach Antelat, which is our temporary destination. If required, we should be able to cover that distance tomorrow. So far we haven't seen any sign of our air support, but that doesn't mean there isn't any. They are very likely working to the north of us.

This evening we received a message from Siwa to say that nearly half of G Patrol had been captured. We don't know the details yet. On the wireless this evening we heard that Derna and Mechili were in our hands and that the Jerries were still running for their lives. The force that captured Jalo are moving north to join up with this force and are first of all going to take Saummu. The Coldstreams are going to take Antelat and the Scots Guards are going to take Msus. Well, it is time I went to bed, as there will probably be an early start tomorrow.

21 December 1941 We set off this morning at 7.30am and are now getting back into more dangerous areas. At 9 o'clock we heard explosions not far from us and thought we were getting bombed. Shortly after, two Lysanders, escorted by fighters, landed close to us. They brought word about Brigadiers Reed's party. The 'bangs' turned out to be Royal Engineers exploding mines or Thermos bombs left from the last push. We are now having lunch, having covering 45 miles so far today.

9.00pm We have now camped for the night after covering another 50 miles. We had three scares this afternoon. One when six bombers went over us, probably ours, another when three Beaufighters came over us, and another when we saw what looked like trucks moving on the horizon, but they turned out to be camels. By now the 11th Hussars and the Scots Guards have probably taken Maus and Sceleidima, and Brig. Reed's party have probably taken Saumnu. Tomorrow this party will take Antelat. After that I don't know what is going to happen. We are now camped about six miles of Saumnu and 15 miles east of Antelat.

22 December 1941 We set off at 6.30 this morning. The convoy is now getting into battle order. We had a downpour of rain last night and I was lucky to get a shot at the stars. After dark last night no fires were allowed and no smoking, so we just had a cold tea.

9.30am We are now within two miles of Antelat and armoured cars in front are scouting around. There is a rise leading up to the place and we can't see it from where we are. Bruce is talking to some of the other officers near two armoured cars, which are in communication with other armoured cars. So far there has been no sign that Antelat is occupied and I wouldn't be a bit surprised if we found it deserted.

10.00am Well, it was deserted all right except for one Libyan who looked harmless enough. There is practically nothing there except a walled-in square and a well. One of our chaps picked up a beautiful sword. We have just heard that Saumnu was occupied and there is a bit of a scrap going on. However, we will hear more details about that later. Having done our job here, we are going back to Brigade HQ which is about 15 miles NE of us.

1.00pm Here we are at Brigade HQ once more. We passed several other parties who wanted directions to different places and we also passed the HQ of the support group where Brig. Campbell was. We had not been there half an hour when two ME 109s came over and machine-gunned us. Once again the LRDG received the brunt of the attack, but none of our trucks were hit. One HQ truck was set on fire.

9.00pm We received a message from Siwa telling us to return there forthwith, as we had work to do away in the west of Tripolitania. We will be off tomorrow morning I expect.

23 December 1941 *10.00am* The party that navigated the Scots Guards have just returned minus Skin Moore, who received a bullet wound through the leg and has been evacuated to hospital. They have been bombed and also machine-gunned from the air.

Skin received his bullet wound when a couple of ME 109s machine-gunned them. They have come back with the news that there are some Jerry tanks about five miles from us. HQ are getting ready to move just in case they happen to come this way. We have to change a truck spring, so as soon as that is done we will be heading for Siwa.

We set off at 11.45am and have now stopped for lunch. A while back we thought we were going to see a plane crash in flames but although it was on fire it did not crash. Somehow the fire went out and the plane continued on its journey.

9.00pm We are now camped for the night, having covered 82 miles over very rough going. We heard Saumnu was occupied by 15 men, and the 11th Hussars soon accounted for them.

[Though the LRDG successfully completed their role as navigators, the Guards operation had ended in failure. On 22 December an enemy covering force, including 30 tanks, held up the outflanking columns in the Sceleidima-Antelat area. This enabled the Axis troops to complete their withdrawal from

T1 Patrol enjoys Christmas dinner and beer in the shade of an oasis.

The Special Air Service's winged dagger cap badge (above) and parachute wings (top). The LRDG and SAS served together on many successful operations behind the lines.

Benghazi. Rommel's Afrika Korps retired from Cyrenaica to strong defence positions among the salt marshes between Agedabia and El Agheila.]

24/25 December 1941 Arrived at Siwa for Christmas Eve. There was extra rum left and a bottle of Chianti, so quite a merry Christmas Eve was spent. We had heard of the wonderful work S Patrol had been doing up north. They attacked two aerodromes [*with the SAS*] and destroyed over 60 planes. They lost two men, who were killed when the patrol was attacked by aircraft on their way home.

The Mayor of [*deleted from diary*] somehow managed to hear about the LRDG and donated £250 to us for Christmas. It was much appreciated by all. We received two tins of beer, 20 cigarettes, Christmas cake and pudding, nuts and 50P each.

26 December 1941 - 1 January 1942 T Patrol stayed at Siwa for several days then went on to Jalo via Giarabub to pick up fuel supplies.

A newly arrived Chevrolet 1533X2 30cwt truck having T Patrol markings painted on its side. Note the sand channel resting against the vehicle and the deep tread on the 10 inch wide sand tyre in the back.

2 January 1942 *9.00pm* There was a frost this morning and if I remember right, there was a frost on the same day last year when we were camped on the Sand Sea about 150 miles south of here.

Well, we arrived in Jalo at 4.30pm and were met with the terrible news that the other half of T Patrol [T2] had gone out on a job and only six men had come back. Apparently they took some parachutists *[SAS]* up to an aerodrome to destroy some planes and the alarm went up before their job was completed. Then they endeavored to make a run for it, but were attacked by Stukas and ME 109s on and off for six hours, and four out of five trucks were set on fire. Even after that the planes still came over and machine-gunned the men hiding in the bushes. The crew of two trucks came back on the remaining truck which, though it was not set on fire, was battle scarred. There were bullet holes all over it, about 30 altogether, so it was purely good luck that the truck got safely back. What the fate is of those men who did not return no one knows. We don't know if they are killed, captured or wounded. All we can do is hope for the best.

3 January 1942 We heard to day that in this push alone, the LRDG together with a few *[SAS]* parachutists destroyed 92 enemy planes on various grounds.

4 January- 24 February *1942 The missing T2 men eventually walked out to safety after an arduous eight-day trek. While at Siwa, T1 Patrol carried out reconnaissance duties and assisted Lieutenant P L Arnold's Heavy Section with supply runs between base and Jalo. On 31 January they had returned to Cairo to begin 10 days leave. As Jopling wrote, "We went straight to Abbassia where we unloaded the trucks and received one pound each, then went to Cairo to get cleaned up and to get a good fed inside us."*

Major Bruce Ballantyne's distinguished service in the LRDG was now over and he returned to his original unit, the NZ Divisional Cavalry. His replacement was Captain C S 'Bing' Morris. Lieutenant N P Wilder became T Patrol's 2 IC and Lieutenant J E Crisp had also joined the patrol.

While in Cairo the LRDG was issued with new trucks, far superior to the Ford F30 V8 4x4s previously used. These were purpose-built Canadian Chevrolet 1533X2 30cwts. Though only two-wheel drive, their extra low ratio of gears along with a six cylinder engine that consumed less petrol, made them ideal for desert work. T1 Patrol returned to Siwa base on 24 February.

Trooper D M Bassett, T2 navigator. This photo was taken shortly after he had completed an arduous eight day desert trek having guided a ten-man party to safety, after four T2 Patrol trucks were shot up and destroyed. He received the Distinguished Conduct Medal for his skilful navigation.

THE ROAD WATCH

The Afrika Korps had broken out of El Agheila on the Gulf of Sirte in Libya and the Middle East HQ desperately needed reliable intelligence for a planned counter-offensive in Cyrenaica. To help gather this information, the LRDG was ordered to establish the 'Road Watch'. This entailed constant observation, day and night between 2 March and 21 July 1942, of the Tripoli-Benghazi road (via Balbia) – 643 kilometres behind enemy lines. Records were taken of all movements of enemy armour, artillery, supplies and troops travelling to or from the front. Considered a very tedious task by the LRDG, it proved to be one of the Group's most important activities. The information gained was invaluable to General Staff Intelligence in assessing the enemy's strength in Cyrenaica.

25 FEBRUARY 1942 This evening I was told to go to the Rest House to discuss future operations and there I learned what the next job was to be. We are to leave here on 2 March and go up to the coast road west of El Agheila and take a census of the traffic going up and down. Half of S Patrol left for there today and we will relieve them on 7 March.

26 FEBRUARY- 2 MARCH 1942 After several days of preparation we are getting ready to move off tomorrow. For some reason the date of our departure has been postponed for one day and now we are all set to leave tomorrow. It is going to be a very ticklish job, as you can well imagine. We will be about 500 miles behind enemy lines and will sit within 100 yards of the main coast road. We will be on the road for seven days, when we will be relieved by R1 Patrol.

3 MARCH 1942 Well, we got off at 10am and had our photos taken by an official movie cameraman, so I suppose we will be on the pictures when our doings are allowed to be made public. I can see that on this trip I am going to have a responsibility on my shoulders, as this time I am the only original member. It is Nick Wilder's first trip with the LRDG and he comes to us for advice. He asked me what route I reckoned was best and I told him. He said, "All right, we'll go that way," so we headed along the Sollum road and had gone 35 miles when one of the trucks developed gearbox trouble. The fitters reckoned it would have to go back to Siwa to get fixed. So Nick sent it back and told them that we would carry on for a while and camp on the road and they could catch us up.

We travelled until we were 65 miles from Siwa, where we are now camped for the night. We sent a message back to Siwa to say where we were camped, and I told them that we would wait until 0800 hours tomorrow morning for the other truck, and if it hadn't arrived by then we would carry on without it.

4 MARCH 1942 The other truck arrived all right last night, so we set off at 7.30pm, crossed through the wire at Washka and then headed SW over good going most of the way. We camped for the night after covering 180 miles. It has been very miserable today as there has been a cold wind and heavy showers.

5 MARCH 1942 We set off this morning at 7.30 in a heavy dust storm and we were just cruising along when we saw five armoured cars. We got all guns ready for action and Nick Wilder had just gone off in his truck to find out if they were friendly or enemy. Fortunately they turned out to be a South African patrol. I certainly didn't expect to see any of our armoured cars as far south-west as this. We got stuck in a very bad place and it took us almost an hour to get all the trucks out again. Tomorrow we will be crossing the Jalo road and it may be patrolled by enemy aircraft every day. So there is a danger of being spotted and on a

In March 1942, to replace the Ford F30s, the LRDG was issued with new purpose-built Canadian right hand drive Chevrolet 1533X2 4x2 30cwt trucks. This T Patrol vehicle and its crew were photographed at Siwa in 1942. The truck is in its bare state – on operations it would normally be heavily laden with weapons, equipment and supplies.

job such as we are to to to do, it would be almost fatal to get seen until the task was finished. However, we hope for the best.

⌖6 March 1942⌖ *12 noon* Last night we received a message saying that we would have to be prepared to stay on the job an extra three days as R1 Patrol will be unable to relieve us as prearranged. We are now having lunch by a row of dunes, which have a very soft approach to them. This afternoon we will probably cross the Marada-El Agheila road, which is a very dangerous part of our trip. It was along that road that Rommel decided to make a stand against our last push, so goodness knows what we might run into along there.

7-8 March 1942 *Two days were spent trying to locate S Patrol's road watch postion. On the evening of the second day they met up with the Rhodesians who were pleased to see them, as they had enough after seven days and said they were sorry for the New Zealanders, who had to do ten. T Patrol set up camp, camouflaged their vehicles and prepared for their first watch the next day.*

⌖9 March 1942⌖ *8.00pm* Well, our first two men went down to the road this morning at 4 o'clock. They have to walk three miles across dead flat country and naturally they have to get there before dawn and find as good a hiding place as possible before daybreak. Once in position they have to stay there until after sundown, hardly moving. After sundown they

R Patrol crew dig out their truck, which has sunk up to its axles. Note the mass of stores in the back and the 'bail out' kits next to the driver's seat.

New Chevrolet 1533X2 30cwt trucks lined up before setting out for road watch operations. Note the Maori names on the T Patrol vehicles. Left is J L D Davis; behind Te Aroha is R W N Lewis; centre is Frank Jopling with his ubiquitous sand goggles; extreme right is Captain N P Wilder, the T Patrol commander.

can stand up and stretch themselves, that is, if they can stand up at all, after lying in the same position for so long.

Up in the wadi here we have had quite an uneventful day, except for a few aircraft flying a bit towards the coast from us, but naturally they are not expecting to see any British troops over here.

10 March 1942 *8.00pm* This morning our second two men went down to the road and the first two returned. They reckoned it wasn't such a bad job. The worst part of it was that there were some workmen working on the road almost opposite to where they were watching from, and once or twice during the day they thought they had been spotted. They also got a shock or two when aircraft boomed over the top of them. Once again things were very quiet all day up here, except for a few aircraft. We do picquet here night and day, one hour on and 12 hours off, but that doesn't worry us much.

11 March 1942 The third party of two men went down to the road this morning and the second party returned. The driver of my truck and myself go down tomorrow morning, so I will then be able to give a more or less running commentary on what it is like down there. There is still nothing of interest to report from here except that we heard on the wireless that Rangoon had fallen.

Mussolini erected this arch (the Areo Philaenorum) as a monument to the Italian colonisation of Libya. Straddling the Tripoli-Benghazi highway, it was situated about eight kilometres from the Road Watch's base camp. It was known to the Allies as the Marble Arch. (MacGibbon)

12 March 1942 Well, this morning at 3 o'clock we loaded up our 'throw out kit', which is a pack that we keep full of emergency rations in case we get attacked and the truck gets blown up and we have to walk. We usually keep some bully and biscuits in it and maybe some chewing gum or something we have had sent out from New Zealand. And, of course, our water bottle is either in it or is very handy to grab in case of emergency. We packed the kit with some food for the day, made sure our water bottles were full and made ourselves a cup of tea.

At 3.45am, after being wished "good luck" by anyone who was awake, we set off for the road accompanied by one of the first two men who went down. He had taken a Tommy gun with him and camouflaged it under a bush. But when the sun had gone down again he went for his Tommy gun and couldn't find it. So he came down with us to see whether he could find it again. After walking about a quarter of a mile we came to the mouth of the wadi and from there we had to walk by compass on a bearing of 40 degrees. It was pitch black and cloudy and it seemed a terrible long walk – actually it was about 3 miles.

We eventually arrived at the roadside at 4.50am and set about trying to find a good hiding place. We soon found out that there wasn't such a place, so we eventually decided on a spot about 120 yards from the road, in a slight hollow. The man who came down with us reckoned we were too close. However, we said we would give it a go here. So we picked a few bushes from round about and camouflaged ourselves as much as possible. The other man had a look round for his Tommy gun, but failed to locate it. Dawn was just about to break, so he had to set off back to camp so as to get back into the wadi before it got light. In the meantime we made ourselves as comfortable a possible, or perhaps I should say, as little uncomfortable as possible.

It is now daylight and so far three trucks have passed us. If only those Ities and Huns knew that not 150 yards away two defenceless New Zealanders were watching them go past and writing that fact down in a notebook.

The workmen have just passed us shouting and talking to each other, but it was all 'Dutch' to me.

10.00am Well, so far so good. It isn't a bad job at all. We got a shock a while ago when I thought another truck was coming along the road but then realised it wasn't on the road at all. In

A well-camouflaged road watch camp. It was essential that the watch operations were not discovered, so the men and trucks were kept well hidden. (Pittaway/Fourie collection)

fact it wasn't even on the ground, but was an aeroplane just hedge-hopping alongside the roadside. We ducked and lay perfectly still, but it passed without seeing us. So far 97 trucks have passed us, mostly big five and ten tonners with big trailers.

Hello! Here is that low-flying plane coming back. It has passed us again.

11.00am Well, I didn't expect to be writing this diary now. I expected to be in 'Campo Concentrato' or at least on my way there. I was looking at the traffic passing when my driver said, "Look Jop, here's a man coming towards us."

"Gosh! Yes! There is!" I replied.

At this time he was about 100 yards away from us. He kept on coming towards us, kicking the bushes as he walked. Then he turned and travelled parallel with us for a while until he was behind us. I told my driver to keep an eye on him. We had no rifle or revolver with us, as we had decided beforehand that if we started shooting it would endanger the lives of the rest of the patrol up in the wadi. If we were caught we were going to say that we had been walking round in the desert for the past week or so, and were just going to give ourselves up anyhow. The Itie who was walking about didn't have a rifle with him, but he could have had a revolver. If he had spotted us we might have been able to overpower him, but the struggle would almost certainly have attracted the attention of the workmen on the road or of passing traffic. So, if he did spot us, although he was only one man against two, I wouldn't have given two pence for our chances of escape.

I was working all this out in my head, and by now the Itie was almost straight behind us about 70 yards away and coming towards us. We kept our eyes on him and every now and then he would look straight at us, until we became almost certain that we had been seen. By this time he was about 40 yards away and still coming towards us, looking straight in our direction every now and again.

He came on and was within 20 yards of us when my driver whispered to me, "We're done, Jop, he has seen us alright."

T1 Patrol men rest in front of a well camouflaged truck while on road watch. Trooper Jopling is third from right.

"It looks like it alright, but maleesh!"

Then I began to picture what it would be like in Campo Concentrato and thought it might not be bad after all. At least we would be fairly certain of getting back to New Zealand, but still I didn't like the idea of it. Well, the Itie came within 30 feet of us and then started to head to where we first saw him.

"He is going away," my driver said.

"Thank heaven for that," I replied, and at 10.45am he had gone.

Well, I have had a few thrills since I have been in this outfit and have been very close to death several times, but that is the closest I have ever been to getting captured. And believe it or not, I reckon it was the most anxious half hour I have ever spent. At other times when I have ever been in any excitement, I have always had something to do to keep me occupied, but this time all I could do was lie perfectly still and wait.

I can't understand how it was possible he didn't see us, and even now he may have gone for some troops or arms and may come back and get us yet. However, we can only hope for the best. We were glad that we didn't take the advice of the men who came down with us and move back, because if we had been any further back than we were, he would have walked right on top of us.

Well, to get back to our job again. There was quite a lot of traffic passing while that Itie was running about, but I'm afraid we didn't keep a very accurate tally of it, so we had to guess the number to a certain extent and so far this morning 199 trucks have passed us.

1.00pm Two hours have gone since the Itie left us and nothing has happened so far, so I suppose he can't have seen us. But all the same, he has spoilt the whole day for us. Half the day has now gone and our elbow and backs are aching all over. But we can't move or else some part of us will be conspicuous from the road. It has been very quiet on the road since 11am and only nine trucks have passed us.

4.00pm There have been five planes over us since 1pm, all flying very low, but they have not worried us much. There is still no sign of the Itie returning. Gosh! We are looking forward to that sun going down so that we can get up and stretch our legs. To make matters worse, the wind is blowing and the sand is flying, so we can hardly keep our eyes open.

There are only about two more hours of daylight to go, but every hour seems like a year. As each truck goes past we have put down the time in our notebook and since 6am this morning I have had my watch out in front of me watching each minute go past. If you can imagine lying on your stomach hardly moving and watching the minute hand of your watch take 12 complete circles you may be able to imagine what we had to go through. So far 225 trucks have passed us.

6.00pm The sun has now gone behind the hill, but it is still too light to get up and walk around, though it won't be long now. I have never longed for the sun to go down as much as I have today. I am aching all over and if I stay in this position much longer I think I will die. So far 274 trucks have passed.

Well, we are just about to get up, and won't I be pleased.

13 March 1942 *7.00am* Well, here I am back in the wadi. It was too dark to write any more yesterday, so I will write the rest now. We had a cup of tea yesterday morning and from the time we left to go to the road until 6.30pm, we never had a bite to eat or a drink of water. So believe me, we felt like something to eat. So the last thing we did when it got dark was to stand up and walk round a while, and then sit down to a tin of bully and some shortbread. We also opened a tin of apple juice that I had in my pack. After that we didn't feel so bad,

Trooper P V Mitford of T1 Patrol notes the passing traffic while on the road watch. This important, though tedious and exhausting duty, was undertaken by two men on 24 hour shifts.

except that it started to get very cold after a while. Only an hour ago we had been longing for the sun to go down, now we were longing for it to come up again so that our day would be finished. We nearly froze during the night and there was a very heavy dew.

We counted 38 trucks during the night and brought our grand total to 336. We set off on our walk back at 4am and believe me, it seemed an awful long three miles, but we eventually arrived here at 6am and set about getting some breakfast in. We have had breakfast and now feel a lot better.

3.00pm About half an hour ago the picquet came down off the hill and reckoned there were two trucks coming across the flat from the road towards us. Immediately Nick went up on the hill and looked through the glasses and ordered all camouflage to be taken off the trucks and for us to prepare for action. It didn't take long before all trucks were loaded up and ready for action.

However, so far nothing has happened, but we are still waiting. If anything other than a tank or an armoured car comes up this wadi, it will have a very short life. We have four trucks here and there are six machine-guns all loaded and pointing at the entrance of the wadi.

4.00pm We have now been told that we can put the camouflage back on the trucks and it is now my turn to go on the hill for picquet, so I had better go.

8.00pm The rest of the day passed without incident, so I don't think those trucks were looking for us.

14 March 1942 *9.00am* One of our chaps went out on the flat at dawn this morning to see if he could see any tracks from those trucks yesterday. He came back to say that he couldn't see any, but that a convoy of about 100 trucks was parked along the road. Nick went up on the hill to have a look at them through his glasses and calmly informed us that they were not trucks, but tanks, and heavy ones too. I went up and had a look and sure enough they were tanks all right.

That means we will have to send a message back to Siwa – a thing we didn't want to do, as we are almost certain to get picked with wireless direction-finding and that means we will have the bombers over. Despite the risk it has to be done, so we will have to make the best of it. However, we can't very well send a message until after dark and we will have to get in touch with the road watch for particulars.

1.00pm Our wireless operator listens in to Siwa twice a day, at 11.30am GMT and again at 5.00pm GMT, to see if they have any messages for us. If they have, he takes it down, but doesn't touch the key himself. Well, today at 11.30 they had a message for us and it told us to let them know immediately if any tanks passed us. They must have found out about these tanks from other sources. Nick decided to estimate the number of these tanks and send a message this afternoon. So we estimated that approximately 100 tanks had gone past along with increased transport activity. Then Nick told us to go about 10 or 15 miles away and send the message and come back at dusk.

5.00pm Well, we have come 15 miles due south and have sent the message. So far there is no sign of bombers. Before we left, Nick told me that if we did get bombed, he would send another truck out to pick us up. We have to wait an hour for a reply. By that time it will probably be too dark to get back to the wadi tonight.

6.15pm We received a message to say that R Patrol would meet us at the hill with two cairns, either at night on the 16th or dawn on the 17th. It was quite a welcome message to receive. It is now dark, but we will go back as far as the hill with two cairns, camp there the night and go into the wadi at dawn in the morning.

15 March 1942 *1.00pm* We arrived back in the wadi shortly after daybreak this morning and immediately we made out another message with fuller details. At 11.30 GMT we received another message from Siwa asking for further details urgently. So we made another message out and we are going only about nine miles to send it. So far there has been no sign of aircraft going over where we sent yesterday's message, so apparently we got away with it.

3.00pm We left this afternoon at 1.30pm and set off up the wadi and out on to the flat that we are getting to know so well. On this flat we can see for about 20 miles, as well as the sea and road, and we are only five miles off the road. Every time we cross it we expect to get spotted, and yet so far we have got away with it every time. We seem to drive around here as though we owned it. However, we crossed it again all right, and now the operator is sending the two messages. This time we are going to get back before it gets dark.

7.00pm We arrived back at 5pm and almost as soon as we got back Nick came round with a hat and asked us to draw a ticket. Everyone had now done a shift on the road and there are still two days to go, so we are drawing for who goes down the second time. This time it will only be 12-hour shifts, as we will relieve them night and morning. Well, my driver and I both drew one and we don't have to go down tomorrow morning, but that doesn't mean to say that I won't be going down tomorrow night.

16 MARCH 1942 *5.15pm* This morning the weather was lovely and fine, and this afternoon it is blowing a gale and the sand is blowing very bad. This afternoon I drew a ticket to go down to the road this evening, so I am now ready to set off. I just had time to listen to the news on the wireless and it said that in Libya our patrols were active in giving information of enemy concentrations. We don't like them broadcasting things like that, not while we are still watching the road anyhow.

This afternoon one of the men who didn't draw a ticket to go down to the road offered me a proposition that he take my watch tonight on the chance that he draws or doesn't draw a ticket to go down tomorrow. But I said no, I would be sure of the night watch rather that risk getting a day watch. However, I have just heard that he drew the ticket and has to relieve us at dawn tomorrow. Thank goodness I didn't take up the proposition.

17 MARCH 1942 *7.00am* Well, we set off down to the road with a strong wind and sand blowing. We went very close to the road and covered our heads with our coats and each truck that went past we could hear long before it got close. During the whole night only ten trucks passed us. Seven travelling E to W and three W to E. At 4am, just as I was setting my compass for our return journey, there was a blinding flash. It gave us quite a shock until we realised it was nothing worse than lightning.

We arrived back here just as it started to rain. We have now had breakfast and it is raining cats and dogs and it looks as though it is going to last all day. We were pleased to see R Patrol arrive this morning, so we will be heading for Siwa at dawn tomorrow. I had another shock this morning when I heard that our wireless operator had been using the key last night. However, we received a message asking for more particulars about the tanks. Gosh! Soon they will want to know how many nuts and bolts are in each one.

2.00pm It rained solidly until midday, but has now cleared up. R Patrol told us that S1 Patrol was up near Benghazi and they had some rain there which washed three of their trucks away. One is a total loss, but they are going to try and salvage the other two. That is the sort of rain we get here at times. Well, we have made out two more messages to send to Siwa and we are just about to go 15 miles away to send them. After that we are coming back to the hill with two cairns and we are all here except Nick and the two men who were on watch during the day. I don't suppose they will arrive here until morning.

18 March 1942 *6.00am* It rained again last night, which made things pretty miserable. However, Nick and the two men who were on watch have arrived and are just having a cup of tea before we move off.

In my opinion we still have the most dangerous job to do and that is to get back to Siwa. We have to cross the Marada-El Agheila road and then cross the roads north of Jalo. R Patrol

A Chevrolet 1311X3 15 cwt exploring spectacular country outside Siwa. (Craw)

tell us that the tracks we made across the Marada El Agheila road have since been mined, so they must be on the lookout for us. However, I hope to get across the Marada road and the Jalo road today. We are about to move off now.

8.30am We are now about 20 miles from the Marada road and we are getting all guns ready for action. I thought I saw a truck over to our left, but I wouldn't be sure. However here goes.

10.00am Well, we travelled about 15 miles towards the road from our last stop when we saw ten trucks to our left. Three of them were coming flat-out towards us. Just then it started to rain heavily, which probably saved us a lot of trouble. We turned south and drove about five miles before turning back to our original course. Every now and then when we looked back we could still see one truck following us. However, that one didn't worry us, it was the nine behind him that we didn't want to meet up with.

When we got near the road we could see some traffic on it and Nick looked through his glasses and said, "It's alright, they're going north."

We were going to cross the road south of them, but we didn't know if there were any more coming up from the south. However, we carried on and crossed the road, only a few chains in front of ten covered vehicles. Having been spotted, we are expecting aircraft over at any time now, but we are now 20 miles east of the road and we haven't seen any yet.

12.30pm We have now stopped for lunch on the edge of the rough country. This afternoon we will be on good going all the way and will cross the Jalo road. We still haven't seen any sign of aircraft looking for us.

8.00pm Just as we approached the Jalo road, we saw a truck and what appeared to be two men sitting beside it. Immediately the action signal was given and we charged down on it, only to find it abandoned and there were two tins alongside it.

We carried on and crossed the road without having any more excitement. We have now camped for the night after covering 245 miles. We are feeling safe again until the next time we go out on a trip. We shot two gazelles just before we stopped, so we will have some fresh meat when we get back to Siwa.

19 March 1942 *1.00pm* We have stopped for lunch after covering 75 miles of rough country. We are sending three long messages to Siwa concerning the traffic we saw on the road, so we will be here for a while yet.

8.00pm We set off at 3pm and have now camped for the night after covering 135 miles for the day. We will arrive in Siwa some time tomorrow afternoon.

20 March 1942 *12 noon* We crossed through the wire at 10am and we are now on the Sollum road, only 64 miles from Siwa.

8.00pm Here we are back in Siwa after arriving at 3.30pm. We are the only patrol here at present. We were told that we would have to go back to the road again on 25th March, which doesn't give us much time here. Today Nick Wilder had to fly to 8th Army HQ to give them all the details of the tanks we saw, but before he left he asked me to complete a report of the trip out and the trip back. So I have been doing that today. On the wireless tonight it said that the Free French under Col. Leclerc were pushing northward and were now NE of Murzuk and 300 miles from the Gulf of Sirte. Not bad I suppose, as he only has a handful of men with him.

21-30 March 1942 *The patrol rested in Siwa for five days and received a message from the C-in-C Middle East congratulating them on the Road Watch, as invaluable information had been obtained. On 25 March they set off again for another turn on the watch and relieved R Patrol on the 28th. Their trucks were camouflaged and Jopling spent the first several days on picquet duties.*

☞**31 March 1942**☜ *9.00am* I am again on picquet on the hill. The two men who came back from the road say that 12 tanks and 6 armoured cars had moved east. This time they were only medium tanks. We are not going to send a message back to Siwa yet. There was a lot more traffic on the road yesterday; 380 vehicles past. There do not seem to be very many going past at present.

8.00pm Today turned out to be another miserable sort of day as the wind rose again and the sand blew. There have been more aircraft over today but we still haven't been spotted.

R2 Patrol truck and crew looking forward to being relieved from the tedium of the road watch.

☞**1 April 1942**☜ *1.00pm* Once again I am on picquet up on the hill. And once again it is a miserable day. The wind is blowing strong and so is the sand. I hope it clears up for tomorrow, because I go down on the road watch tomorrow at dawn. It seems fairly quiet down on the road at present.

8.00pm Well, my 'throw out' kit is packed and I am all ready to go down to the road early tomorrow morning.

☞**2 April 1942**☜ *6.00am* We had a cup of tea and an omelet at 3.30 this morning. We bought the eggs at Siwa before we left, and we set off for the road at 3.45am. This time we went on a bearing of 15 degrees and travelled a bit more than three miles, but we have found a far better place than we had last time. We are on top of a hill in a slit trench only about 150 yards off the road. We can move around in here comfortably without being seen from the road, and yet we can see the road for miles each side. So far only three trucks have passed, all going eastwards.

7.30am I don't suppose the rest of the patrol will believe this, but once again an Itie has been round us, though this time we didn't have quite such an anxious time as the last. For one reason we have a revolver with us and for another he didn't come any closer than 100 yards, and he did not wander round kicking each bush as he came to it. He came off the road to our right and headed out at right angles from there. When he was about 100 yards behind us, he turned to his right and went parallel to the road, passing behind us and heading straight for an old Jerry camp site. He was walking very fast and sometimes broke into a run, so he didn't worry us very much, but we kept an eye on him all the time. After roaming round the camp site for a while, he turned back into the road again and headed westward. Well, so far 47 trucks have passed us, 34 westward and 13 eastward.

8.00am We have just seen two planes take off from the aerodrome just to our left. One of them came zooming along the road flying very low and the other must have passed very close to the wadi where the rest of the patrol is camped. However, they both went straight past, so can't have spotted anything. So far 76 vehicles have passed us, 57 westward and 19 eastward.

9.30am The wind is getting up again and the sand is starting to blow. A convoy of 36 trucks has just passed us, travelling eastward. 28 of them were five ton Lancias, all heavily laden, some with boxes of stuff, one with a load of tyres and others with sides so high that we couldn't see inside them. So far, 72 have gone westward and 74 eastward, only three in the last half hour.

12 noon Well, we have just had lunch, which consisted of a tin of fruit and a tin of beer which we bought at the canteen back in Siwa. Now 98 vehicles have passed westward and 89 eastward. Half the day has now gone and we feel a lot more comfortable then we did at 12 noon the last time we were down here.

3.00pm So far 119 vehicles have passed westward and 128 eastward, and we can now see a very long convoy coming from the west going east.

4.00pm There were 61 trucks in that convoy. The majority of them were loaded with troops. At a guess I should say at least 600 troops went past, mostly Itie. While this convoy was passing, 17 went the other way so I was kept pretty busy. So far 136 have gone westward and 189 eastward.

6.30pm Well, here we were at the end of another day of watching the road. We have still the night to fill in, but we don't mind that so long as it doesn't get too cold. So far 180 vehicles have travelled westward and eastward, making a total of 379. We went another 21 to bring the tally up to 400, which will be a record for this patrol. Well, it is getting dark now, so I will close down again until tomorrow morning.

3 APRIL 1942 *7.00am* Here we are back in camp again and our total tally was 202 vehicles going westward and 211 travelling eastward, making a total of 413. Last night after dark we went down on the road and walked along it for a little way. We saw some trucks coming, so we lay down a few yards off the road until they passed. It wasn't nearly such a cold night as the last time we were down, and together we had quite a good day.

9.00am We had just finished breakfast when one of the boys went to fold up the cover he had been sleeping on. He let out an exclamation and said, "Look at this!" There was a 5ft 6in long snake coiled up under the cover that he had been sleeping on all night. We grabbed a shovel. Just as we were going to kill it, it sat up ready to strike and blew out its hood. I don't know much about snakes, but it must have been some kind of cobra. However, when we get back to Cairo I will endeavour to find out. It was certainly a poisonous snake, because we drained the poison out of its fangs.

8.00pm This evening one truck went up the hill with two cairns to meet G2 Patrol who are going to relieve us, and should be here either tonight or tomorrow morning. Our last two men go down to the road at dawn tomorrow and will return after dark in the evening. We will set off back to Siwa as soon as the moon gets up tomorrow night, so as to cross the Marada road before daylight if possible.

4-8 APRIL 1942 *T1 Patrol, having been relieved by G2 Patrol, returned to Siwa via Giarabub to pick mail and supplies.*

9-27 APRIL 1942 We are still in Siwa, but we have had orders to leave early in the morning of 29 April. We don't know yet what our job will be. During the past two weeks we have had no work in the mornings or in the evenings, so in the mornings we have been shooting every day and in the evening we have been playing baseball against another patrol.

About a week ago it came out in Routine Orders that in future all navigators are to receive 1/- a day extra pay. So Bing Morris went to see the NZ Administration Office and they told him that the New Zealand government wouldn't pay extra for navigators. The position at present is that all Tommy navigators are getting 1/- per day extra while we don't get anything extra, which seems to be a very unsatisfactory state of affairs to me.

We have had the option of having Siwa as our base for the summer, or going up on the coast near Bug Bug, but we all wanted to stay here. One of the main reasons is that B Squadron [G, Y, and S Patrols] were going up to Bug Bug and if we stay here we will be on our own. Four days after we arrived in Cairo, T1 Patrol went to relieve G2 Patrol watching the road, and a week ago S Patrol set out to relieve T2 Patrol.

28-30 APRIL 1942 *T1 Patrol was to return to the road watch, but that order was cancelled when Colonel Prendergast proposed another operation. First though, they had to learn how to make bombs.*

CONVOY ATTACKS

⁌ **1 May 1942** ⁍   Four of us had to attend a lecture on bombs today. We learned all about plastic explosives, Nobel's 808 gelignite, thermite, electron fillings, detonators, fuses and time pencils, etc. It appears that we plan to go to the coast road and do what seems to me at present to be the most impossible thing we have yet undertaken. We are going on to the road at night to put some obstacle across it, so as to slow down the traffic. As the trucks go past we are to throw bombs into the back of them. These will be set to go off four hours later. Well, we'll try anything once.

⁌ **2 May 1942** ⁍   Today we received another lecture on the different types of explosives. This evening we saw an experiment, or rather three experiments. Three bombs were tried out. The first with 1lb of Nobel's 808 and 1½ oz of electron fillings and a beer tin of benzine. Another was 2 lb. of 808 and 3 oz of electron fillings and one beer tin of benzine, and the third was 808 [1lb] with a ½ lb of thermite and a beer tin of benzine. Col. Prendergast decided that the 2 lb of 808 and 2 oz of electron fillings with the beer tin of benzine was the best, so that is what we are going to make and use.

⁌ **3 May 1942** ⁍   This morning we had the first church service we have ever had in Siwa and only the second we have ever had in the LRDG. After church we went to another lecture on explosives.

⁌ **4 May 1942** ⁍   Today four of us were shown how to make bombs and this evening we started to make them ourselves. After handling Nobel's 808 for a while you get a severe headache. Each of us had to make six bombs and this evening I made my sixth, and believe me, I certainly developed a headache. So did everyone else who made their sixth bomb.

⁌ **5 May 1942** ⁍   Well, today we saw the most wonderful sight I have ever seen in the desert. We had just had tea and had gone outside in the cool when we saw a long thick cloud in the horizon. It reminded me straight away of the sight we just saw as we were leaving Murzuk 36 months ago. So I said, "Look at this dust storm coming!" but no one would believe me. They all thought it was an ordinary cloud. At the time there wasn't a breath of wind blowing. Half an hour later the cloud was a lot closer and one or two distant hills vanished.

I said, "Do you believe me when I say it is a dust storm coming now?" And one or two started to become a bit suspicious. After a while we could see what looked like thick clouds of smoke pushing through each other in the cloud. And after a while again some of the nearer hills vanished in the cloud. But the best sight of all was as it came across the oasis. It looked as though an enormous dam had broken through and was crashing down on us. As it came across the palms and over the hill of ruins we could hear the wind, and just before it came upon us, the wind got up. Well, I have never seen a dust storm like it. It was far thicker than the Murzuk one. Everything went dark and a dull orange color and we couldn't see more than ten yards ahead of us. Sand and dust got everywhere, but in spite of the discomfort it as a sight I would very much like to see again. Words cannot describe it. It had to be seen to be believed.

⁓6 May 1942⁓ Today the remainder of the bombs were completed, and we have 70 to dispose of when the time comes. This evening after dark we went out and practiced putting the bombs on our own trucks. Provided we don't put a bomb on top of someone in the back

A dramatic dust storm approaching Siwa, May 1942. (Craw)

of one the Itie trucks, I don't see why we shouldn't get away with this new 'impossibility'.

7 May 1942 Today we filled the beer tins with benzine and had them soldered up. This evening we went out again to practice putting them on the trucks.

8 May 1942 Today we fixed up the time pencils, fuses and detonators, and this evening we went out practicing again. The way we have got things worked out at present is this: We place something on the road to slow the traffic up. About 50 yards before that spot, one man is lying down about ten yards off the road, holding one end of a piece of string about 30 yards long. At the other end of the string, nearer to the road stop, two men are lying down 15 to 20 yards off the road. One man is holding the bomb while the other is holding the string.

T1 Patrol at Siwa in 1942. Back row, L-R: T Scriven (British radio operator attached to patrol), R E Hay, K Kelly, S D Parker, H D Mackay, K E Tippett. Centre row, L-R: B F Shepherd, A H C Nutt, R W N Lewis, Captain N P Wilder (patrol commander), M H Craw, T E Ritchie, F W Jopling. Front, L-R: E Sanders, T B Dobson, T A Milburn, J L D Davis, P V Mitford. (Craw)

When a tank or a truck comes along, the man furthermost from the road stop sees whether there are any troops in the back of the truck, if so, he tugs the string. The man at the other end tells his mate with the bomb to stay where he is and the vehicles goes past unmolested. But if there is no tug on the string that means that there are no troops visible in the truck, and as soon as the lights of the vehicle have passed the man with the bomb, he rushes out to catch the truck and drops the bomb inside.

It sounds a bit fantastic I know, but we have received our orders, and we will carry them out to the best of our ability. We are leaving the day after tomorrow and we are going between Agedabia and Benghazi, which in my opinion is about the most dangerous part of the coast road. G1 left today with 70 bombs. They are going near Sirte and we are both going to start putting the bombs onto trucks on the night of the 14th.

9-14 May *T 1 Patrol undertook the four day journey to the coast road and arrived on the 14th. They set up camp and prepared for their new operation.*

⌒15 May 1942⌒ Well, here I am again. While I was on picquet last evening I saw a wog with a camel not far away, and also one with a donkey. When Nick Wilder relieved me I pointed them out to him, but we didn't take much notice of them as there are hundreds of wogs around here and all are pro-British. I then had my tea and at 6pm Nick came down from the hill with the news that a German staff car had pulled up at the mouth of the wadi and the wogs with the donkey and camel had gone up and spoken to the occupant. However, the staff car went away and at about 6.45pm we set off for the coast road, all of us wondering what was in store for us between now and tomorrow morning.

We arrived at the road at 8pm having crossed 23 miles of perfectly flat country which is occupied by a lot of wogs who had been chased out of Benghazi by the RAF bombings. Shortly after we had reached the road, we saw a glare of headlights to the west, so drove the trucks about 100 yards off the road and got some bombs ready for action.

We decided to try the first truck that came along without any road block at all. So three men lay down at the edge of the road and waited for the truck to arrive. When it did, it turned out to be a large tanker towing a tanker trailer. What a beautiful target for a spot of gunplay. But that was not our job – our job was to put our bombs on them. So as the tanker was passing, one man got up and tried to put his bomb on it, but couldn't catch it as it was going too fast.

After that, two trucks passed going west and I was picked out to try and fix this one up. I got a bomb ready and then lay down at the side of the road and waited. As the lights came close they seemed to shine straight on to me and it seemed as though I must have been seen. As it came closer still, I realised it was a motor bike, so I just lay still while it passed five feet away from me.

After that there was a long spell with only two vehicles going westward and none going east. At midnight we saw another glare coming towards us from the west. So this time we decided to put a 44 gal drum on the road to try and slow him down a bit. Once again three men went down on the road and when the truck came along and his headlights shone on the drum, he never even bothered to change gear. He just swerved round it without slowing down at all and once again our men couldn't catch up to put the bomb on board.

By this time we were all getting rather sick of the job, as we hadn't had any success and there was practically no traffic on the road. We couldn't go to sleep, so were getting very tired and to top everything off, a dust storm was blowing. We had quite decided by now that those two wogs we had seen talking to the occupant of the staff car had given us away, and consequently most of the traffic had been stopped. However, next time we decided to try two drums lying almost right across the road. If that didn't slow them down, nothing would.

Well, it was about 1.30am before we again saw the headlights in the west, and once again we got the stage all set. This time there were two sets of headlights coming, and as they got closer we could see that the back truck was rapidly catching up on the first truck and that they were going to pass very close on our road block. As it happened, a smaller 15 cwt. overtook the big truck about 50 yards from the road block. We couldn't attempt to put anything on the 15 cwt, as the lights on the back truck would shine on anyone chasing after it.

We waited for the next, but as before, it still didn't slow down enough for anyone to catch up to it after it had passed. So Nick said, "Right oh! We'll shoot up the next one that comes along and then get out of it."

At 2.30am when the next set of headlights came into view, three trucks, including my own, lined up about 50 yards from the road and waited for the truck to arrive. When he came level with us, three machine-guns opened up on him. I have never seen anyone stop a truck and switch off the lights so fast in my life.

When he had stopped we drove up and shouted for the occupant to "Kamerad!" However there was no reply. We carefully went up to the truck, but there was no sign of the driver or anyone in or near the vehicle. It was a big ten ton Lancia and trailer, but unfortunately empty. We set about destroying it completely by putting three bombs in it with ten-minute time pencils attached to them. We put one in the engine, one above the benzine tank and the other one in the trailer, then set off back to the escarpment. We hadn't gone far when a flash lit up the whole countryside and then 'Wooff!' Which meant that the first bomb had gone off. Then another flash and 'Wooff!' And then a third. All that was left of that truck and trailer wouldn't be much use to the enemy.

After travelling 20 miles due east, we knew we must be getting near the escarpment, and as it would be almost impossible to find a way up in the darkness, we decided to wait until dawn. So we had about one hour's sleep and then carried on. Our idea was to go to a mud flat we had crossed on our way out, where there were some fairly high bushes. This was

Highlight of the day: mealtime in the cool of an oasis. The LRDG enjoyed the best rations in the Eighth Army.

about 45 miles from the coast road. There we would hide for the day and think up a new plan of campaign.

After we had travelled 40 miles, we were crossing the Msus-Saunmu Road, which at some time or other had been muddy and had some fairly deep ruts. My truck went over these ruts too fast and bent the steering column. We couldn't fix it in the middle of the road, so we towed it for the remaining five miles. We are now on the mud flat which at present is dry, but there is a lake about a mile to the south which is about three miles long. We have had breakfast and the fitter is trying to straighten our steering. Another truck has sheared off the rivets where the back spring fits on to the chassis, so Nick has decided to send the two damaged trucks and the fitter's truck back to Siwa, while his truck and the other one have look round and see what they can see or do. He is sending me to navigate the three trucks back to Siwa.

10.00am Well, the steering is fixed and although is fairly stiff, at least the truck can carry on under its own power. So now we are about to set off for Siwa.

12 noon We have now stopped for lunch and are 18 miles from the Trigh el Abd. So far on this trip we have not seen a single plane, which is amazing.

9.00pm We have now camped for the night after travelling 120 miles since leaving the other two trucks. I had just got the theodolite set up and was about to shoot the stars when a strong dust storm got up, which made it hopeless, so I had to give up the idea.

⁓ **16 May 1942** ⁓ *12 noon* We had a bit of a lie-in this morning and did not get started until 9am. We have now stopped for lunch by a crashed German plane, a JU88 that is absolutely riddled with bullet holes.

7.00pm We passed some South African armoured cars this afternoon. They don't seem to think much of their job, as they never see anything. We have now camped for the night only 60 miles from Washka and we hope to arrive in Siwa tomorrow afternoon.

17-26 May 1942 T1 Patrol returned to Siwa to rest and reorganise and prepare for their next job.

⁓ **27 May 1942** ⁓ *12 noon* Nick came in just before lunch and told us that we had to get all our trucks loaded up with benzine, rations and water for 1,000 miles over three weeks. When loaded we had to be ready to move out at half an hour's notice. That has come very suddenly, as we didn't expect to be leaving until at least 4 June.

6.30pm This afternoon we loaded up the trucks with benzine, rations and water and we have now heard what all this is about. The Germans started a push this morning, only two or three days before we were going to start one. The Jerries are apparently pushing in the south of the battlefront and this patrol has to be ready to move at half an hour's notice. We also have to have a picquet on at night in case German parachutists come over. On the news from Daventry this evening we heard that a big tank battle is going on at present near Bir Hacheim. We are now going to a dinner and smoke concert as a farewell to Major Don Steele, our squadron commander, who has to return to the Division.

⁓ **28 May 1942** ⁓ The dinner etc, was a great success. We had toheroa soup, roast mutton, mint sauce, green peas and roast potatoes, followed by apricot pie, beer and rum. This evening we heard that a tank battle was still being fought round Bir Hacheim and El Adem and that we had the enemy force surrounded.

⁓ **29 May 1942** ⁓ This morning we had another explosives demonstration and this afternoon part of T1 arrived back with two sick men. According to the BBC, a big tank battle is being fought 20 miles south of Tobruk. According to General Ritchie the position is satisfactory. In my opinion the Huns will retreat to Agedabia, where they have been building large-scale defences.

⁓ **30 May 1942** ⁓ This morning we went swimming and had one or two races and this afternoon we had our final lecture on explosives. G1 Patrol arrived today. They had been near Sirte to throw bombs on westbound trucks and one of their men was killed. Apparently they went down to the road and found a natural roadblock and while down there, captured two Itie prisoners. After searching them, they let them go! Why, I don't know.

They reckoned that the natural road block would slow the traffic down nicely but to make sure, they put a couple of petrol drums there too! Why, I don't know. When the next truck came along and saw the drums, it hardly slowed down at all, but went for its life. So did all the other trucks that came along. They didn't get any bombs on at all.

The next day at lunch time an Itie patrol came along and shot them up a bit, although they reckon that there were several Itie casualties. They brought back two baby cheetahs. The tank battle is still going satisfactorily. It appears that the Huns are now trying to retreat, but the order has been issued that they must not be allowed to travel any further west at all costs.

31 May 1942 We are now T1 Patrol once again. Major Don Steele who is OC A (NZ)

T2 Patrol in Kufra, 1942. Back row, L-R: M W Stewart, (unknown), G C Garven, R F McLeod, J L Reid, E Ellis. Middle row, L-R: A G Ferguson, C A Dornbush, (unknown), A G Biddle (British radio operator attached to patrol), K Kelly, D M Bassett. Front, L-R: T E Ritchie, C B McKenzie, W H Burgess, R F White. (Ellis.)

Squadron, has gone back to the Division, and Bing Morris, who was OC T2 Patrol, has gone up to OC A Squadron. Nick Wilder, who was OC T2 Patrol is now OC T1 Patrol.

1-3 June 1942   *T patrol prepared for its next operation, which would be attacks on enemy road convoys.*

◦**4 June 1942**◦   Needless to say, we have been very busy getting ready to depart tomorrow morning. However, we are about ready now. We are going out this time as a full patrol, i.e. T1 and T2 together. As far as I can gather, we will be splitting up when we get out on the job. The whole of the LRDG except R Patrol is going to attack in different places at once. Our area is the same district we were in last time, between Agedabia and Benghazi. We have a roving commission and can do what we like in our area, so you can bet your life we are going to see some excitement before we get back to Siwa again.

◦**5 June 1942**◦   *7.00pm*   We set off this morning at 9am travelling slowly, as we have a heavy load on this time. In benzine alone we have over 250 gallons per truck as well as three weeks supply of rations and water. Also mines plus bombs for blowing up the trucks that we shoot up. We are now camped near the wire at Washka and tomorrow morning we will make for Etla where there is a dump. We have to count how much benzine is there and wireless back our report.

◦**6 June 1942**◦   *12 noon*   We are now at Etla and have checked over the benzine. We are about to have lunch and will then carry on westward.

8.00pm   We are 58 miles west of Etla and are camped for the night. It is cloudy tonight, but I think I will be able to get a shot at the stars later on. We have about 100 miles to do tomorrow morning, to a place where we are going to make a dump of surplus benzine etc. We want to be as light as possible when we make our attacks. Our first attack will be tomorrow night on the coast road between Agedabia and Benghazi.

◦**7 June 1942**◦   *1.30pm*   We are now at the place where we are dumping some benzine and rations. We had just started to scatter the trucks out to make separate dumps when we heard a bang. A cloud of dust and smoke rose up from of T2's trucks. He'd run over a thermos bomb which burst both front tyres and did a bit of other damage. They are now fixing it and they reckon they will be able to move off again shortly after 2pm. We have dumped our benzine etc and are keeping about 90 gallons on board. It is another 95 miles to the coast road and we will cover about 45 miles and then do the rest after tea, to arrive on the coast at dusk. There are two more thermos bombs around here, but we're keeping well away from them. The driver of one truck got a bit of shrapnel in his hand, but nothing serious. He was not in the truck that ran over the bomb, but was driving another one about a chain away.

4.30pm Well, we didn't get started until 3.20pm and the two patrols were then separated, T2 going north of us. We are now about to have tea and still have about 75 miles to get to the road. I'm afraid it will be dark long before we get there.

8 JUNE 1942 *7.30am* It was dark when we arrived at the escarpment and we were still

Members of T2 Patrol at Siwa with their truck-mounted Italian 20 mm Breda automatic gun. These replaced the cumbersome 37mm Bofors. The Breda guns proved very effective against ground targets and were used with great success on many operations. Left to right:
I G McCulloch,
A G Ferguson,
C A Dornbush,
C B McKenzie, unknown.

25 miles away from the road. But we carried on and arrived at the Magrun-Solluch road at 11pm. We placed six mines there and connected all the telephone wires together to short them. We had decided to shoot up Magrun, which was marked on the map as being on the left of the road, so we had placed all the guns ready for shooting on the left of the truck. When we got to Magrun we found it was on the right of the road.

There was a checkpost there and we were ordered to stop, but we ignored them and drove straight on. After driving about a mile past the checkpost, we stopped and again joined all the telephone wires together to prevent that checkpost telephoning the next one, which we were also going to attack. After connecting the wires together we travelled on again and had done about six kilometres when our last truck overtook us and informed Nick that two trucks were following us. While driving past the checkpost and along the road we had our headlights on, and as soon as Nick heard about the two trucks, we switched out all the lights, pulled off to the side of the road and waited with guns ready.

While we were waiting, one man went again and connected all the telephone wires. When the trucks arrived, the leading truck was allowed to almost pass all our patrol before we opened fire on them, so as the second truck could get within range. But when we did open up on them, what a barrage! After both trucks were set on fire, we set off down the road again. I have never seen a truck put up such a firework display as those two trucks did. They must have had almost every kind of explosives imaginable from .20 mm bullets up to bombs.

Well, we got on to the road again, but had only travelled two kilometres before we saw some heavily laden big trucks camped on the side of the road. We made a semi circle round them and opened up. After firing for about 30 seconds and receiving no answer, we went up to them and found one man with splinter wounds all up his arm, which we bandaged before letting him go. He told us that all the other Ities who had been there had gone for their lives as soon as we had opened up on the first two trucks, two km away. We found three large trucks and one large trailer loaded up with timber and food. We then set about blowing them up.

An Italian convoy protection truck. The effectiveness of the machine-gun may well have been limited, with the wine barrel evidently being considered more important.

By this time it was 3am and as we wanted to get back to the escarpment by dawn, we decided that six loaded vehicles wasn't a bad night's work and we should be satisfied with that. So we then headed back to the escarpment, arriving just as dawn was breaking. We then carried on for another 27 miles east of the escarpment to a mud flat where were are supposed to meet T2. We are now at the mud flat, but so far there has been no sign of T2. I am now going to endeavour to get a bit of sleep.

1.00pm We received a message from T2 today that their operations last night were a washout and that they would try again tonight. They are going to try to contact us at 3.30pm. So far this morningwe have heard four planes, but have only seen one of them, which came right over the top of us. It was fairly high and apparently didn't see us.

7.00pm T2 did not locate us this afternoon, so they will probably be on their way to the coast by now. We saw 4 enemy trucks about 3 miles away this afternoon. Two of them seemed to have big guns on the back and two looked like infantry trucks, but they were too far away and the country too flat to chase after them. This evening we are going to camp on the Antelat-Msus road, just in case anything happens to come along. We will have one man on picquet and he will wake us all up if he sees a light coming.

🔹**9 June 1942**🔹 *9.00am* Well, there was no traffic on that road last night and we have moved back to our hiding place. We were just about to have breakfast when we saw T2 Patrol come over a rise about half a mile away, so we signalled them to come to us. When they arrived they told us their story. In short, they told us that for two nights they tried to get to the coast road and both times they failed to get there. How they failed to get there, I don't know. They have now gone into some bushes about half a mile away. This evening they will go up and camp where we camped last night. We are going on to the Antelat-Saleidims road, and if we don't see anything there by dark, we will again go down to the coast road.

4.00pm We received a message to say that Gus Holliman *[Capt. C A Holliman, S Patrol commander]* and Gurdon *[Lt. R B Gurdon, G2 Patrol commander]* are going into the Benghazi area and that if possible, we should postpone our next shoot-up until the night of the 10th-11th, which is tomorrow night. So we are not going down to the east road tonight, but will watch the same roads as we did last night. T2 will go to the Solluch-Msus road.

🔹**10 June 1942**🔹 *8.00am* We are once again back in our hiding place after another quiet night. T2 arrived a while ago and they saw nothing on their road; however they mined it. The flies are very bad here and they almost drove me crazy. There have been planes around us most of the morning, but I have seen only two of them. A short while ago a wog rode a camel into our hiding place. He dismounted and came over to one of our trucks for food, water and cigarettes. I asked him where he had come from and he said Saumnu and also that he was going to Bir Hamed. However, we don't like the look of him, as you don't often

T1 Patrol members line up in front of their Chevrolet trucks, 1942. On the left, Corporal Merlyn Craw's truck Te Paki III is equipped with twin aircraft .303 Brownings. Recovered from a crashed Hurricane fighter, they gave devastating firepower against soft targets such as enemy truck convoys. Back, L-R: W G Gerrard, (unknown), A H C Nutt, Captain N P Wilder, J L D Davis, B F Shepherd, F W Jopling. Front, L-R: M H Craw, R W N Lewis, T A Milburn, E Sanders, (unknown).

see one man and one camel roaming around the desert. We have been given away by spies before and we don't want to be caught again, so we are going to hang on to him. Two trucks are going back to Siwa today with two malaria cases, so the wog will go back with them.

4.00pm Well, we are going down to the coast road again tonight and are going to shoot up a checkpost. We are now about to have tea and we are leaving here at 4.45pm.

11 June 1942 *1.00pm* We set off last night at 4.45pm, reached the escarpment shortly after 6pm and headed down a wadi which led down to the flat. Just below the escarpment there is a road leading from Antelat to Sceleidima, and we had just got to the south of the wadi when we saw a truck loaded with troops going away from us towards Antelat. It was too far away to chase after. We waited until it was out of sight and were just about to set off across the flat when we saw a cloud of dust coming towards us from Antelat. We decided to wait, and attack it. As it came closer we could see that this one also had troops on board. We decided that we would try and get them to surrender without a shot being fired. So when it came almost opposite us, we drove out of the wadi and started to encircle it. Unfortunately, they opened fire first with a 20 mm Breda and a little Breda, so we had no option but to return fire. Naturally it was only a short and one-sided battle. By the time they had given up they had two men killed and one wounded in three places. Their truck was already burning when they surrendered. We captured one officer and five other ranks.

It wasn't until after we had left the wadi to attack the truck that we saw a staff car and motor cycle coming towards us from the same direction, but of course when they saw us they turned around and went for their lives. If we had seen them sooner, we would have let

T 2 Patrol during a halt. Note the commander's Willys Jeep in front of the column. (Ellis)

the truck go and attacked the staff car as we might have been able to take someone worth having. All these men we have captured were Ities.

As we had been spotted in the area, we decided that it wouldn't be advisable to carry on down to the coast road, so we chose to be satisfied with what we had already done. Corporal Craw *[Cpl. M H Craw]* dressed an Italian's wounds, which were not serious as there were no bones broken, and then we set off eastwards in darkness. We arrived back at our hiding place shortly after 11pm and had a tot of rum, as we were carrying on towards the dump we had made further south. One of our men can speak a bit of Italian and he learned from a prisoner that they were on patrol and that they had already seen us. Thinking we were not going to attack just then, they came back to have a look at us. That motor bike we saw has gone back to put some fighter planes on our tail.

We carried on until 1pm, when we camped for the remainder of the night. I shot our position and soon after daybreak we were on our way again. We arrived at the dump at 10.30am. Here we took our empty benzine tins off and made the load up to 20 full tins again. It was decided that T2 would take the prisoners back to Siwa and they set off at 11.45am. Just as they moved off, a plane came over. He must have seen us although he showed no sigh of it. Nevertheless, we will find out this afternoon if he did or not.

We are present hiding up about five miles SE of the dump and will be staying here for the night.

6.00pm Three fighters passed just to the north of us this afternoon, but luckily they didn't spot our patrol. That reconnaissance plane must have seen us after all. But I don't think we will be troubled any more tonight, and tomorrow morning we will be moving south-west from here.

Rhodesian S Patrol trucks ready for action and prepared for a long patrol. Note the heavy loads of stores, equipment and weapons. (Pittaway/Fourie collection)

An S Patrol truck carefully negotiates the downwards slide on a sand dune. (Pittaway/Fourie collection)

12 June 1942 *8.00am* At daylight this morning we set off SW and we are now camped and camouflaged in a wadi 118 miles from where we were camped yesterday. This evening I believe we are going to attack the Agedabia-Antelat road.

4.30pm We are just about to move off for the Agedabia-Antelat road. If we are successful tonight we will head straight back to Siwa. I developed flu yesterday and it is making me very miserable, but it takes more than a flu to stop a navigator doing his work out in the middle of the desert.

13-16 June 1942 T Patrol returned to base. Preparations were being made for A [NZ] Squadron LRDG to leave Siwa, as Rommel's forces were gaining the upper hand. In the meantime Jopling recorded several observations.

17 June 1942 We had to re-load our trucks today so that we could be ready for any emergency. On the wireless we heard that the Allies had evacuated El Adem and Sidi Rezegh

☞ **18 June 1942** ☜ S1 Patrol arrived back today, having taken *[SAS]* paratroopers to Derna, where they destroyed 50 planes on the ground.

☞ **19 June 1942** ☜ Today we heard we had retreated back to the Egyptian frontier, which means that after two years of war out here, neither side is any further ahead than they were when they started. A lot of men are going sick with malaria and sandfly fever, so the sooner we leave Siwa the better.

☞ **20 June 1942** ☜ This afternoon, for the first time, a Wellington bomber landed on Siwa airfield, which is only 300 yards long. But it made a perfect landing and a good take-off.

T2 left this afternoon to pick up some RAF personnel who had crashed in the desert. We have picked up nearly 100 RAF men to date.

☞ **21 June 1942** ☜ Today we heard that we may leave Siwa soon and camp up on the coast. Also, we heard on the wireless this evening that Tobruk and Bardia had fallen.

☞ **22 June 1942** ☜ We had just had breakfast when Nick Wilder arrived to tell us that we

Field Marshall Erwin Rommel of the Africa Korps shares a toast with an Italian officer. The LRDG and SAS attacks on the Axis supply columns and airfields proved a real thorn in the side of Rommel's forces, who had believed they were safe within their own lines. Consequently, Rommel was compelled to commit additional troops to these areas, not knowing where the raiders were going to strike next. Of the LRDG Rommel wrote, "The LRDG caused us more damage than any other British unit of equal strength." (Rutherford)

will be moving out to go on leave in Cairo for ten days, after which we will go straight to Kufra. So now we have all shaved our beards off and are ready to depart early tomorrow morning.

23 June 1942 We left Siwa this morning at 7.15am with 24 trucks: T1, T2, R1 and A Squadron HQ. Travelling has been very slow, as we can only travel as fast as the slowest truck. When we were about 20 miles from Mersa Matruh we were diverted on a new track, because we were not allowed on the coast road near Matruh. This is because the 9th Army is taking over from the 8th Army and there is a lot of traffic on the road.

24 June-3 July Jopling spent his leave in Cairo, staying in the New Zealand Club. The the military situation was causing constraints, as he described on 28 June:

Today we heard that Mersu Matruh had fallen and that all troops had to be out of Cairo by 8pm and back at Maadi camp. However, after a lot of wangling, Bing Morris managed to get permission for LRDG personnel to stay in Cairo. But we were not allowed to walk in the streets after 8pm. So it spoiled our leave.

The New Zealand Forces Club in Cairo.

⌒**4 July 1942**⌒ We heard today we are going down to Fayoum. Why we are going there I don't know, because it is only 30 miles out from Cairo, so we might as well work from there. The fighting is still around El Alamein and the situation is still very serious, though it has improved.

⌒**5 July 1942**⌒ Well, we set off at 2.30pm for Fayoum and arrived there at 5pm after stopping for a cup of tea at Mona. LRDG HQ is here, as well as G1 and S1 Patrols.

⌒**6 July 1942**⌒ The mosquitoes last night were worse than I had ever seen, and we are all eaten by them. Luckily we hear there is no malaria around here.

We received a wireless message today from No. 3 Hospital telling us that one of our chaps, Cpl. Dick Lewis [Cpl. R W N Lewis] was dangerously ill, and would we send someone up to make arrangements for him. It sounds bad when they send messages like that.

The fighting is still around El Alamein, but captured Huns say that they are only getting half a water bottle per day and a lot of them are surrendering because they are dying of thirst.

⌒**7 July 1942**⌒ This morning we were told to be ready to leave this afternoon. Naturally

Corporal Dick Lewis

All hands help push out a Chevrolet 1533X2 stuck in a salt marsh. (Craw)

we all wanted to know where we were going and we got a big surprise when we heard we were going to Tobruk. We still have the hardest part to do though – that is to get there. Siwa and Giarabub are in Jerry hands, so he has control of the whole wire. All the gaps will be mined and there is sure to be an air patrol up and down the wire.

We have to contact our own forces up near Daba and then go through the wire south of Maddelena. Well, we left Fayoum at 2.30pm and we are now camped for the night at the south end of the Rattaniya Dunes.

⌒**8 July 1942**⌒ *12 noon* We carried on this morning at 7am in a NW direction and we have stopped for lunch 30 miles south of El Alamein, where the battle is at present being fought. We are near a hill called Garet Sonara.

6.00pm We set off again at 1.30pm and, after travelling for ten miles, we climbed a high escarpment on the northern end of the Qattara Depression. From there on we passed a number of derelict vehicles, all British. We had a bit of a shock ourselves at one stage when 12 fighters came straight for us. We wasted no time putting out our air recognition signal, which is a sand mat painted red and white. When they arrived overhead at about 100 feet up, we saw that they were Kittyhawks.

Shortly after that we came across an enormous dump with about 15 abandoned vehicles. Some of the trucks were in perfect order. All that was wrong with them was that they had become stuck in the dump. Some still carried rifles.

Then we saw five vehicles coming towards us and decided we had better find out if they were friend or foe. They turned out to be friend. We then carried on west until we came to

Waves in a sea of sand – some of the 'impassable' country negotiated by the patrols. Special navigation and driving skills were required to successfully cross the sand seas.

Weis where we met some Indians who had been to raid Fuka aerodrome. They reckoned they had a hard job to come back, as they were being fired at most of the way. We also heard that there was a strong enemy force on the road running along the top of the escarpment on the border of the Qattara Depression. That was the way we had intended to travel. However, as it was getting late we decided to return a couple of miles eastward and camp for the night. There are two messages for us from Fayoum, but we are unable to receive them as the atmospherics are too bad, so we will receive them in the morning.

9 July 1942 *12 noon* The messages were to tell us to join Major Stirling at Bir Quseir, where we will be under his orders. Also to report any enemy air or ground activity. As it appears to be impossible to travel west to the north of Qattara Depression without being stopped, we are going to cross the Depression. We have now halted for lunch. It has been fairly soft going so far, but not too bad.

10 July 1942 *12 noon* We set off this morning at 7am and followed the telegraph wires across the salt marsh. It was hard going all the way across to Ras Qattara, but so far there has been no show of getting up the escarpment. We travelled west alongside the escarpment and came to Qattara spring, but the water there is too salty to drink. We carried on and tried to take a shortcut, but got stuck in the salt marsh. We then turned back and kept to the edge of

Corporal M H Craw, T1 Patrol, 1942. He poses draped in machine-gun belts in front of an old 1938 Ford V8 used as a base runabout at Siwa. He went on to win the Military Medal after personally destroying ten aircraft with homemade bombs at the Barce Raid. Craw was captured, but escaped a year later. (Craw)

the escarpment. We have now stopped for lunch. It is very hot in the Depression, as there is no breeze at all.

6.00pm Well, at least we have got up the escarpment, but we had to go within 12 miles of Qara Oasis before we could do it. We followed up the road from Qara to Mersa Matruh and we have now camped for the night, just off the track.

11 July 1942 *11.00am* We had an early cup of tea at 4am and then set off on a bearing of 15°. We had only travelled 15 miles when a thick fog swept on us. Because the country is very hilly and rough, we were unable to carry on until it cleared. That was the first time I have seen fog in the desert. It cleared by 8am and then we got into some absolutely impassable country. We had been trying to get through all morning and finally we found a camel track and managed to get up by following it.

We are now in fairly open country, but it is still rough and it is another 25 miles to our rendezvous. We are now about to have lunch and will probably move off about 1pm. In mid summer between 11am and 1pm, the sun compass is inaccurate as the sun is almost straight overhead of us and the needle doesn't throw a long enough shadow.

6.00pm We are approximately at our rendezvous, but so far have seen no sign of Major Stirling and his SAS party. So I will shoot the stars tonight and we will move on in the morning.

12 July 1942 *7.00am* We again had an early cup of tea and moved off as soon as it got light. We are now at the rendezvous, but no-one was here to meet us. We had just arrived here when we got the same type of fog we had yesterday, and a very wet fog it is too. We are now about to have breakfast and will stay here till someone meets us or we get word to go somewhere else.

The Jopling diary entries for 13 July to 13 September have not been located by the editor. They may have been lost. However, T1 Patrol's story continued when Captain Nick Wilder and his men met up with Stirling's SAS, and supported them in their raid on the Sidi Haneish airfield in the Fuka area. Though the patrol didn't participate in the actual attack, due to being cut off by a tank trap, they observed the grand night-time spectacle of 18 SAS jeeps speeding down the centre of the runway with all guns blazing. The German aircraft lined up on either side made easy targets, and 40 were destroyed. As Corporal Merlyn Craw, Jopling's NCO, later observed, "We fired a few rounds, but were too far away to be effective, so could only watch. It was up till then the best sight I had seen in the war."
The next day the SAS and T1 Patrol were being sought by German forces, so had to spend most of the day hiding out. However, Wilder was almost captured by the enemy when he was sighted while out on a foot patrol. He had to be rescued by Corporal Craw, who picked him up in his truck while under fire. Also a Fiesler Storch spotter plane had landed close by to where Troopers K E Tippett and T B Dobson

had concealed their truck. As the plane was taking off they shot at it with a Tommy-gun, causing it to stall and land again. They captured the pilot and a medical officer with the rank of colonel, then poured petrol over the plane and set it alight. By this time German reinforcements were arriving, so the patrol decided to make a run for it. Before they could properly desperse, they were being closely pursued by an enemy column. Therefore Gunner E Sanders, to give the rest of the patrol a better chance of escape, sat behind the 20mm Breda gun mounted in the back of his truck and coolly targeted the advancing Germans. Before he withdrew he managed to knock out two half-tracks mounting 50mm Flak guns and two troop-carrying transports. All of T1 eventually returned to base unscathed. Tippett, Dobson, and Sanders earned the Military Medal for their roles in this action. Frank Jopling also took part in this operation, and his account of events would have been interesting.

T1 Patrol's next mission was to be Operation Caravan, a raid on the Axis-controlled airfield and town at Barce in Cyrenaica. In early September 1942, a month before the second battle of Alamein, a force under the command of Major J R Easonsmith set out from its base at Fayoum. There was a LRDG HQ unit and two patrols: T1, led by Captain N P Wilder, and G1 under Captain J A L Timpson. A total of 47 men in 12 trucks and five jeeps made the outward 13-day, 1,860 kilometre journey, which included the arduous crossing of the Egyptian and Kalansho sand seas. During the first crossing, Timpson's jeep capsized over the edge of a razorback dune, throwing the occupants out and rolling over them. Timpson fractured his skull, while his gunner, Guardsman T Wann, injured his spine and was paralysed from the waist down. They were fortunate that they were still close enough to be airlifted back to Cairo.

Jopling's diary starts again on 13 September, when the patrols had already arrived at the outskirts of Barce.

BARCE RAID

13 September 1942 I have only just managed to procure a notebook, so in parts I will not be able to give a day-by-day description. However, I will do my best and will start this diary from September 13th at 5pm.

We travelled 12 miles this morning over impossible country: deep wadis and high steep rocky hills with trees growing on them. We arrived at this spot at lunch time and we are staying here until evening. We are now only about three miles off the Barce road and about 16 miles in a direct line to Barce. Our job is to attack the town, destroy as much equipment as possible and then come out. At the same time, one party is going up to attack Benghazi and another will attack Tobruk. It is the largest guerrilla operation ever carried out in the Middle East. We are setting off at 6pm, so as to get onto the road before dark. We have sent in two Arabs who we brought with us to fish out any information, and we are to meet them at a spot along the road. We received a wireless message to say that yesterday there were 18 planes on the aerodrome and we are hoping that they are still there.

T1 Patrol trucks lined up at the edge of the Great Sand Sea before the Barce raid in September 1942. The Chevrolet on the right is Te Anau II T6, the fitter's truck. It was the only one of the 17 vehicles to return from the raid. (Craw)

The first page of a captured Italian notebook in which Jopling recorded the Barce raid and the incredible 12 day trek that followed. His fortitude was reflected in a determination to complete the journal, despite the extreme privations and suffering on a journey that ended in his capture.

T1 Patrol rests under the trees at Gebel Akhar on the outskirts of Barce, while Captain Nick Wilder explains the attack. The bald headed man sitting left is Major Vladimir Peniakoff of Popski's Private Army fame. Peniakoff participated in this operation.

6.30pm We had intended to set off at 6pm, but there are a lot of low-flying aircraft over us, so it isn't safe to move yet.

9.30pm We eventually set off at 7pm, so it was dark by the time we arrived at the road. We hadn't been travelling long before we heard a shout to halt. We stopped, and our leading truck shone his lights onto a building on our left, from which an Itie was coming towards us. The leading truck opened up and received no answering fire, so we drove up to the building and threw a couple of hand grenades into it. There was a stable full of horses, but we didn't touch them. We captured one of the police *[Tripolitanian troops under Italian officers]* and took him away with us. We set off again and had only travelled about half a mile when we came across two more buildings, one on each side of the road. We received fire from the buildings but we soon silenced them. However, when we stopped, our Breda gun truck bumped into the truck in front of him and knocked its radiator in. After taking a few necessary things off the gun truck, we left it on the side of the road. Three miles further on, one of the G Patrol trucks hit a boulder and broke its sump. After taking the necessary things off that truck and putting them on other vehicles, we set off again.

Until then we hadn't been using our lights, but they were switched on when we arrived at the spot where we are supposed to meet the Arabs who had been sent in previously. They haven't turned up yet. The prisoner we captured says there are 160 men in that police post,

Captain Wilder talking with his men before the Barce raid. The men are looking somewhat apprehensive, as an enemy aircraft had just flown overhead. (Craw)

so we will probably get some 'hurry up' from them on our way back. We cut the telephone wires on both sides of the post, so they can't warn anyone of our approach. We are staying here until 11.30pm, so I am going to try and get a bit of sleep. The plan is for T1 Patrol to attack the aerodrome, while G1 Patrol targets the barracks and Major Easonsmith looks after the streets in the town.

14 SEPTEMBER 1942 *8.00am* The Arabs we sent in yesterday never turned up and we set off for Barce at 11.30pm. After travelling about five miles, we came onto the main bitumen road, eight miles from the town. We travelled straight down the road, and when we were about two miles from Barce we saw two light Italian tanks, one on each side of the road. They opened up on us and we replied. After that they were silent.

When we arrived at Barce itself, all was quiet so G Patrol set off towards the barracks and we headed for the aerodrome at the other end of town. We didn't have a shot fired at us until we arrived at the entrance to the aerodrome, where two guns opened up on us. The entrance had an iron rail across the road which lifted up like some of the old fashioned railway crossing gates. Captain Wilder, in the leading truck, opened the gate while the rest of us kept the enemy guns quiet. We then drove through and came across several trucks loaded with drums of benzine. We fired one burst into each and they went up in smoke. The next thing we came across was the hangar and that also went up in smoke. Then we came onto the drome proper and there were three planes straight in front of us. Needless to say they went up in smoke too. We then turned left and headed clockwise around the airfield.

My one ambition in this war has been to set a plane on fire, because then you know you've done some damage. Well, I certainly achieved my ambition last night, as I know for certain I set five planes on fire and possibly several more. Altogether we burned 25 to 30 planes, some by bombs and others by machine-gun fire with incendiary bullets. We were

G1 Patrol on the way to Barce. Guardsman Duncalfe behind the twin .303 Vickers K machine-guns, with Sergeant Jack Dennis at the wheel. Dennis led the Guards patrol after his officer, Captain J A L Timpson, was injured after crashing his jeep over a razorback dune. Sergeant Dennis won the Military Medal for his role in this action. (Craw)

on the drome for about an hour and were fired at from several quarters, but as I have always said, the Ities are terrible shots and they didn't hit any of us. By the time we had destroyed all those planes, most of our magazines were empty and we had used most of the bombs. Knowing that before we could get away we would have a lot more shooting to do, the patrol set off for the rendezvous. However, it was not going to be quite so easy as it was coming in.

As we drew near to the exit of the drome, we were met with heavy fire from machine-guns, rifles and 47mm guns. Just near the exit, our leading truck driven by Captain Wilder got off the track and became stuck on a soft mound with a ditch on the other side. We stopped and pushed him back and meanwhile, all the enemy guns and mortars were giving us everything they could. But as I've said before, the Ities are terrible shots and again they didn't hit any of us.

Once we were out of the airfield we thought we were fairly safe, even though we had to go through the town again. However, when we got into the main street it was found to be lined with tanks and armoured cars. Well – I never thought for a minute that we had a show of getting past them. There were eight or nine, and all of their guns were pointing straight down the street towards us. There were also machine-guns firing at us from various other places.

We were the second vehicle after Nick Wilder's truck, which had rammed straight into a light tank to clear a way through. We came to a halt right beside another one, so we put a hand grenade underneath it and one in the turret, which ought to have quietened it down a bit. A jeep picked up the crew of the leading truck, so we set off again with the enemy two-pounders still firing at us. How they missed us beats me. Nonetheless, we dodged past the armoured vehicles – each one in turn – and eventually passed the last one. We had to turn left at the end of the street and turned a bit too soon, because we found ourselves in a rubbish dump. However, we turned right and ran parallel with the main street and, as luck would have it, came out onto the main Tobruk road. We then turned left and went flat-out.

We had gone about two miles when we came across two small tanks on the road with their guns pointing towards Barce, but they didn't fire at us. They just about blocked the road, and as we managed to squeeze past, we hit one heavily, tearing off our left mudguard, a spare tyre and a sand tray. We still kept going and joined Major Easonsmith's party just before turning off the main road. We were the first T Patrol truck to arrive back and he asked if we were OK. I told him the position and said that some probably wouldn't get away. He said, "You seem to have done a good job anyhow."

From here we had a great view of the fires and it looked wonderful. The whole place seemed to be alight. All our other trucks arrived back except Wilder's one that had rammed the tank, and T5, with Corporal Merlyn Craw and his crew, *[Tprs. K Yealands, T A Milburn, R E Hay]* all of whom are missing. Two other men are missing. *[L/Cpl. A H C Nutt, Tpr. H T R Holland; all these men were captured.]*

Bruce Dobson *[Tpr. T B Dobson],* in the back of my truck, received a wound in the hand when we were coming through Barce. Several times we asked him how it was, and he would say, "Oh it's nothing much, it's OK," so we didn't worry. But when we stopped, he clambered down off the truck and said, "Water, water" very weakly and collapsed. We called the medical orderly, who examined him and pronounced him dead. Shortly after that the 'dead' man opened his eyes and said, "I'm OK now." We got him up onto the truck and once again we set off for the rendezvous.

We turned off the main road and had travelled about three miles when one of the Guards' trucks went off the road. While trying to get back, it tipped over, so a G Patrol truck and Major Easonsmith went back to try to right it again. We hadn't gone much further when we got a puncture. Unfortunately our good spare wheel had been torn off when we hit the

Captain R.P Lawson, LRDG Medical Officer. Following the Barce raid he was kept busy looking after six wounded men under very difficult circumstances, including air attacks. His bravery and devotion to duty earned him the Military Cross.

tanks. The only one we had left was badly ripped, yet it was better than nothing so we changed the tyres.

15 SEPTEMBER 1942 Setting off again, we arrived at the rendezvous at 3.30am. Dr Lawson *[Capt. R P Lawson, RAMC]* was there, dressing the wounded. Soon afterwards, Major Easonsmith and the G Patrol trucks arrived with the vehicle that had tipped over, not much worse for its experience. We only had one man seriously wounded, *[Tpr. S D Parker]* who had been hit in the leg and a bullet had passed through his stomach. When the doctor had finished dressing the wounds we set off once again, our object being to get as far from Barce as possible before daylight.

The patrol still had to pass the police post where we expected to meet some opposition. It was 4am when we set off, which didn't leave much travelling time in the darkness. When we arrived at the abandoned G Patrol truck we towed it. By then, only about three miles from the post, the road began to narrow. It was only wide enough for one truck and on each side were tree-covered hills – an ideal place for an ambush.

Sure enough, we had only gone another few hundred yards when we were fired at from both sides of the road. Talk about running the gauntlet! We couldn't see them, but they could see us. All we could do was fire in the direction of the flashes. After three miles of this, we came opposite the buildings and the Breda gun truck, which we also put on tow.

While hooking up, one of our trucks arrived with a puncture, so Major Easonsmith told them to change the tyre. As luck would have it, the enemy had no machine-guns in this section, but plenty of rifles were firing at us. It took about ten minutes to change the wheel, but incredibly, not a man or truck was hit.

We set off again and ran the gauntlet for another two miles. About the last shot that was fired, hit me in the left leg. I thought it was shattered – you would almost swear that it had broken the bone. Well, by this time it was daylight and we knew that aircraft would be looking for us at the first opportunity, so we travelled another six miles and hid up among trees, where we are now. When we stopped I had to be carried to the doctor as I couldn't walk. The wound has now been cleaned and dressed and we have had breakfast.

10.00am We hadn't finished breakfast more than half an hour ago when were fired on again. They were police from Sidi Bu Raui who had followed us up. There were quite a few aircraft flying around, but luckily at this moment they were a long way away. The police tried to attract their attention by setting off smoke bombs. Fortunately they were unsuccessful and we soon managed to chase them away, but we decided that we couldn't stay in that position. We were unable to carry on towing the two broken down vehicles. So after unloading and transferring everything to other trucks, we placed bombs in them set with two hour time pencils.

After that we made for Cheda bu Maun where we were supposed to meet Colonel

Stirling's party, which had attacked Benghazi. We had only travelled a few miles when the the bolts at the back axle of G Patrol's wireless truck sheared off and the axle dropped out. They've decided to try and fix it, but it could be a long job as they have to drill all the ends of the bolts out. We are now under some trees waiting for them to do the repairs. The truck with the broken axle is not under cover, so we hope aircraft don't come over.

12 noon Well, there has been a CR 42 *[a Fiat Italian fighter aircraft]* looking for us for the last hour, and he eventually spotted the broken-down truck. He dived straight at it, but did not fire and then circled around several times and must have seen us. He has gone back to Barce and it is only a matter of time before he brings back some of his pals to deal with us. We are all carrying 'bailing out' kits which contain some bully beef, and other rations, plus our water bottles, so we are waiting for the worst.

3.00pm Well, the worst certainly came. Six CR 42s came over and dived on us continually with their guns blazing, for two solid hours. I never knew a fighter could carry so much

February 1942: the newly-issued T9 (Te Aroha III), a Chevrolet 1533X2, at base preparing to set out on patrol. This truck was later lost on the Barce raid. Trooper Jopling stands to the right. The driver, Private T E Ritchie and the man standing on truck, Signalman T. Scriven, did not participate in the September action. (Imperial War Museum)

ammunition. My truck was the first to go up in smoke and we were unable to salvage anything. None of the other trucks were burnt, but most were damaged beyond repair. Only two 30 cwts and one jeep were still operational.

One thing I will always remember is our medical officer, Dr. Lawson, who throughout the attack sat on top of the truck with 'Snow' Parker who had a bullet through his stomach. As luck would have it, that truck was one of the 30 cwts which was untouched. Nick Wilder, our officer, was wounded in the face and both legs and a Guardsman was hit in the leg. Those are the only casualties that I know of, because as soon as the planes had gone we were ordered to take the movable trucks well away, and for everyone to take their 'bailing out' kits and get well away from the vehicles. So we took the two trucks about a mile away and again camouflaged them up. We are now about 200 yards from them, and the doctor is dressing the newly wounded.

15 September 1942 To carry on the story from last night – just as the sun was going down, we heard shooting over where the derelict trucks were, and on looking around we saw a column of vehicles. I was absolutely unarmed, so it was no use my going to investigate. Instead I got out of their sight in a wadi where our trucks would almost certainly have to come through, if they came at all. When they came, we would be able to stop them and jump on.

When it got dark there were ten of us in the wadi and we waited until about 9pm. We decided that they couldn't be coming and that everyone must be captured. If one of the trucks had started up and didn't come this way we would have certainly heard it, but we never heard a sound, except that of gunfire, which had stopped just before dark.

We decided to set off walking to Cheda bu Maun, where Stirling is supposed to be on the 15th. I didn't know whether I could make it or not with the wound in my leg, but I was determined to give it a go. It is 20 miles and we had to get there by the night of the 15th. I was the only New Zealander and the only navigator, so the direction was left to me. I had no compass and only a very small and inadequate 'escape map'. Cheda bu Maun was not marked on it, so I had to go by memory, having seen it marked on the larger map in my truck.

We set off at about 9pm and my leg wasn't feeling too good. On level going it wasn't too bad, but got very painful while travelling downhill, and after sitting down for a while, it was very sore when I started walking again. We were all very tired after a very difficult 24 hours and after about five miles we decided to try to get some sleep. It gets very cold at night and as I had no blanket or overcoat, believe me I was cold. We set off again just before dawn, and as it got light we saw four Arab tents, so we decided to call in and fill ourselves with water. They gave us some water and we set off with about three gallons among the ten of us. We travelled about a mile further and decided to have a bit of breakfast. This consisted of a fifth of a tin of bully each, and we boiled a fruit tin of water in which we melted a bar of chocolate and divided it into ten. We are now about to move off again.

12 noon Most of this morning seems to have been spent ducking for cover from aircraft. They certainly seem to be determined that no one escapes, even on foot. One plane dropped bombs in the wadi next to us. What they were bombing for I don't know, because there were certainly no trucks there. At 10am, just as the heat was becoming unbearable for walking, we came across a herd of camels, so we knew there must be an Arab somewhere looking after them. It was some time before we found him and when we asked him for water he took us to a well. A very welcome sight it was too. We drank as much as we could and filled all our containers.

There were some more Arabs at the well and we asked them where Cheda Bu Maun was. They told us about three miles west, which wasn't bad, considering we had made a very twisted journey by keeping to the wadis to dodge aircraft as much as possible. It was now too hot to do any walking, and none of us felt much like travelling those three miles when there was a possibility no-one was there and we'd have to walk all the way back. One of the Arabs offered to go on a donkey, so we gave him a note for Stirling and off he went.

7.00pm In the meantime we got into the shade of a big bush and settled ourselves down for the afternoon, though it was too hot to sleep. One Arab brought us some eggs, cups and a tin to boil up some more chocolate. He said he would bring us some bread after the sun went down. They were celebrating Ramadan which is a period of 28 days during which they don't eat, drink or smoke between sunrise and sunset.

Sure enough, at 6.30pm he came along with some bread, which we ate with water. The Arab who had gone to Cheda Bu Maun returned and informed us that there was no one there. We had all expected this, so weren't unduly disappointed. However, that leaves us with only one alternative and that is to head for the truck which we had left behind on the Msus-Mechili track, about 60 miles from here. It made me sick to think of walking so far with the wound in my leg, and I honestly thought I would never make it, but decided to do my best. The road is marked on the map, but just what part of the road the truck is on I again had to work out from memory, and then guess the bearing, as I had no protractor. We are going to have a few hours sleep and then get going.

16 SEPTEMBER 1942 *12 noon* We slept much longer than we intended and it was just about breaking dawn when we set off. We had five gallons of water among us, and we reckoned it would take three days to do the 60 miles, which meant that we could have one pint of water a day each. It isn't much to trek 20 miles a day on. We would walk for an hour and sit down for about ten minutes. Every time I restarted it was agony, but after the first 100 yards or so it wasn't so bad. We had to duck from a few aircraft, but not nearly so many as yesterday.

Corporal M H Craw, T1 Patrol. He earned the Military Medal after personally destroying 10 bombers during the Barce raid. He and his crew were later captured as they were trying to escape the town.

By 10am we were all very hot, very dry and very tired. We had been looking for some shade to get under for the last hour. Half an hour ago we saw a few big bushes ahead, but after half an hour's walking they still seemed to be as far away as ever. So we decided to sit down and make the best of the little shade from a few little bushes. They were absolutely inadequate. Two members of the party then saw some goats near the large bushes. Where there are goats there must be Arabs, so they set off to find out if there was any water, while we lay down again. Presently an Arab came and told us that our two mates were at the big bushes and there would be plenty of water over there at five o'clock. I for one had a good drink from my water bottle before heading for the big bushes, where we are now.

We had no sooner sat down in the shade than the Arab made a roof over us with his shawl and made us very comfortable. He told us that last night three men in a jeep had camped here, and from his description we thought they were Major Easonsmith, Sgt. Dennis and Cranstone, none of whom are New Zealanders. They had bought a sheep – there were sheep among the goats – and had left at dawn. We were annoyed with ourselves because if we had left last night when we had intended, we would probably have got this far by dawn. But they had gone, so it was no good crying over spilt milk.

3.30pm Well, we ate another fifth of a tin of bully each, made another brew of chocolate and carried on drinking our water, as the Arab assured there would be plenty of water at 5pm. Since leaving the last well, we had drunk about four gallons of water, leaving us with only about a gallon.

Shortly after 5pm three more Arabs joined us and they were definitely pro-Italian. When they heard that 'our' Arab was going to give us water they made a dickens of a row and said we couldn't have any. The argument go so hot that one of them set off for Charruba, which is an Italian outpost about eight miles away. In the finish they gave us about one gallon and told us to keep going all night because tomorrow the Italians would be out looking for us. So now we have two gallons to last ten men perhaps three days or maybe more. Who knows?

17 September 1942 *12 noon* As soon as we got the water yesterday we set off again travelling until about 11pm, when we lay down and had a sleep. At dawn we drank half a bully tin of water each before setting off. About two hours later we came across a derelict Italian truck. We thought there must be some water in the radiator and were looking forward to a good drink. However, the water was undrinkable. I tried some and it seemed to dry out all my mouth. Someone said it had anti-freeze stuff in it.

We carried on until 9.30am and there wasn't a decent sized bush as far as the eye could see, so we made as good a shelter as possible on a hillside. Gosh, how we hate and dread these long hot hours between 9.30am and 4.30pm. Just to lie here and shelter from the midday heat and unable to touch our water. Since we arrived here we have had a spoonful of water each and can't afford to touch anymore. My mouth is dry and very uncomfortable and my leg is much the same. It gives me hell when I start off after each rest, but after the first 100 yards or so it is not too bad. From here we can see a rock formation very similar to where we left the truck, but I think it is raising false hopes to even think that it is the correct place, as I reckoned it was further away than that.

8.00pm No, it wasn't the spot, but one of the party who was watching on the Msus-Mechili road for two weeks where we left the truck, says he recognises the countryside and he reckons we are about eight miles from the truck. Well – he may be right, but in my opinion we still have 20 or 30 miles to do.

They are travelling too fast for me, now that they think they are getting so close. They are going too fast for another man too. One of the first rules of walking in the desert is, 'Never try to hurry'. My mouth is dry and the saliva dries in my mouth and I have to scratch my lips, tongue and the roof of my mouth with my fingernails to scrape it off. Oh well, we will see what happens tomorrow, now we are going to have a bit of sleep.

Major J R Easonsmith, the highly regarded commander of the Barce raid (Operation Caravan), where he earned the Distinguished Service Order. In October 1943 he became the Officer Commanding LRDG, but was killed in action a month later while on operations in the Dodecanese Islands.

∽**18 September**∽ We hadn't been travelling long this morning before we came across two new sets of jeep tracks – the same jeep travelling both ways. They decided to follow the tracks, and after walking all morning until 9.30 the tracks came to an end and went back the way they had come. Just beside the tracks we found two keffiyehs *[LRDG issue Arab headdresses]*, so it was definitely LRDG. We also found a pack with some food in which must have fallen off the jeep, but we can't eat food without water so it wasn't much good to us.

My throat is dry and I have been doing a lot of retching, but nothing comes up. We now have less than a gallon of water among ten of us, and only have a spoonful every two hours. If we find the place where we left the truck and it isn't there, or if we don't find the place where we left it, I don't know how we will get on, as we will be three days from the nearest water. We are now resting near a road which is about 15 miles from where we left the truck. Now we are all getting thin and very weak, and being so dry make things almost unbearable.

8.00pm We set off this evening before the heat had gone out of the sun. Not only that, they went far too fast, too fast for another man and myself. We hadn't been going long before we had to sit down and rather to my surprise the others carried on.

We hadn't been resting long when my mate *[Guardsman Gutheridge]* said to me, "You go on Jop and leave me here." That will give some idea of the condition we were in and we are still a long way from any water. I wouldn't leave him, and we had a bit of sleep. However, I was weighing the chances of finding the truck. Maybe someone had got to it first and taken it away. I also thought of the other eight men who now have no navigator. But if they don't want to wait for a wounded navigator they must reckon they can manage OK.

∽**19 September 1942**∽ Last night, after a bit of rest, we set off northward without a drop of WATER!! By taking things easy we must have walked further this morning that ever we walked before. My tongue is very sore. Maybe we will see some Arabs tomorrow who will give us some water.

8.00pm Carried on for a while and now hope to get a bit of sleep.

20 September 1942 We set off at dawn this morning and were just heading for some bushes for shade when we spotted an Arab on a camel. Our excitement rose as high as it was possible for excitement to rise in the condition we were in and we immediately turned to head him off. For quite a while we couldn't see whether we were getting any closer to him or not, it certainly didn't look like it. Eventually however, we got within quarter of a mile and shouted out. After several efforts we at last made him hear us and he stopped. When we finally arrived alongside of him and asked for water, he told us he didn't have any. We could have cried. We told him what we had been through, that we hadn't had any water for two days and hardly any for three days before that, but he still said he had no water and there was none around here.

With that he set off, while we got into the shade of a bush to spend the remainder of the day. We hadn't been lying down for long however, before we saw the same man and camel coming back. He told us there was a well about eight miles eastward and if we came along now he would take us there. It was then about 11.00am, the sun was scorching and we were dry as a bone, but we were determined to give it a try. We had to sit down and rest about every quarter mile. My mate nearly gave up and told me to go on without him, but I kept him going with the thought of water at the other end. Stops became more frequent and the Arab became tired of this and asked if we had any money. When we told him we hadn't, he went off and left us. So now we are spending the remainder of the day in the shade.

How we have been getting on for water for the last couple of days I leave to the reader's imagination, but whatever we did, it saved our lives.

12 midnight When it had cooled down a bit we set off northward, thinking it was better to keep heading to where there are plenty of wells, rather than trying to find one well in the dark. We hadn't been travelling long when we heard a dog barking away in the distance to our right. Now every Arab camp has one or more dogs in it, and it is habit of the dogs to keep barking all night. When an Arab is travelling from one camp to another and is not sure where the camp is, he waits until darkness falls and follows the bark of the dogs.

Well, this dog was barking in the direction that the Arab was taking us this morning, so we turned right and followed the bark. Gradually the bark got louder and we walked for four hours in the direction of the dog before we eventually saw the animal. That gives an idea of how far you can hear a dog barking. He was standing on top of a rise and as we approached he came running towards us looking very fierce. They all do, but I've never heard of anyone being bitten by one. We weren't worrying very much about the dog though, for we knew that within a 100 yards there must be an Arab camp and water.

When we arrived on top of the rise we saw a glow from a fire. No one can ever realise how we felt as we made our way to that glow, and I'm afraid I couldn't describe it. When we arrived there we asked an old man for some water which he immediately gave us. Both of us only had a very little to start with and gradually took more, until we decided that we had better not have any more, and we asked the Arab if it would be all right to sleep under some bushes not far away. We made ourselves more comfortable than we had felt for a very long time.

21 SEPTEMBER 1942 We hadn't been asleep long when we were awakened by the Arab and invited to have some food – bread and tea. The tea was especially welcome, but it was surprising how little food we could eat. We just didn't feel like it, in spite of having had practically nothing to eat for the past five days. There were two Arabs at the fire and a herd of goats all round. It was strange that although we had now drunk a lot of water we felt very dry soon after each drink. I suppose it was being absorbed into the body as fast as we drank it. After we had again our fill of water we slept until daylight.

The first thing we thought of when we woke up was water, and again filled ourselves up. After that we could more or less take notice of things, and I realised my leg was poisoned, as it was very sore and I had a lump in my groin. We were still about a 100 miles from anywhere I could get medical treatment. I had a field dressing in my kit, so I boiled up some water and bathed and bandaged my leg. One of the Arabs said there was an Arab doctor near his home, where he will take us when the sun goes down.

I thought his home was about five miles away, but after walking about 12 miles we are settling down for the night.

22 SEPTEMBER 1942 I now need a stick to walk with and I am slowing down the trip. After ten miles and about a mile from the Mechili-El Abiar road we met some more Arabs who filled our tins with goats milk. It was great. God! What agony it is to set off, and what pain it is to keep going. Shortly we came upon an empty well about four feet deep which opened into a room about 20ft by 12 ft. It was nice and cool and we were able to rest until the sun became cooler. We have already travelled about 30 miles with this Arab and apparently still have a fair distance to go. I am sure if it hadn't been for the kind attention he gave me I would never had come so far.

At 4.00pm we headed for another well, where we had a wash and received some more milk. While we were sitting there, about 50 German planes came over, flying very low, from east to west. At dusk we reached some Arab huts and were made welcome, then given a kind of milk pudding which was very nice too. We joined the Arabs round a camp fire and drank tea and told yarns, which is known as 'falkering.'

⁍ **23 September 1942** ⁌ *11.00am* We are now sheltering in a cave. I'm afraid I can't walk much further. Every time we set off after sitting down, I tell the others not to watch me start, but to keep going. I am certain that if we didn't have the Arab with us I would have failed to start long before now. My leg has swollen very big and it stinks.

4.30pm After another hour of travel we were climbing a hill, I was about 100 yards behind the other two, and was just about to shout out that I couldn't possibly go any further when my mate shouted back that he could see the Arab tents about 100 yards away. I gritted my teeth and carried on, but had it been another 100 yards I am sure I would never have made it.

⁍ **24 September 1942** ⁌ This morning I was unable to walk, and the Arab brought me a donkey and put me on it. He said he would take us to the doctor, where we duly arrived about midday. The doctor had a look at my leg, bathed it and put the bandage back on again. He said nothing to me, but my Arab friend told me he would take me to another doctor tomorrow, so we are staying here tonight.

⁍ **25 September 1942** ⁌ This morning there was a white horse ready for me outside the tent. They lifted me on and away we went, my mate walking with the Arab leading the horse. We had been travelling about two hours when two trucks came over a rise and drove straight up to us. They were obviously expecting us. It was then that the Arab told me that the doctor had told him that he couldn't do anything for me, and that if I didn't get to a proper doctor quickly I would lose my leg, if not my life. He thought this was the best way out. There were about a dozen Ities on the trucks. They lifted me on board, and my mate and the Arab climbed on and away we went to an Italian outpost.

When we arrived, an officer who asked me a few questions through an Arab interpreter – such as where we had come from, how long we had been walking etc. Then we were put on a truck again and taken to Barce. I wondered what sort of reception we would get, however when I told them we had been on the raid there, they seemed glad to meet us. Seven hours after I was captured they took me to a first aid post, which was just across the road. The Italian medical orderly there made a good job of cleaning and bandaging my leg, although it was very painful. When he had finished he gave me some brandy, which was very welcome. When I asked them here how many planes were destroyed, they said 27.

At 4pm they put us on another truck and took us to Benghazi. There my mate and I had to split up. He was marched off to prison camp and they took me to the hospital. I was taken to a room where there were two doctors – one German and one Italian. I still had the Arab interpreter there and through him they asked me how long it was since I received the wound and how long it was since I had medical attention. They shook their heads and said it would have to come off. I asked them to have another look at it and if there was any show to try and save it, so they looked at it again and talked to each other for a while and then said, "Alright, we'll give it a go, but one more day and it would have to come off."

The raid on the airfield and town of Barce cost the Italians four killed, 15 wounded and one taken prisoner. In addition, 24 valuable aircraft were destroyed or damaged, along with fuel dumps and a number of vehicles. Ten of the aircraft were wrecked by Corporal M H Craw, who at great personal risk placed homemade bombs on those not already burning as a result of the machine-gun fire from the circling trucks.

The patrols lost six men wounded. All of them recovered. Ten men were captured, while 16 vehicles were destroyed or broken down. Miraculously, none of the men were killed despite the mayhem and firepower directed at them. The LRDG losses were insignificant when measured against the material and psychological damage such a small force had inflicted on the enemy. The raid had relieved some the pressure on the Eighth Army as it prepared for the El Alamein offensive.

Only one LRDG vehicle, Te Anau II, returned to base and all the men who walked were eventually rescued. Up to the time of their capture, Trooper Jopling and Guardsman Gutheridge had trekked a remarkable 240 kilometres during 12 days of hardship and suffering.

For their roles in the operation, Major Easonsmith and Captain Wilder received the Distinguished Service Order, Captain Lawson the Military Cross. Sergeant Dennis who led G Patrol, and Corporal Craw of T1 Patrol, both earned the Military Medal.

POSTSCRIPT

Despite suffering the early stages of gangrene as a result of a small entry bullet wound that left a large exit laceration, Jopling kept his leg and recovered as a POW. One of the main factors contributing to the survival of both he and Gutheridge was that during his Cairo leave some two years before, he chose to spend time learning Arabic while his comrades visited the bars and saw the sights. Consequently, on the trek he was able to communicate with the Arabs, who in turn became more well disposed towards him. In addition, it was through an Arab interpreter that Jopling was able to talk to the German and Italian doctors who, without his protests, would probably have amputated his leg.

He was listed as missing until December 1942, when notice was received that he was safely interned at a hospital POW camp at Udine in northern Italy, close to the Yugoslavian border.

Back in New Zealand, Lieutenant E H McCormick, the officer in charge of Military Archives, heard that Jopling was a prisoner of war and wrote to Frank's fiancee Irene Gwyer in March 1943. His letter included:

"Frank is one of the most regular and vivid diarists I have ever come across. I had the pleasure of meeting Trooper Jopling and hearing of his experiences. I was sorry to learn that he has been taken prisoner after so many adventures and near escapes. One thing I am fairly certain is that he will be continuing his diary, wherever he may be."

Jopling's diaries up to his capture were safe. However, as a POW he was only able to continue his journals by writing on the paper side of wrappings in cigarette packets. To keep his writings out of sight, he rolled the wrappings together and plaited them into a belt which he wore around his waist.

In the confusion of the Italian capitulation in September 1943, Jopling along with many others, escaped from the camp. He made his way to the south of Italy sheltering with friendly Italians on the way. On one occasion the Germans visited the farm where he was staying. He was spotted and his hosts were asked who he was. They replied that he was family, but was unable to speak. Because Jopling had spent so much time outdoors and had developed a dark swarthy skin, the Germans were convinced he was an Italian and left.

After evading the enemy for six weeks he reached the outskirts of the Allied lines. Unfortunately, before he could cross over to freedom he was picked up by a German patrol. In the resulting personal search, they took his plaited belt, so his wrapping paper diaries were lost. He was sent on to a POW camp in Germany where he remained until the end of the war. However, before his camp was finally liberated he managed to escape and found a bicycle. He cycled towards the advancing Allies and was picked by the Americans.

In August 1945, soon after returning from Europe, Jopling married his fiancee Irene Gwyer. He went back to farming as a contractor, but the muscle damage from his old leg wound, combined with a shoulder injury aggravated by farm work, made it difficult for him to continue on the land. He settled in Auckland and found a job as first mate on the inner harbour ferries that crossed the Waitemata Harbour between the city and the North Shore suburb of Devonport. He went on to study for his master's ticket, became a skipper and spent the next 20 years working for the ferry company. Interestingly, at one time his first mate was Norman Kirk, who later became Prime Minister of NZ in the early 1970s. Following his retirement, Jopling found further employment in the electrical workshops at the NZ Naval dockyard in Devonport.

After a full and active life which included a keen interest in sport, Frank Jopling died on 15 March 1987, aged 74. He was survived by his wife Irene, two sons (Bill and Bruce) and three granddaughters – Cheryl, Janine and Hayley.

Perhaps the best summary of Frank's time in the LRDG was in a letter he wrote to Irene during the war: "You asked me if I would rather be with the Division or with the LRDG. The answer is definitely with the LRDG. In between the unpleasant experiences, we have a great time as far as the army goes."

Captain Frank Jopling with his ship's cats, at the wheel of the Devonport Ferry, Auckland, 1970

APPENDIX I

GUARDSMAN EASTON

Frank Jopling commented in a letter to his fiancée Irene, about an article in the Auckland Star newspaper that claimed that Guardsman Easton had died 'raving mad' after the long trek led by Trooper Moore (see page 100). Frank's letter, dated 31 January 1941, said:

> "The man who died was the bravest man you would ever see and to say that he was raving mad when he died is not only a terrible thing to say, but is absolutely untrue. That man walked nearly 200 miles with a bullet in his throat, and without food and only one and a half gallons of water between four of them for 10 days. He kept walking until he was too weak to move. When he was picked up he was just alive and they tested his blood and there wasn't any left in his body, just water. To publish in the paper that a man as game as that "died raving mad" is an absolute crime and you can tell them that from me."

APPENDIX II

THE LONG RANGE PATROL BADGE

In March 1941 Frank wrote to Irene about the striking of a Long Range Patrol badge. Before this, the LRP had no specific insignia, apart from their parent unit badges.

"You say that it is in the paper that we have been given a especially struck medal and that there was a photo of it, is it anything like this? *[Frank included a drawing.]* Because if it is, it isn't a medal. We wanted to have an official hat badge for this unit, so one of the boys *[Cpl. C O 'Bluely' Grimsey]* made a sketch and took it to a jeweller to get it made into a badge.

The first one they didn't like, so we took it back and told them we wanted a better job made of them, so we got the one we have now. The circle and lettering are in silver and the scorpion gold plated. It looks very good and we wear it as a hat badge now.

"However, they are to make an official issue hat badge now, as the other we had made for the original New Zealanders who had formed the LRP, now known as the LRDG. Apparently when a new unit is formed during a war that unit is not allowed to have its initials on the hat badge until after the war. So the issue is going to be a scorpion inside the circle and a crown on top. We are also getting LRDG shoulder titles too."

When the official brass LRDG badge was adopted in early 1942, there was no crown on top and the LRDG initials were included in the circle.

Left: the silver Long Range Patrol badge. Right: the official brass LRDG badge introduced in early 1942. This badge was slightly bigger than the LRP badge.

APPENDIX III

T PATROL TRUCK NAMES

Te Anau
Te Ariki
Te Aroha
Te Auti
Te Aute
Te Awa
Te Hai
Te Hau
Te Pa
Te Paki
Te Puke
Te Rangi
Te Roti
Te Taniwha
Te Wanaka
Taipo
Taupo
Tirau
Tutira

The trucks were given Maori names, painted along the side of the vehicle bonnets in white letters, usually against black, though against dark green on some LRP vehicles. Replacement trucks often carried on the same name, so they became Te Anau II or Te Paki III. By 1943 the naming of new trucks was discontinued.

APPENDIX IV

New Zealand members of T and T1 & T2 Patrols who served with Frank Jopling at some time between July 1940 and September 1942. These men would have shared similar experiences to those recorded in Jopling's diaries.

LRP = Long Range Patrol
KIA = killed in action
POW = prisoner of war

Name	Service No.	Comment
Adams, W R	1074	LRP
Aislabie, W P	1014	LRP
Ballantyne, L B	1398	LRP
Barrett, D	1062	LRP
Bassett, D M	12518	
Beech, F R	1093	LRP; KIA 31/01/41
Brown, F S	1127	
Browne, L H	4444	LRP
Burgess, W H	14351	
Burke, P J	17545	Barce raid
Burnnand, W D	1179	LRP
Campbell, N R	12071	
Carter, E G	1131	LRP
Cleaver, H H	1195	LRP
Cramond, A R	23051	
Craw, M H	37112	Barce raid
Crawford, A B	15263	

Name	Service No.	Comment
Crisp, J E	7689	
Croucher, C H B	8803	LRP
Davies, J	1302	LRP
Davis, J L D	37293	Barce raid
Davison, G L	1349	LRP
Dobson, T B	1203	Barce raid
Dobson, E J	12958	Died while POW, 4/04/45
Dornbush, C A	29533	
Edmundson, F B	991	LRP
Ellingham, S W	30972	
Ellis, E	16503	
Ellis, L A	1135	LRP
Eyre, C W	1305	LRP
Ferguson, A G	2441	
Ferguson, I C	1371	LRP
Forbes, W D S	35079	
Garland, P L	1366	LRP
Garven, G C	1307	LRP
Gerrard, W G	16606	
Hankins, A E	7891	LRP
Hawkins, L J	7377	LRP
Hay, R E	15302	Barce raid
Heard, V J	29568	
Hewson, C D	1030	LRP; KIA 11/01/41
Hobson, N W	14324	
Holland, H T R	34194	Barce raid
Hood, A W	1041	LRP
Hughes, L T	3862	LRP
Hutchinson, E Y M	34264	
Job, A J	508	LRP
Johnstone, L R B	1141	

Name	Service No.	Comment
Kelly, K	17625	
Kendall, F	1019	LRP
Kitney, E W R	3863	LRP
Lewis, R W N	12053	
Macassey, J L P	15250	
Mackay, H D	17668	
Martin, A C	21956	
McCorkindale, A	2676	LRP
McCulloch, I G	12001	
McGarry, T J	1214	LRP
McInnes, D J	9651	
McInnes, I H	1052	LRP
McIver, L A	37404	Died while POW, 16/2/45
McKenzie, C B	17536	
McLeod, A F	3388	LRP
McLeod, R F	439511	
McNeil, T B	1253	LRP
McQueen, R B	1401	LRP
Milburn, T A	17850	Barce raid
Mitford, P V	12002	Barce raid
Moore, R J	1248	LRP
Morris, C S	1072	
Nutt, A H C	14550	Barce raid
Ormond, A R W	1256	LRP
Parker, S D	21963	Barce raid
Payne, L	29781	
Porter, R T	14265	
Rail, W H	1262	Barce raid
Ramsay, R A	1325	
Reid, J L	31121	
Rhodes, F D	1331	LRP

Name	Service No.	Comment
Richards, J	1357	LRP
Ritchie, T E	29441	
Roderick, L	1113	LRP
Sanders, E	598	LRP; Barce raid
Shepherd, B F	5365	
Shepherd, J R	1328	LRP
Simonsen, J M	46071	
Simpson, R A	29613	
Smith, E B	1065	LRP
Smith, G T	29792	
Spain, V C	1149	LRP
Spedding, A J	1023	LRP
Stewart, M W	14355	
Stutterd, E C	24964	
Tant, R D	16650	
Thompson, J H	37409	
Tinker, R A	7483	LRP
Tippett, K A	20441	Barce raid
Vincent, A	16913	Barce raid
Walsh, T E	28796	
Warbrick, D P	21884	Barce raid
White, R F	1174	
Wilder, N P	21988	
Wright, O W	29935	
Wynne, J E	1151	LRP
Yealands, K	10736	Barce raid
Zimmerman, J	1392	LRP

SOURCES

Jopling, Frank, T Patrol LRP/LRDG. Personal diaries written between February 1940 and September 1942.

Jopling, Irene (widow of Frank Jopling). Interviews between 2001 and 2002.

Wartime correspondence between Frank and Irene Jopling.

Kay, R L , *The Long Range Desert Group in Libya 1940-1941*, NZ Official History, 1949.

Kay, R L , *The Long Range Desert Group in the Mediterranean*, NZ Official History, 1950.

Nominal Rolls and Establishment Lists of the LRDG, dated 1 December 1940, 28 December 1940, 31 March 1941 and March 1942. Kindly loaned by the LRDG (NZ) Association.

O'Carroll, Brendan, *Kiwi Scorpions, The Story of the New Zealanders in the Long Range Desert Group*, Token Publishing, 2000.

INDEX

Abbassia, 14, 18-19, 22, 24, 30, 33, 36-37, 39, 40, 46, 120, 148
Abbots Gulch, 93-94, 98
Abd el Galil, Sheikh, 53, 56-57, 63, 65, 74
Adams, Tpr. W R, 60, 86, 87
Afrika Korps, 12, 124, 148, 150
Agedabia, 144, 145, 148, 169, 172, 174, 180
Ain Dalla, 34, 35, 40, 44, 45, 52, 56, 103, 104
Aislabie, Tpr. W B, 51
Antelat, 145-147, 176-178, 180
Arnold, Lt. P L, 149
Auto-Saharan Company, 82, 85, 87, 89, 93
Aircraft:
   CR 42, 195
   Fiesler Storch, 186
   Ghibli, 61, 85, 104, 105
   Heinkel, 100, 133
   Hurricane, 131, 137, 138, 177
   Ju 88, 172
   Kittyhawk, 184
   Lysander, 98, 104, 107, 146
   Messerschmitt Me 109, 133, 137-138, 146-147, 149
   Messerschmitt Me 110, 139
   Savoia Marchetti SM, 79, 85, 104, 129
   Savoia Marchetti SM, 82, 132
   Stuka, Ju 87, 133, 138-143, 149
   Tomahawk, 138
   Vickers Valentia, 40-41, 105, 108
   Waco, 105-106, 113, 119, 122-123, 126
   Wellington, 181
Bagnold, Maj. R A, 9, 11, 14, 28-29, 33, 37, 39, 47, 69, 74, 90, 102-103, 114, 119
Ballantyne, Lt. L B, 22, 53, 57, 59, 67, 84-94, 96, 102, 108, 111, 117, 119, 120, 131, 133, 149
Barce, 6, 17, 185-203
Bardia, 55, 91, 133, 181
Bassett, Tpr. D M, 102, 149, 173
Barker, Sgt. R F T, 123, 126

Beech, Cpl. F R, 60, 78, 85
Benghazi, 90, 100-101, 111-112, 123-124, 137, 145-160, 169, 174, 177, 188, 195, 202
Bishara, 81-82, 86
Big Cairn, 106, 41, 50
Bir El Gubba, 128
Bir El Hacheim, 128-130, 133, 142
Bloquet, Sgt. 54
Bourrat, Sgt. 54
Browne Cpl. L H, 29, 37, 55, 63, 70, 86, 93, 107, 112, 114
Bruce, Pte. J, 83, 112
Carabinieri, 63-65
Cairo, 9, 13-15, 33-41, 45-48, 50-51, 53, 67, 69, 75, 81, 87-88, 90-91, 99-102, 108, 111, 114-117, 119-123, 126, 143, 149, 165, 181-182, 187, 204
Chad, 28, 48, 53
Cheda bu Maun, 194, 196-197
Citadel, 18, 39-40, 48, 52, 54-55, 63, 65, 67, 75, 78, 91, 108
Clayton, Maj. P A, 18, 39-40, 48, 52, 54-55, 63, 65, 67, 75, 78, 91, 108
Cleaver, Tpr. H H, 112-113
Costello, Lt. P, 122
Craw, Cpl. M H, 6, 99, 102, 168, 177, 179, 185-186, 193, 197, 203
Crisp, Lt. J E, 149
Croucher Lt. C H B, 90, 105 128, 136
Cyrenaica, 116, 144
Crichton-Stuart, Capt. M D, 47-48, 52-53, 58, 65, 87-88
Daventry, 100, 133, 172
Dennis, Sgt. J, 192, 198, 203
Derna, 143, 145, 180
Dobson, Tpr. T B, 168, 186-187, 193
Easonsmith, Maj. J R, 126, 187-199, 203
Easton, Gdsm. J, 83, 91, 100-101, 206
Edmundson, Lt. F B, 10, 32-33, 53, 67
Eggenspiller, Lt. 54

Egyptian Sand Sea, 44, 50- 51, 104
El Adem, 140, 143, 172, 180
El Agheila, 148, 150, 152, 161-162
El Alamein, 182-184, 203
Ellingham, Lt. S W, 91,93, 116, 122
Faya, 53, 69, 72, 75, 77, 80, 105
Fayoum, 182, 184-185, 187
Ferguson, Tpr. I C, 73, 173, 175
Fezzan, 48-54, 60, 66, 90, 100
Fort Lamy, 54, 78
Free French, 54, 62-63, 67-68, 70-71, 73, 78, 87, 104-106, 163
Freyberg, Maj. Gen. B C, 11, 12, 39, 46, 107, 122
Freyberg, Lt.. P, 122-124, 126, 127, 141
G Patrol, 48-53, 65, 67, 70, 75-76, 79-80, 86, 88, 100-101, 145, 190-191, 193-195, 203
Garven, Tpr. G C, 112, 114, 173
Gatrun, 53, 65
Gebel Sherif, 82, 84-86, 100, 108
Giarabub, 91, 92-101, 123, 125, 127-130, 148, 165, 183
Gibbs, Lt.. M A, 48, 86
Grimsey, Cpl. C O, 207
Gurdon, Lt. R B, 177
Gutheridge, Gdsm. 199, 203-204
Gwyer, Irene, 13, 15, 204-205
Hay, Tpr. R E, 168, 193
Heavy Section, 9, 20, 29, 49, 97, 106, 118, 149
Hewson, Sgt. C D, 30, 44, 61-63
Holland, Tpr. H T R, 193
Holliman, Capt. C A, 177
Hopu Hopu, 13, 38
Hunter, Capt. A D, 128, 129, 135-136
Jalo, 40, 42, 51, 96-97, 101, 111, 116-117, 136, 145, 148-149, 151, 161-162
Kalansho Sand Sea, 48, 187
Kayugi, 52, 54
Kennedy Shaw, Capt. W B, 11, 41, 52, 67, 114, 116-117, 130, 136
Kharga, 53, 88, 90
Kendall, Cpl. F, 32, 118

Kufra, 23-24, 40-41, 44, 48, 51, 54, 75, 78, 81-82, 87, 93, 101-110, 114-119, 123, 126, 173, 181
Lawson, Capt. R P, 193-194, 196, 203
Libyan Sand Sea, 41, 44, 51
Leclerc, Col. 87, 105-106, 163
Lewis, Sgt. R W N, 99, 153, 168, 177, 183
McCormick, Lt. E H, 204
McGarry, Tpr. T J, 32-33
McInnes, Pte. D J, 23
McInnes, Tpr. I H, 61, 70, 83-84, 93, 114, 123, 136
McIver, Tpr. L A, 99, 135
McNeil, Tpr. T B, 83
McQueen, 'Mary' Lt. R B, 19-22, 24, 27, 31-32, 42, 44-47
Maadi, 13-14, 91, 101, 120-121, 182
Maddalena, 137-138, 142-143
Marada, 115-116, 152, 161-162, 165
Marble Arch, 154
Massu, Capt. 54, 63, 67, 68
Matmata Hills, 9
Mechili, 135, 145, 197, 199, 201
Mersa Matruh, 23, 130, 182, 185
Milburn, Tpr. T A, 168, 177, 193
Mitford, Maj. E C, 39
Moore, Tpr. R J, 23, 25, 83, 85, 88, 91, 100-101, 146, 206
Morris, Lt. C S, 135-137, 149, 165, 173, 182
Msus, 145, 171, 176-177, 197, 199
Mushroom Rock, 15, 18, 37, 40, 45
Murzuk, 48, 53-55, 57-70, 87, 92, 114, 163, 166-167
Naarten Bisciara, 23
New Zealand Forces Club, 119, 182
Nutt, L/Cpl. A H C, 168, 177, 193
Ormond, Sgt. A R W, 16, 24, 30, 45
d'Ornano Col. J C, 54, 55, 62, 63
Parker, Tpr. S D, 168, 194, 196
Peniakoff, Lt. Col. V, 11, 190
Porter, L/Cpl. R T, 99, 135
Prendergast, Maj. G L, 105, 119, 122, 135, 142-143, 165, 166

R Patrol, 16-18, 21-22, 29-30, 32, 39, 41-44, 91-93, 102, 109, 111, 123, 126, 128, 136, 145, 152, 159, 160-161, 163, 174, 183
Rawnsley, Pilot Officer D, 124, 126
Ritchie, Tpr. T E, 99, 102
Rhodesians, 10-11, 110, 152
Road Watch, 150-165
Roderick Cpl. L, 43, 61, 86, 87
Rommel, Field Marshal E, 12, 144, 148, 152-154 158-159, 163, 165
S Patrol, 110, 114-119, 123, 148-152, 165, 177-180
Sanders, Gnr. E, 102, 168, 177
Sarazac, Capt. 55, 67
Sarra, 26, 78, 80-81, 86-87, 91, 100-101
Sceleidima, 145-146, 178
Senegalese, 30, 72, 105
Shepherd, Cpl J R, 29, 96
Shepherd, Tpr. B F, 177, 168
Sutherland, Lt. J H, 50
Sidi Rezegh, 180
Sirte, 116, 150, 163, 169, 172
Siwa, 18-20, 22, 26-27, 92, 96, 106, 111, 122-135, 137, 142-151, 159-168, 171-172, 174-175, 178-183, 185
Sollum, 23, 96, 105, 127, 150, 162
Solluch, 175, 177
Smith, Tpr. E B, 51, 85
Spain, Tpr. V C, 86
Special Air Service (SAS), 10, 123, 137, 148-149, 180-181, 186
Spedding, Cpl. A J, 16
Steele, Maj. D G, 39, 92, 111, 137, 172-173
Stirling, Lt. Col. D, 123, 185-186, 195-197
T Patrol, 16, 18-19, 21, 29, 47,51-53, 55, 62-65, 68, 74-75, 77, 84-85, 87, 91, 93-94, 96-100, 105, 107-110, 112, 114-115, 117-120, 123, 127-130, 133-136, 139, 141, 148-153, 174, 180, 193,
Tazerbo, 101, 106, 109, 110
Tejerri, 53, 55, 65, 67-68
Tibbus, 80, 57, 67
Tibesti Mountains, 48, 54-55
Tighe Pte. A, 84, 91, 100-101
Timpson, Capt. J A L, 187, 192
Tinker, Cpl R A, 145
Tippett, Tpr. K E, 168, 186-187
Tobruk, 55, 105, 138, 172, 181, 183, 188, 193
Traghen, 63-65
Tripoli, 9, 100, 115-116, 146, 150, 154, 190
Umm el Arenab, 29, 64
Uweinat, 29, 30-33, 41, 53, 87-88
Vehicles, LRDG
  Chevrolet WB, 53, 66, 68, 74, 85, 93, 101, 103
  Chevrolet 1311X3, 15 cwt, 161
  Chevrolet 1533X2, 148-153, 177, 183, 195
  Ford F8, 111, 133-135
  Ford 01, 15 cwt, 10, 16, 53, 60, 67-70, 75, 89, 123, 185
  Ford F30, 92, 96, 101-104, 113, 115, 117-118, 120, 131, 149, 151
  Jeep, 10, 123, 178, 186-187, 192-193, 196-199
  Marmon-Herrington, 20, 29, 36, 45, 144
  White, 49, 97, 106
W Patrol, 16-17, 29, 31-33, 39, 41, 47, 50, 111
Wadi Halfa, 87-88, 105, 107
Walsh, Gnr. T E, 102
Wann, Gdsm. T, 187
Washka, 151, 172, 174
Wavell, Gen. A, 15, 39, 46
Weapons:
  Breda, 10, 82- 83, 135, 175, 178, 186, 190, 194
  Bofors, 10, 84, 88, 94, 97, 102, 109, 119-120, 135, 137, 175
  Boys anti-tank gun, 23, 38, 53, 59, 85, 93
  Lewis gun, 23, 38, 53, 59, 85, 93
Wilder, Capt. N P, 9, 149-151, 153, 163, 168-169, 174, 177, 181, 186, 187, 190-193, 196, 203
Willcox, Tpr. L A, 50
Winchester, Gdsm. A, 83, 91, 100
Y Patrol, 100-101, 123
Yealands, Tpr. K, 193
Zighen, 109-111
Zouar, 68, 71-73, 76, 79, 89, 105